Instructor's Manual

to accompany

THE STUDY OF LAW
A Critical Thinking Approach

Katherine A. Currier
Thomas E. Eimermann

D1520847

Katherine A. Currier, J.D.

PUBLISHERS

111 Eighth Avenue, New York, NY 10011
www.aspenpublishers.com

ISBN 0 – 7355 –5254 – 1

This manual is made available as a courtesy to law teachers with the understanding that it will not be reproduced, quoted or cited, except as where indicated. In the event that anyone would like to cite the manual for thoughts drawn from it, a reference to the relevant page number of the materials text (with the formula "suggested by") may be appropriate.

Copies of this manual are available on computer diskette. Teachers who have adopted the casebook may obtain a copy of the diskette, free of charge, by calling the Aspen Publishers sales assistant at 1 – 800 – 950 – 5259.

Permissions
Aspen Publishers
111 Eighth Avenue
New York, NY 10011

1 2 3 4 5

Table of Contents

Preface to this Manual

Preface

This course is incredibly fun to teach. The students are eager and full of curiosity about how the legal system works. Because the main emphasis is on learning reasoning skills, as opposed to rote memorization, you and your students will have engaging, thought-provoking classroom discussions.

This is also a course that is a lot of work to teach. Because everything is new to the students, at times they tend to get frustrated by their lack of knowledge and what can seem like an overwhelming new vocabulary. I have found that the best way to handle this is through a number of short, building block type assignments that reinforce what they are learning in class.

The structure of this book was designed to make it interactive. Ideally, you should have to spend very little classroom time on straight lecture. Rather, at the beginning of each class, you can briefly establish the framework for that day's lesson and then move on to presenting most of the material through interaction with the students by relying on the review and discussion questions, the legal analysis exercises, the practical tips, and the ethics alerts. In fact, we purposely dispersed these throughout the chapters so that the students would be encouraged to think about them while the material is fresh from recent reading and so as to be readily available to you to use as springboards for classroom discussion. While we did relegate the review questions to the end of each chapter, we have labeled them with the pages they cover so that you can easily assign just part of a chapter with its accompanying review questions.

This course can be taught in either one or two semesters. Ideally, the material should be divided over two semesters, with the first semester focusing on building a sound legal vocabulary, developing an appreciation for and an understanding of our legal system, and on acquiring sound analytical skills. The second semester can then focus more on the substantive law. The substantive law chapters are not meant to substitute for full courses in these subject matter areas. Rather, the emphasis in these chapters is on giving practical, basic knowledge with an appreciation for how rapidly the law is changing, especially in the areas of tort, family, and criminal law.

Finally, I always tell my students that there is no way they can become an expert or even competent in all areas of the law. The law is vast and is always changing — what they learn today may be outdated tomorrow. The goal is to give them a solid foundation upon which they can build, so that they can become self-learners with an understanding of the techniques necessary to learn about and update any area of the law.

In this Teacher's Manual you will find suggested answers to all of the following:
Discussion Questions
Case Discussion Questions
Legal Reasoning Exercises
Review Questions

In addition, throughout you will notice short 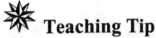 **Teaching Tip** suggestions on how you might want to approach a particular topic. Following the presentation of the material in the chapters, I have included two sample syllabi — one for a two semester course and one for a one semester course. Also included are sample assignments along with their grading sheets. Finally, you will find selected figures and exhibits that you can use for creating overhead transparencies for use in the classroom.

✳ Teaching Tip

You will find Netnotes throughout the text. At the time of publication, I checked all of the web addresses for accuracy. But as you know, the web is a constantly changing environment. Therefore, be sure to double-check the addresses yourself and alert the students as some of the addresses may have changed by the time they are using the book.

✳ Teaching Tip

I have found that even when grading a subjective assignment, such as is required when doing legal analysis, that the students and you benefit from following as objective a grading method as possible. For example, whenever I grade a case brief, I assign a set number of points for each of the parts of the brief. This helps the students to see very graphically where their weak and strong areas are. It also helps you when a student comes to complain about that "B" that the student thought should be an "A." You can look at your grading sheet and explain very clearly to the student exactly where improvement is needed. I have included such grading sheets for many of the suggested assignments.

Chapter 1

Introduction to the Study of Law and the Legal Profession

We believe that it is more important for students to learn how to think critically about the law and to develop an appreciation for the need for constant re-education than it is for them to learn black letter law in specific substantive areas. Therefore, while this book teaches students the fundamentals of the American legal system and certain basic legal tenets, the emphasis is upon teaching students how to think. As an instructor in this course faced with entry level students, you will face the difficulty of convincing them that without researching the law and then carefully applying it to the specific facts, there is no easy answer. In this first chapter we introduce basic principles that we will be discussing in more depth throughout the book.

Students really enjoy discussing the material in this chapter. Therefore, you may find yourself having to do some traffic control to keep the conversation within a manageable amount of time. Sometimes I think we could spend the whole semester on the legal reasoning issues raised in this chapter. If you let them, the students will talk and get very involved in these cases. While you do not want to stifle their enthusiasm, you should be aware that this can get out of hand.

 **Teaching Tip**

In this first class I always try to do the following:
1. Introduction to the course and the instructor.
2. Learn something about the students. (I always hand out index cards and ask the students to write their names and a couple of sentences about their goals upon graduation. I collect the cards and then talk with each student briefly. I am awful with names, and I have found this is a great way to start making the connection between name and face early in the semester.)
3. Overview of the course: Write on the board —
   Legal Reasoning ---- Legal Research --- Legal Writing
   and use an example client problem to walk the students through the three stages. Draw arrows to show how the process is circular.
4. Discuss why the study of law is important to everyone, whether the ultimate goal is law school, to work as a paralegal, or simply to be a more informed citizen.

Page 4, Case 1: The Distressed Grandfather and page 5, Case 2: The Harassed Student
We think it is very important that legal principles be illustrated through case stories. We encourage you to add to those in the text by including more examples in your classroom lectures or in additional assignments.

Page 7: Emphasize that not everything is "against the law," but that law is constantly changing. Also, be sure that they see for there to be a valid cause of actions, the client must be able to show both the requisite facts and the law.

DISCUSSION QUESTIONS, page 7
1. Why do you suppose there are certain types of harm, such as the humiliation Ms. Smith felt when the construction workers whistled at her, that courts will not help individuals resolve?
The purpose of this question is to encourage students to see that we have become such a litigious society that sometimes we just assume everything should be handled by the courts. But courts can be expensive, not only in terms of money but also in regards to the litigants' time and emotions. Also, there may be some harms that are simply part of living and that cannot be altered.

       For example, ask whether the students think someone who's fiancee has called off their engagement should be able to sue for the hurt it causes? Ask if any of them have heard of other "outrageous" law claims?

       You can also explore whether they think it is good for people to always turn to the courts instead of relying on themselves. For example, some have suggested that the demise of the extended family is a reason for why people today need to go to third parties for help in resolving their problems.

2. Do you think it is right that employees can go to court and sue their bosses for sexual harassment? Why? If the harasser were a co-worker instead of a boss, how would you view the situation?
This will encourage more thinking about who and why people should be able to sue. Have them try to decide whether a co-worker is more like a boss or more like the stranger (construction worker). What of a customer?

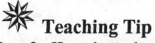 **Teaching Tip**
Page 9: Have the students discuss the similarities and differences they see between Mr. Drake's situation and the two prior cases. Write the ideas on the board. Ask the students whether it would matter what type of relationship Mr. Drake had with his grandson — for example, only occasional visits versus acting as the primary care giver. The purpose here is to help students start to understand that the goal is not to come up with the "right" answer but to learn how to develop arguments to support their answer.

Legal Reasoning Exercises, pages 9-10

1. What kind of problems do you think this might raise? Personal, medical, moral, religious, legal? If you think this is a problem that the legal system should address, should such practices be made illegal? Should they be legal, but regulated by the government?

Of course, this raises all sorts of potential problems. The mother might decide to keep the child; the parents might decide not to take the child; the child might be born with disabilities. All of these potential problems could be viewed as presenting personal, medical, moral, and religious questions. From the point of view of the parents, this should also be seen as a legal problem. They will want a contract so that both sides will know the terms and so that the surrogate cannot back out. This is one purpose of law — to enhance predictability and reliability. From society's point of view, again this should be seen as a legal problem. Perhaps society does not think this sort of arrangement is a good idea and so wants to outlaw it. Alternatively, society may think it is a good idea but that there should be restrictions on it.

2. What do you think of these contractual arrangements? Are they fair to both parties? Which, if any, of these provisions do you find objectionable? Why?

A contract will not necessary protect the couple. It depends on the status of these kinds of contracts. Point out that the law varies from state to state and a lawyer would not necessarily know the answer. Remind them that no one can know the answer to a legal problem without first researching both the facts and the law (no cocktail party questions).

Reassure the students that from law school, the attorney would know the basics of contract law but remind them that unless he had this type of problem before, he probably could not give the client an answer on the spot regarding surrogacy contracts. First, he would have to engage in legal research.

Several provisions of the contract are questionable, especially the ones regarding the decision to abort, relinquishment of parental rights, and the $8000 payment per month.

3. What do you think the court did in that situation? Do you think the court ordered the man to continue the payments?

At this point, you may want to take a bit of a sidetrack into the basics of contract law — for a contract to be valid three things must be satisfied. There must be an offer, it must be accepted, and there must be consideration. In this case the man offered the money and the woman accepted. The tricky part is whether or not there was consideration. Tell them that consideration just means something of value, and for the contract to be valid each party must be giving up something of value. Here the man was giving up $500 a month, clearly something of value. You can ask them what they think the woman gave in return. If the court found that she gave her time and companionship, the court would see this as something of value, so there probably was a valid contract.

However, let them know that even when there is a valid contract, the court will listen to any good reasons one party might have for not fulfilling his or her side of the bargain. (This is a good time to give them their first taste of the differences between the plaintiff's prima facie case and defenses.) For example, if one of the parties was underage when he signed the contract, that might provide a valid defense. Another valid

defense is to argue that the contract is against public policy. A court might see this as essentially a contract for prostitution, and hence against public policy. If however, it was simply a contract for companionship, then it probably is enforceable.

4   What are the implications of this case for the Hardlucks? Do you see any similarities between their case and that of the live-in couple? Is the surrogacy contract a contract for prostitution? How do you define that term? Even if it is not a contract for prostitution, is a surrogacy contract against public policy?

Emphasize the importance of being able to answer "why?" something is important rather than worrying about whether or not they have reached the correct answer.

If they see the cases as different, show them that means this contract is enforceable. A good argument is that it is not for prostitution, but rather for the creation of life. If they see the cases as the same, then the contract is not enforceable. Arguably, in both cases, a woman's body is for sale. Point out that even after they have done legal research, they often will not know a definitive answer to the client's case. Law is not just a bunch of rules that you can memorize and then know the answers. You must take those rules and see how they apply to your client's particular facts.

NOTE: This hypothetical is similar to the case of *In the Matter of Baby M*, 537 A.2d 1227 (N.J. 1988), excerpted in chapter 14, beginning on page 522.

Page 11, Ethics Alert
Although there is no code of paralegal ethics (yet), as legal professionals, paralegals must be made aware of potential ethical problems. To encourage students to see ethics as an on-going concern, rather than simply as a separate chapter topic, we have placed ethics alerts throughout the chapters. We suggest you regularly set aside some class time to discuss them with your students.

DISCUSSION QUESTIONS, page 13
3.   If paralegals **are** working under the supervision of an attorney, do you think they should be allowed to give legal advice to clients? What if they are **not** working under the supervision of an attorney?
This should spark a good discussion. Discuss the need for low income people to receive legal services at an affordable price, but also the dangers of nonlawyer practice.

4.   Some argue that paralegals should be licensed, following a process similar to that used for attorneys. Do you agree?
You might discuss the parallels to the medical model. For example, in some states nurses can "practice medicine" to some extent and even prescribe drugs. Should there be limited paralegal practice?

REVIEW QUESTIONS, page 14

1. Why does the study of law involve more than simply memorizing rules?
- **The list of rules is too long to be memorized.**
- **Law is ever changing and so the rules are changing.**
- **There may be no law that applies a to client's case.**
- **Every case is unique and you can't determine the answer without engaging in legal reasoning: applying law to the facts.**

2. What is legal reasoning?
Legal reasoning involves applying the law to the facts.

3. What is the doctrine of stare decisis and why is it important?
It means let the decision stand; *all things being equal* a court will decide the same way that courts have in the past by looking to precedent; it supplies stability as well as the ability to change.

4. Why is it important to know if a client's facts are analogous to or distinguishable from prior court decisions?
If they are analogous, then following stare decisis, a court will probably decide as courts have in the prior decisions. If they are distinguishable, a court need not decide as courts have in the prior decisions.

5. What is a cause of action? What does it mean to say that a person does not have a valid cause of action?
A cause of action is a claim based upon the law and facts sufficient to support a lawsuit. If a plaintiff does not have a valid cause of action, a court will not even listen to the facts of the case. If the does have a valid cause of action, the court will listen, and if it agrees with the plaintiff's view of the facts, then the plaintiff will recover.

6. Why does law change? Should it?
Law changes because societal views change. The students may express some concern that if law can change — where are the limits? This can lead into a discussion of how no one judge makes the law, the check by appellate courts, the federal versus state system, and the legislative branch. But without change, law would cease to serve us.

7. Why is there no one "right" answer to a legal problem?
There can be no one "right" answer because the job of lawyers and paralegals is to make their best prediction as to what a court will do. Until the court acts, there is no "right" answer. But even a court decision can be incorrect in a more global sense. And it is important to realize that even though there is no right answer, there are better and worse arguments.

8. Should it be the attorney or the paralegal who sings a letter that analyzes the law? Why?
The attorney must sign the letter, or it is the unauthorized practice of law.

9. What are the requirements for becoming an attorney? A paralegal?

Becoming a licensed attorney involves attaining a bachelor's degree (not required in all states, but most attorneys have one), a graduate legal education (normally three years if attending full-time or four years part-time), passing a state bar exam, and passing a morals/character check. In some states to practice law, attorneys must also join their state bar association and fulfill annual continuing education requirements. Unlike the qualifications for becoming an attorney, most states have no requirements for becoming a paralegal.

Chapter 2

Functions and
Sources of Law

Although most students will have heard of the various sources of the law, many will not really understand the differences among the various sources nor why those differences matter. For example, students often think that the United States Supreme Court always has the last say on all issues. That another source of law, the legislature, can amend a statute if it does not like the way the Court has interpreted it, is a novel concept that takes some getting used to. Also, although they have certainly heard of administrative regulations, they often to not know how agencies get their powers nor where administrative regulations fit in relation to statutory and case law.

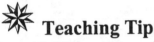 **Teaching Tip**

Page 15: The students will meet Diane Dobbs again in a later chapter so you may want to spend a bit of extra time going over her story.

A. Functions and Theories of Law, pages 16-19

If you are on a tight schedule, you may want to have the students just skim over this section. However, it is a good reference for when they later hear or read about various judicial philosophies.

If you would like to explore this topic in more depth with the students, one approach would be to give the students a more concrete feel for the legal realists approach by previewing with them the discussion they will be reading in Chapter 6 when we study statutory interpretation. There, we will see how, despite their best efforts, legislators often write statutes containing ambiguous language. For example, an ordinance forbidding vehicles on park pathways would clearly prohibit motorcycles. Would it also prohibit a six-year-old child from pushing her doll's carriage down the path? To answer that question, a judge would have to go beyond the precise language used and try to determine the purpose behind the statute. Therefore, the language alone cannot answer the problem.

A second point raised by the realists relates to the problem that often there is at least arguably more than one rule that could apply to a situation. For example, in Chapter 11, we include a case where the litigants asked the judge to resolve a case where a contractor had installed the wrong brand of pipes. In functionality, the pipes were identical with those requested in the contract, and by the time the mistake was found, the pipes were already encased within the walls. Therefore, their removal would mean the demolition of substantial parts of the completed structure. One rule of contract law states that the parties have a right to get what the contract states. If this rule were to be applied, the contractor would have to remove all of the pipes and replace them with the correct brand. However, another rule states that if the deviation from the contract requirements is insignificant, then the correct outcome would be to leave the pipes in place but to require that the contractor pay the difference in value between what was contracted for and what was received. The realists' response to this dilemma would be to acknowledge that one rule is no more "correct" than the other. To determine the just result, the judge must consider the consequences of choosing one rule over another.[1]

DISCUSSION QUESTIONS, pages 19-20

1. Do you agree with the statement "laws are necessary"? Many believe we have too many laws today. Do you agree? If you do, which laws should be eliminated? Do we need additional laws in some areas?

To get this discussion started, you could ask them what they would think about a law that outlawed smoking in all restaurants — places of work — everywhere. Another possibility is a law requiring everyone to wear a seat belt or a motorcycle helmet.

2. Can you think of ways, other than those mentioned in the text, that natural law theory has influenced the development of American law?

One example is the Preamble to the U.S. Constitution.

3. One of the basic principles of the natural law theory is that people should not have to obey and unjust law. Should it be left to the individual or to a judge to determine when a man-made law is unjust? If it is left to the judge, what criteria should the judge use?

Some argue that the Civil Rights movement would never have made the progress it did, if it had had to resort solely to the court system.

4. Which of the theories of jurisprudence discussed in the text do you think best explains how law should work?

The formalist approach is the theory that most closely parallels the doctrine of stare decisis. However, point out that many judges use a blend of theories.

5. Would you expect to hear a follower of natural law, legal positivism, legal realism, or Critical Legal Studies making the following statements?

    a. The killing of another human is wrong.

       Any of the theories might make this statement.

    b. The penalty for first degree murder is life imprisonment or death.

       A legal positivist.

---

[1]To learn how the court resolved this dilemma, see *Jacob & Youngs, Inc. v. Kent*, 230 N.Y. 239, 129 N.E. 889 (1921), excerpted beginning on page 394.

c. Studies have shown that a disproportionate number of minority men are sentenced to the death penalty.

Either a legal realist or someone from the Critical Legal Studies movement.

6. There is an old joke about a lawyer who was asked, "What is two plus two?" The lawyer responded, "What do you want it to be?" Which legal theory does this best exemplify? Is it necessarily a bad thing that we live in a world where two plus two does not always have to be four?

This exemplifies one of the beliefs of the legal realists, i.e., that the English language is sufficiently vague so as to allow for multiple interpretations. Therefore, it is more important to look to the consequences of any given result.

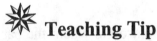 Teaching Tip

B. Sources of Law, pages 20-27

Page 21: I always find it worthwhile to spend some time retelling the story of how judicial review came to be. One approach is to spend some time (not a lot) letting them look for this power in the Constitution before telling the story.

Page 23: Contrast the breadth of scope of the statute, Title VII, with the narrow focus of the EEOC guideline, pages 24-25. Discuss the various elements of the EEOC guideline. Sexual harassment can consist of either:

1. sexual advances, or
2. requests for sexual favors, or
3. verbal conduct of a sexual nature, or
4. physical conduct of a sexual nature,

when any one of the following is present.

1. the behavior is made a term or condition of employment, or
2. submission or rejection of the conduct is used as a basis for employment decision, or
3. such conduct unreasonably interferes with work performance, or
4. such conduct creates an intimidating, hostile, or offensive working environment.

The first two types are what is known as quid pro quo discrimination. For Ms. Dobbs to have a claim she would first have to show that the physical conduct was of a sexual nature, and second, that it created an intimidating, hostile, or offensive working environment. As this was a one time incident, it would be difficult to prove the latter.

DISCUSSION QUESTIONS, page 27

7. Assume Congress enacted a statute making it a federal crime for "anyone" to kidnap children and take them across state lines. Assume further that the U.S. Supreme Court decided that the word *anyone* did not include a parent. If it wanted to do so, could Congress amend the statute to say that the word *anyone* does include parents? Why?

Yes, because Congress and not the courts has the last say on the meaning of legislation.

9

8. Assume Congress enacted a statute making it a federal crime to have an abortion. Assume further that the Supreme Court declared the statute to be unconstitutional as interfering with a woman's Constitutional right to privacy. If it wanted to do so, could the executive branch prosecute women for violating the statute? In other words, does Congress or the Supreme Court have the final word on what is Constitutional? Why?

The Supreme Court has the final say on what is constitutional because of the power of judicial review.

9. For each of the following, which source of law — a constitution, a statute, an administrative regulation, or a court opinion — would be best able to handle the problem and why?

    a. A requirement that all motorcycle riders wear helmets.

Statute — covers a general class of persons. Probably no need for the particularity that a regulation would give.

    b. A rule making a bar owner liable for any injuries caused by a patron to whom the bar sold drinks.

Statute or court rule; traditionally covered by common law tort law; if a statute, would probably also need regulations to cover each individual situation (size of bar, public versus private, etc.) so perhaps better left to courts to handle on a case by case basis.

    c. A rule that all semi-trailers traveling on interstate highways use concave mud flaps.

Probably a regulation as there are many details as to what vehicles travelling on interstate highways can and cannot do. Also, because the science of highway safety changes, it might be preferable to put these rules into a regulation that can be more easily updated than a statute.

    d. A requirement that employers not discriminate on the basis of religion or sexual orientation.

Statute as this governs a broad class of people, but would need to be fleshed out with regulations.

    e. A requirement that no more than a certain percentage of a known pollutant be released by factory smoke stacks.

Regulation as this will require a lot of detail as to the type of pollutant, and the regulations may need to change frequently as we learn more about pollutants.

    f. A question as to whether a person not wearing a seat belt should be able to recover for injuries that person sustained in an automobile accident that was not his fault.

Statute or court rule; traditionally has been handled by common law tort law but as it covers a broad category of people it could also be handled by legislation.

g. A law prohibiting government from interfering with an individual's right to freedom of speech.

Constitution as it goes to controlling the government's interference with our individual freedoms.

REVIEW QUESTIONS, page 29

1. What are the two primary functions of the U.S. Constitution?
First, to establish the organization of the government.
 -the three branches
 -federal versus state powers
Second, to protect us from governmental overreaching.

2. What is the power of judicial review, and why is it so important to our legal system?
Judicial review means that the courts have the final say on whether a statute is constitutional. This is important because many Constitutional provisions are ambiguous and without one source for authoritative interpretation, we would have chaos with all three branches conceivably having a different view of what the Constitution means.

3. Read the excerpts from the U.S. Constitution and the Bill of Rights located in Appendix A. Then answer the following questions.
 a. Which article deals specifically with the legislature? **Article I**
 With the executive? **Article II**
 With the judiciary? **Article III** (This may seem like trivia necessary only for Jeopardy contestants, but lawyers often refer to Article I, Article II, or Article III powers.)

 b. Which amendment states that the powers not specifically delegated to the federal government are reserved to the states?
 The Tenth Amendment

 c. Make a list of the rights protected by the first ten Amendments.
 First - No law respecting an establishment of religion; prohibiting free exercise of religion; abridging freedom of speech; abridging right to peaceably assemble or to petition the government.

 Second - Right to keep and bear arms.

 Third - Must consent to quartering solders in peace time.

 Fourth - No unreasonable search and seizures; warrants only upon probable cause.

 Fifth - Capital crimes require a grand jury indictment; no double jeopardy; no self-incrimination; due process of law required before deprivation of life, liberty or property; no taking of private property without just compensation.

Sixth - Right to a speedy trial; to a impartial jury; to be informed of the nature of the accusation; to be confronted by witnesses; to obtain witness; and to an attorney.

Seventh - Right to civil jury trials.

Eighth - No excessive bail; no cruel and unusual punishment.

Ninth - Retention of other rights not named.

Tenth - Rights reserved to the states and people.

4. Why do constitutions and statutes frequently include ambiguous language?
The possibilities include sloppy draftsmanship; the inability to anticipate future circumstances; and deliberate glossing over to avoid conflict.

5. How do courts become involved in the legislative process?
When a statute includes ambiguous language, it is the court's role to interpret it. If it does so in a way the legislature did not intend, the legislature can amend the statute.

6. Who has the final say as to what a statute means, the legislature or the courts?
The legislature has the final say.

7. Who has the final say as to the constitutionality of a statute, the legislature or the courts?
The courts have the final say.

8. How are statutes and administrative regulations similar? How do they differ?
They are similar in that they are forward looking, that is, they are meant to govern future conduct. They are different in that statutes are usually broader in scope and are enacted by legislatures. Regulations are promulgated by agencies.

9. Why are administrative agencies referred to as the fourth branch of government?
Administrative agencies are referred to as the fourth branch of government because they combine legislative, executive, and judicial functions.

10. What impact did the Norman Conquest have on the American legal system?
The Norman Conquest gave us French and Latin vocabulary. More importantly, it also established the common law system and the doctrine of stare decisis.

11. What is the common law?
The common law is court created law.

12. Why were equity courts created, and what special powers were they given?
Because litigants sometimes want something other than money damages, equity courts can order someone to do something or stop doing something (injunction) or to fulfill a contract (specific performance). Today most courts have both law and equity powers.

Chapter 3

Classification
of the Law

In the second part of this book, the students will be exposed to separate chapters on torts, contracts, property, and criminal law. Therefore, the purpose of this chapter is simply to give an overview of these areas.

 Teaching Tip

I usually begin the discussion by pointing out that clients are people, not entities to be boxed and categorized. Having said that, however, in order to understand their legal problems, the students have to become proficient in classifying their legal problems along the lines outlined in Figure 3-1, page 32.

In class discussion of this chapter I try to continually emphasize four themes:

1. that the concepts of a plaintiff needing to prove a prima facie case and the defendant needing to raise defenses are applicable no matter the specific area of the law;
2. the differences between civil and criminal law;
3. how some activities can be covered by both federal and state law, while others are governed exclusively by either federal or state law; and
4. how procedural issues often need to be resolved before anyone can even begin to discuss the substantive law issues.

DISCUSSION QUESTIONS, pages 37-38

1. For each question determine whether you think the law involved is federal, state, or both.
   a. A person is liable for slander if that person intentionally says that someone is a thief when she knows it is not true.
   State slander law but also governed by U.S. Constitutional provisions protecting freedom of speech.

   b. To be valid a contract for the sale of real estate must be in writing.
   State.

   c. Trucks traveling on interstate highways must be equipped with concave mud flaps.
   Federal — an example of preemption under the Interstate Commerce Clause.

d. No employer with ten or more employees may discriminate on the basis of race, color, religion, sex, or national origin.
State because Title VII only applies when there are fifteen or more employees. This is a good time to remind the students that no law can be a federal law unless Congress has the power under the Constitution to enact laws in that area. Presumably, an employer with fifteen or more employees will be engaging in activities that implicate interstate commerce and hence Congress has the power to regulate their activities.

e. A manufacturer of inherently dangerous products will be liable for any defective product that causes injury.
Currently, products liability law is predominately state law, but there are proposals to make at least some aspects of products liability laws national.

2. Can you think of areas of the law that are not now regulated on a federal level but should be?
Students will probably think of several examples, such as, seatbelt and anti-smoking laws.

3. Are there any areas of the law that you think should be left solely to the states?
Some students may think that those same areas discussed above should be left to the states because of a belief that impinging upon personal freedom — that is, the ability of each person to choose (for example, whether or not to smoke) should be left to the states to determine.

4. Should there be less variation in the law from one state to the next? Do the advantages of diversity outweigh the disadvantages?
Some interesting areas to discuss include gambling, divorce, and prostitution.

DISCUSSION QUESTIONS, page 42
5. What do you think of the differences between judges' and jurors' definitions of "beyond a reasonable doubt" and a "preponderance of the evidence? Do you think this causes any problems for our legal system?
The study quoted on page 39 did not show much of a disparity in how jurors and judges interpreted beyond a reasonable doubt. For civil cases, however, the study indicates that plaintiffs will have a much more difficult time convincing jurors than judges.

6. Take a moment to read the following Massachusetts statute regarding larceny.

Whoever steals . . . and with intent to steal . . . the property of another . . . shall be guilty of larceny . . . .[2]

a. Assume Alan got into a car, knowing that it is not his, "hot wired" it, and then drove off in it. Is he guilty of violating the statute? Why?
Yes, because Alan had the requisite bad intent and did the requisite bad act.

b. Assume Bill approached a car that he intended to steal, but he was scared away by a passerby. Is he guilty of violating the statute? Why?
No, although Bill did have bad intent, he never committed the act.

c. Assume Charles got into a car, thinking he was getting into his friend's car, "hot wired" it, but only meant to borrow it. Is he guilty of violating the statute? Why?
No, Charles did not have the intent to steal. However, he might be guilty of violating some other statute. (Note: that someone could have done something "wrong" and still not be guilty of violating a particular statute is a difficult concept for beginning students to grasp. It reassures them if you let them know that while he cannot be found guilty of this particular crime because its specific elements were not satisfied, there may be another statute that covers his situation. This is also a great time to illustrate for them why it is that law changes. For example, as criminals find new ways of doing "bad" things, the legislature is forced to enact new crimes to cover those situations. A good example is the first time a court was faced with someone stealing computer time and had to find that person not guilty of larceny as larceny was defined as the theft of tangible personal property.)

DISCUSSION QUESTIONS, page 47-48

7. For each question, decide if the facts raise an issue of tort, contract, or property law or more than one area of law.

a. You buy a new car. Two days later as you are driving, the brakes fail, and you go off the road, hitting a telephone pole. Luckily you are unhurt, but the car is badly damaged.
Tort — negligence or strict liability.
Contract law — breach of warranty.

b. You rent an apartment. One night as you are leaving the building through the central stairway, the railing gives way, and you fall down breaking your leg.
Tort — negligence because arguably the landlord acted unreasonably.
Contract — because it involves a lease.
Property — traditionally this has come under landlord-tenant law.

---

[2] Mass. Gen. Laws ch. 266, § 30.

16

8. For each of the following situations, decide if you think liability should be found based on an intentional tort, negligence, strict liability or whether no liability should be found.

a. Sally was angry with Martha. One night after leaving class, she deliberately drove her car into the side of Martha's car.
Intentional tort.

b. One night after leaving class, Sally was in a hurry. When she arrived at the stop sign at the end of the student parking lot entrance to Main Street, she did a "rolling stop." Martha was driving by on Main Street. Sally's auto hit the side of Martha's car.
Negligence.

c. One night after leaving class, Sally got into her brand new Dodge van. When she arrived at the stop sign at the end of the student parking lot entrance to Main Street, she pressed on the brakes, but nothing happened. Martha was driving by on Main Street. Sally's auto hit the side of Martha's car.
Strict liability against manufacturer; no liability against Sally.

d. One night after leaving class, Sally got into her car. When she arrived at the stop sign at the end of the student parking entrance to Main Street, she suddenly got a tremendous cramp in her side and momentarily lost control of her car. Martha was driving by on Main Street. Sally's auto hit the side of Martha's car.
No liability, unless had similar episodes in past and had taken no precautions.

DISCUSSION QUESTION, p. 49
9. Review the hypothetical case that began Chapter 2. How would you categorize Diane's legal problems?
Substantive versus Procedural
   No obvious procedural issues.

State versus Federal
   Could be both state and federal laws regarding her firing if based on discriminatory grounds.

Civil versus Criminal
   Tort of battery; also crime of battery - touching her
   Tort of conversion and crime of larceny - keeping her possessions

REVIEW QUESTIONS, pages 49-50
1. What are the three major ways in which attorneys categorize the law?
Attorneys categorize the law as state or federal, procedural or substantive, and criminal or civil.

2. What is the difference between substantive and procedural law?
Substantive law governs our legal rights and duties. Procedural law governs how the legal system operates.

3. In terms of the type of harm caused, what is the difference between civil and criminal law?
Civil law deals with personal harm. Criminal law deals with harm against society.

4. What is federalism?
Under federalism, the authority to govern is split between a national and regional (state) governments.

5. True or false: Every state must have the same laws regarding gambling? Why?
False. If an area is not given to the federal government by the Constitution, the states are free to regulate in that area. (Have the students take a look at the Tenth Amendment in Appendix A.)

6. What does it mean to say that the federal government is a government of limited powers?
The federal government is a government of limited powers because unless the federal Constitution gives the federal government the power to do something, that power is reserved to the states under the Tenth Amendment.

7. Do you think Congress could (not should) enact a national divorce statute? Why?
Congress could not enact a national divorce statute because nothing in the Constitution gives it power to do so. Be sure to discuss *United States v. Lopez* and *United States v. Morrison,* on pages 35-36, with your students.

8. Why are some areas of the law preempted by the federal government?
Some areas are preempted because there is a need for uniformity among the states. One example is the use of concave versus convex mud flaps on trucks traveling on interstate highways.

9. Name at least four ways in which civil law differs from criminal law.
(See Figure 3-2, page 39)
- **Type of Harm: private injury versus societal harm**
- **Names of the Parties: plaintiff/defendant versus state/defendant**
- **Party who brings the claim: an individual versus the state**
- **Standard of Proof: preponderance of the evidence versus beyond a reasonable doubt**
- **Judgment: liable/not liable versus guilty/not guilty**
- **Remedies: damages/injunction versus imprisonment/fines/death**
- **Source of law: common law/statutes versus statutes**

10. When is the burden of proof "beyond a reasonable doubt" and when is it "a preponderance of the evidence"? What is the difference between them?
In civil cases you use a preponderance of the evidence — more likely than not.
In criminal cases you use beyond a reasonable doubt — no reasonable doubt in the jurors' minds. This does not mean there can be no doubt.

11. In a civil case if a jury is evenly split, leaning equally toward the plaintiff's and the defendant's views of the facts, who will win, the plaintiff or the defendant? Why?
If the jury is evenly divided, the defendant will prevail because to win the plaintiff must convince the jury that its version of the facts is more likely than the defendant's view.

12. What two basic elements must be established for the government to prove the prima facie case in a criminal case?
The two basic elements of every criminal case are mens rea and actus reus.

13. Why can the same act constitute several different crimes?
Because the same act can be accompanied by different states of mind, it can constitute different crimes. A good example is the killing of another (the act) with differing levels of intent — such as, purposefully versus recklessly.

14. What are the two basic defenses to a criminal action?
Some defenses justify the act while others negate the intent.

15. In a criminal case does the government or the defendant present its case first? Why?
The government goes first because if it cannot prove its prima facia case, the defendant must be found not guilty. Defendants are presumed innocent.

16. What is the general definition of a civil cause of action?
A civil cause of action is a claim that based upon the law and the facts is sufficient to demand judicial action.

17. In a civil case does the plaintiff or the defendant present its case first? Why?
The plaintiff goes first because it must first show that it has a valid cause of action. If it cannot, it will lose before the defendant has to present its case.

18. What are the three types of damages available in a civil case?
Civil damages include compensatory, punitive, and nominal.

19. In addition to damages, what might a plaintiff seek in a civil case?
In addition to damages, a plaintiff might seek an injunction or specific performance.

20. What must be present for a contract to be valid?
Every valid contract must consist of an offer, acceptance, and consideration.

21. What is the basic difference between a contract and a gift?
A gift is one sided; a contract requires something of value passing between both parties.

22. What are the three main areas of tort law?
The three main areas of tort law are intentional, negligence, and strict liability.

23. Give the general definition of negligence, and list the elements necessary to prove a prima facie case.
Negligence is the failure to act as a reasonable person under the circumstances. The elements are duty, breach, cause, and harm.

24. What are the main defenses to negligence?
The main defenses to negligence are contributory negligence (comparative negligence) and assumption of the risk.

Chapter 4

Structure of the Court System

Besides introducing students to the concept of separate federal and state court systems, in this chapter I like to emphasize that in every case there are two separate questions. One is: What law, federal or state, governs this case? The second is: What court, federal or state, will hear this case? The students tend to see these as the same question. To dramatize the difference, I often start class by drawing a heavy vertical line down the middle of the blackboard. Then on the left I write — State or Federal Law? — and remind them that is what we just discussed in the last chapter. Then on the right-hand side of the board, I write — State or Federal Court? I then tell them that just because something, for example, is under State Law on the left-hand side of the board that does not mean it automatically goes under State Court on the right-hand side of the board. As a class, we then go through a series of examples that illustrates how the answer on one side of the board impacts on the choice of board on the other side of the board.

DISCUSSION QUESTIONS, pages 55-56
1. Do you think it is a good or bad idea that only questions of law can be appealed?
Generally, this is viewed as a good idea because otherwise you would need to retry the whole case at the appellate level: re-examining witnesses, introducing evidence, etc. This would duplicate the trial court's efforts. Also, it would undercut the jury system if appellate courts could second guess juries.

2. Can you think of a situation when an appellate judge might reverse and remand a case? When a judge might reserve but not remand a case?
An appellate court would reverse and remand a case if evidence was introduced that should not have been admitted so that the case can be retried without that evidence. However, the court might simply reverse if the trial judge's interpretation of the underlying law was wrong. For example, if the appellate court thought that undercover officers buying the same drug they had sold to the defendant was entrapment, there would be no reason for a new trial, and the court would simply reverse the conviction.

3. It is not always easy to know when something is a question of fact or a question of law. In fact, there have been cases when the issue on appeal was whether something was a question of fact or a question of law. That question is itself a question of law. To see how that can happen, assume that there was a negligence trial in which a grocer was sued when a customer slipped and fell. The customer testified that she slipped on a banana peel in the produce

section. The grocery store owner testified that when he came to the assistance of the customer, there was no peel on the floor. One of the store employees also testified that he had mopped the floor in that area just five minutes before the accident and that there were no banana peels on the floor. Nonetheless, the jury found the store liable. Can the store appeal on the grounds that it was telling the truth and the customer was lying? Why? Can the store appeal on the grounds that the jury should not have found it acted negligently because even if there was a banana peel, such hazards are to be expected in the produce section and the store had done all it could to make the area safe? Is that issue — that is, whether the store acted as a reasonable store should — a question of fact or a question of law?

You cannot appeal on the basis of who was lying because that is a question of fact. Whether the store acted reasonably could be seen as either a question of fact — that is, what did they do, or a question of law — that is, what should any reasonable store would do.

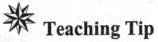 **Teaching Tip**

Page 60: U.S. Supreme Court picture
I always spend some time discussing the various Court members. This helps to bring the Court and its work to life.

DISCUSSION QUESTIONS, page 61
4. Why do you think the framers of the Constitution chose to give federal judges lifetime tenure and to protect them from salary reduction? Do you think that was a wise decision?
They gave federal judges lifetime tenure and protected them from salary reduction so that the political process could not influence their decision making. If judges do not take their responsibilities seriously, theoretically this could become a problem.

5. Do you think it is appropriate that the Supreme Court hears no more than 200 of the approximately 4,000 requests it receives each year? What criteria should the Court use in deciding which cases it will hear?
Obviously, the Court could not hear 4,000 cases every year and still have the time to give serious consideration to each case. In any case, it should be the primary job of the lower courts to resolve most disputes. On the other hand, because the Court denies certiorari in most case, that does deprive litigants of a final decision by the Supreme Court.

DISCUSSION QUESTION, pages 66-67
6. For each of these situations determine whether you think the matter should be heard in state or federal *court*. Also, decide whether you think a court would apply state or federal *law*.
    a.   A wife wants to divorce her husband.
       State court and state law.

b. Martha, a Massachusetts resident, wants to sue Susan, a Massachusetts resident, for $80,000 based on breach of contract.
State court and state law.

c. Sam, a Massachusetts resident, wants to sue Jill, a Vermont resident, for $80,000 based on breach of contract.
State or federal court (diversity jurisdiction) and state law.

d. A teacher in a public school wants to challenge a state law requiring all teachers to start each day of class with a minute of silent prayer.
State or federal court (federal question). Because the state law was challenged as unconstitutional under the federal constitution, both federal and state law apply.

REVIEW QUESTIONS, pages 68-69

1. What are the two basic functions of trial courts?
To ascertain the facts and apply the law.

2. What is the difference between questions of law and questions of fact? Why is it important to know the difference?
Questions of fact relate to what happened. Questions of law relate to how the law should be interpreted or how the trial should be conducted. Only questions of law can be appealed.

3. Give an example of a question of fact that might arise during a murder trial. Give an example of a question of law that might arise in that same trial.
Questions of fact — was the defendant at the scene of the crime; did the defendant kill the victim. Questions of law — should certain evidence, such as DNA evidence, be admitted.

4. What is the difference between a bench and a jury trial?
A bench trial is without a jury so that the judge acts as both the fact finder and the interpreter of the law.

5. What will an appellate court usually do if it finds that the trial court made a harmless error?
Let the trial court decision stand.

6. What is the difference between reversing and remanding a case?
Reversing is to change the lower court decision. Remanding is to send the case back to the trial court for further proceedings.

7. What is the difference between a dissenting and a concurring opinion?
A dissenting opinion disagrees with the result and reasoning. A concurring opinion agrees with the result but not with the reasoning.

8. List the major differences between trial and appellate courts.
(See Figure 4-1, p. 55)
- **Names of the parties: plaintiff/defendant versus appellant or petitioner/appellee or respondent.**
- **Who decides: judge or judge and jury versus panel of judges**
- **Attorney arguments are heard in both.**
- **There is no witness testimony nor evidence introduced on appeal.**
- **Questions of law and fact are decided by trial courts; only questions of law by appellate courts.**

9. In the federal court system what names are given to
   a. the highest appellate court,
      Supreme Court
   b. the intermediate appellate court, and
      Courts of Appeals
   c. the trial courts?
      District Courts

10. Look at the map in Figure 4-3. How many district courts are there in your state? In which circuit is your state located?
Answer will vary based on state.

11. If you hear that "cert." has been denied in a case, what does that mean?
Denial of cert. means that four of the Supreme Court justices have not agreed to hear the case. It does not mean that they agree with the lower court ruling; simply that they do not want to hear the case.

12. In the federal system, what are the "inferior courts"?
The inferior courts are the courts of appeals and the district courts.

13. Describe a typical state court system. Find out how our court system is similar to or different from the "typical" state system.
A typical system has trial courts of both general and limited jurisdiction, an intermediate appellate court, and a highest appellate court.

14. True or false: In every state the highest appellate court is called the supreme court.
False. For example, in New York, the trial courts are called the supreme courts.

15. Jurisdiction refers to the power a court has to hear a case. Define each of the following types of jurisdiction:
   a. general jurisdiction,
      Can hear any type of case

   b. limited jurisdiction,
      Can only hear certain types of cases

c. original jurisdiction,
   Hears cases for the first time

d. appellate jurisdiction,
   Reviews actions of other courts

e. exclusive jurisdiction, and
   Only court that can hear that type of case

f. concurrent jurisdiction.
   Two or more courts have the power to hear the case

16. What are the two major grounds for gaining federal court jurisdiction?
The two major grounds for gaining federal court jurisdiction are federal question and diversity jurisdiction.

Chapter 5

Civil Litigation and Its Alternatives

If your students will be taking at least one other course in the principles of litigation, you may want to touch on this chapter only lightly. However, for your students to be able to understand the procedural history of the cases they will be reading in this book, the following concepts are particularly important:

1. the purposes and differences between motions to dismiss and summary judgment motions; and

2. state versus federal court jurisdiction.

DISCUSSION QUESTIONS, page 75

In Mr. Drake's case, assume that Massachusetts courts have allowed mothers and fathers to recover in situations similar to that experienced by Mr. Drake but have never spoken about whether they would extend the rule to allow recovery by grandparents. Several other states, however, that have directly confronted this issue, have ruled against grandparents. The most common reason for not allowing recovery is the fear that to do so would encourage people to bring too many potentially frivolous lawsuits.

1. With that as the legal precedent, do you think Mr. Drake's attorney should feel any concern in signing her name to the complaint? Why?
No, this would be a "nonfrivolous argument for the extension . . . of existing law."

2. Which language do you prefer: "that to the best of his knowledge, information, and belief there is good ground to support" the claim or "that to the best of the person's knowledge, information, and belief, formed after an inquiry reasonable under the circumstances," the claim is warranted. Why?
The first is more of a subjective standard. The second would seem to require more action on the attorney's part.

3. Assume Mary was injured in an automobile accident while vacationing in California. Joe was driving the car that hit her. Mary is a resident of Michigan. Joe is a resident of Florida. In which state(s) may Mary bring suit? Why?

In California — where the accident happened.

In Florida — where the defendant lives.

4. For years the federal courts have been trying to persuade Congress to eliminate diversity jurisdiction. Do you think that would be a wise decision? What purpose do you suppose diversity jurisdiction was originally meant to serve? If diversity jurisdiction is maintained, should it be tied to any jurisdiction amount, and if so, how much? Why?

Originally diversity jurisdiction was meant to protect citizens of one state from the prejudices of a state court in another state. Many argue this protection is no longer needed and that the best arbiter of state law is the state courts. Eliminating diversity jurisdiction would also lighten the case load of the federal courts.

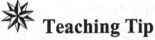 Teaching Tip

Page 80, Figure 5-3: I find it very helpful to either draw this figure on the board or to put it up on an overhead. Students have little trouble understanding the function of the complaint and answer, but tend to get a bit lost with cross-claims and counterclaims. This gives them a very visual method to see who uses which pleading and against whom.

5. Does it seem fair to you that plaintiffs should be allowed to plead in the alternative? Why?

The main argument in favor of allowing plaintiffs to argue in the alternative is that at the pleading stage it is too early to limit the plaintiff's options. For example, until a plaintiff's attorney completes discovery in a motor vehicle accident case, that attorney may not even know for sure who was driving the car, or whether the behavior was negligent, reckless, or even intentional.

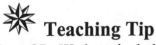 Teaching Tip

Page 87: We have included a number of the Rules of Civil Procedure verbatim because we think it is very important to impress on students the need to know and follow the Rules. I always spend a fair amount of time going over Rule 12 and comparing and contrasting it to a summary judgment motion.

DISCUSSION QUESTIONS, page 93

6. If expense and time were not obstacles, would you prefer to use interrogatories or depositions? Why?

Many prefer to use depositions because they elicit the deponent's and not the attorney's response. They are more spontaneous and the attorney is able to follow up on areas of questioning as the need develops.

7. Some have likened the current discovery process to a guessing game whereby one side tries to guess what information the other side has and attempts to ferret it out through the clever use of interrogatories and depositions. Do you think the system would work better if all parties were automatically required to hand over all relevant information at the beginning of the lawsuit? Do you think that would be a workable system? A fair system? Recently the federal rules were amended to require automatic disclosure in certain circumstances. The change is contained in Rule 26(a)(1). It is too early to tell if the attempt to increase voluntary cooperation among attorneys will be successful.

There is the problem of not always knowing what information the other side will need. Therefore, it may create an extra burden on each party to guess what the other party will want. On the other hand, it should speed up discovery, at least in routine cases.

8. If you were doing the discovery plan for Mr. Drake, what methods of discovery would you prefer? Why? Would your answer change if you were representing Mrs. Small? Why?

This should lead into a general discussion of the types and purposes of the various forms of discovery.

DISCUSSION QUESTIONS, page 96

9. Many people argue that life and lawsuits have become too complex for the average juror. For example, how can anyone but an economist understand the intricacies of an antitrust lawsuit or anyone but a computer expert comprehend the concept of reverse engineering? Do you think there are certain types of lawsuits where the jury should be composed only of experts in that field? Should jury trials be eliminated entirely in some areas of the law?

This raises the issue of who is "a jury of your peers" when experts are on trial or when the issues involved require expert knowledge.

10. When litigants have sufficient money, they often hire jury experts, people who specialize in studying the characteristics of various groups. The theory is that certain types of people will be more likely, for example, in a medical malpractice case to lean towards the doctor, while others will favor the patient. Can you think of any groups that you could characterize in this way? Do you think this is a valid approach to choosing a jury? Even if valid, should it be used?

Studies indicate that jury experts are of assistance. Perhaps it is just an extreme case of challenging for cause, but the cause may be too subtle to name.

11. Do you agree with the rule that only experts should be allowed to state their opinions? What should it matter if a witness who saw Mrs. Small stumble just before she entered her car and testifies that "Mrs. Small was drunker than a skunk"?

Yes, because only experts are trained to reach conclusions.

12. One of the all-time famous leading questions is "So, when did you stop beating your wife"? What is the problem with asking your witness this type of question during direct examination?

The problem is that there is no way to answer it, and it presupposes facts not in evidence.

13. If two disputants want to settle their differences other than by going to court, what options do they have?

They can use mediation, arbitration, summary jury trial, or traditional out-of-court settlement.

14. If you were involved in a dispute, which alternative dispute resolution method would you prefer?

The answer will depend on whether the students want the decision to substitute for the judge's decision as in binding arbitration, or whether they simply want to see if they can first voluntarily reach a compromise through mediation, with the option of still going to court otherwise.

15. Do you think either mediation or arbitration would be appropriate in Mr. Drake's case? Why?

Mediation might be appropriate if the parties agree on negligence, but simply need help determining the amount of damages.

REVIEW QUESTIONS, pages 118-19

1. What are the three basic stages to civil litigation?

The three basic stages to civil litigation are pretrial, trial, and appeal.

2. What rules govern civil litigation in federal courts?

The rules that govern civil litigation in federal courts are the Federal Rules of Civil Procedure.

3. What issues have to be considered in deciding who should be sued?

The issues to consider in deciding who to sue include whether the defendant is judgment proof; whether the defendant is capable of being sued; whether there is compulsory joinder.

4. How does a class action lawsuit differ from one brought by and on behalf of one individual?

In a class action suit a named individual represents a group of people similarly injured.

5. If someone says that a particular court does not have jurisdiction over a lawsuit, what is meant by that?

It does not have power to hear the case.

6. What is the difference between subject matter jurisdiction and personal jurisdiction?

Subject matter jurisdiction relates to the power of the court to hear that type of case. Personal jurisdiction relates to the power of the court to force a person to appear before it.

7. What is the purpose of requiring litigants to first exhaust their administrative remedies?

The purpose is to conserve the court's time by letting an expert agency try to deal with the problem first.

8. What is the purpose of each of the following pleadings:
   a. the complaint,
      states the allegations that form the basis of the plaintiff's complaint
   b. the answer,
      forms the defendant's response
   c. a counterclaim,
      a counter-suit by the defendant against the plaintiff
   d. a cross-claim, and
      defendants or plaintiffs suing each other
   e. a third party claim?
      a suit by a defendant against someone not originally a party.

9. Under the federal rules what three items must be included in a complaint?

Rule 8 requires a jurisdictional statement, a short and plain statement of the claim showing that the pleader is entitled to relief, and demand for judgment.

10. What is a caption?

The caption is the section at the top of a pleading that identifies the court, the parties, and the docket number.

11. Who must sign all pleadings? Why?

An attorney (or if a person is proceeding without an attorney, by that person) must sign all pleadings. Otherwise it is the unauthorized practice of law.

12. What is the purpose of a summons?

The purpose of the summons is to o notify the defendant of the complaint and to alert the defendant to the time within which he or she has to respond.

13. What is the danger to the defendant in failing to answer a complaint?

The danger is having a default judgment entered against him or her.

14. What are the five basic ways that a defendant can respond to a complaint, and what is the purpose of each?

1. Deny the facts to undercut the claim.

2. Assert that the facts do not provide the plaintiff with a remedy.

3. Raise an affirmative defense to completely eliminate the plaintiff's claim or at least to reduce damages.

4. Allege there are procedural defects; if they are substantial, they could result in the complaint being dismissed.

5. Countersue or bring in another defendant.

15. What are the grounds for a 12(b)(6) motion, and what is its purpose?

The grounds for a 12(b)(6) motion are failure to state a claim upon which relief can be granted. Its purpose is to avoid a trial if there is no way that the trial court can legitimately find for the plaintiff even assuming all of the facts in the complaint are true.

16. What is the difference between a 12(b)(6) motion and a summary judgment motion?

The main difference is that in summary judgment you can look to documents other than the pleadings. Also, plaintiffs as well as defendants can bring summary judgment motions.

17. What is the main goal of discovery?

The main goal of discovery is to help each side find out as much information as possible to fairly evaluate the case and aid in settlement.

18. What are interrogatories and depositions, and how do they differ?

Both interrogatories and depositions are discovery tools. Interrogatories are written questions that can only be sent to the other party. Depositions are oral examinations of parties or nonparties.

19. Besides interrogatories and depositions, what are the main discovery tools available to the parties?

Other discovery tools include requests for admissions, requests for documents, and requests for physical examinations.

20. What is the purpose of a pretrial conference?

The purpose of the pretrial conference is to focus the issues before trial and to encourage the parties to agree to matters not in dispute; if possible, to encourage settlement.

21. What is the function of the jury?

The jury determines the facts and applies the law to those facts.

22. What is a voir dire, and what is its purpose?

The voir dire is the questioning of the jury to determine if anyone is unfit to serve as a juror in that particular case.

23. What are the differences between challenges for cause and peremptory challenges, and what is the function of each?
Challenges for cause are unlimited and the purpose is to exclude biased jurors. Peremptory challenges are limited in number and their purpose is to allow the attorneys the opportunity to exclude jurors without giving a reason.

24. What do attorneys hope to accomplish in their opening statements?
In their opening statements, attorneys hope to outline the evidence for the jurors and to convince them to see the evidence in the light most favorable to their client.

25. Who presents its evidence first, the plaintiff or the defendant, and why?
The plaintiff presents its evidence first because the plaintiff has the burden of proof. If the plaintiff does not meet that burden, at the close of the plaintiff's case, the defendant can move for a directed verdict.

26. When can either side move for a directed verdict? What is the purpose of that motion?
Either side can move for a directed verdict when the other side has not met its burden of proof. Its purpose is to end the trial in favor of the moving party.

27. What is the difference between a verdict and a judgment?
A jury brings in a verdict; a judge announces the judgment.

28. What is the difference between the motion for a judgment notwithstanding the verdict (a judgment N.O.V.) and a motion for a new trial? Give an example of when each could be used.
The motion for a judgment notwithstanding the verdict, also known as a judgment N.O.V. (judgment non obstante veredicto), is a request to the judge to reverse the jury's decision on the basis that the evidence was legally insufficient to support its verdict. If the judge grants the motion, the case is over, and the moving party has won. For example, in a negligence case, if the plaintiff's attorney forgot to introduce evidence of causation, the defendant could move for a jundment N.O.V.

An attorney usually bases the motion for a new trial on the assertion that some procedural error has tainted the outcome. The losing party might argue, for example, that some piece of evidence was admitted that should not have been admitted or that someone made improper contacts with a juror on the case. If the court grants the motion, the case has to be retried.

29. Describe the limitations on a litigant's right to appeal.
Usually there is only one right to appeal. An appeal must be based on a legal issue first raised in the trial court.

30. What is the difference between a harmless error and a reversible error?
A harmless error will not cause the appellate court to reverse the trial court. A reversible error will.

31. Why must some disputes to be taken to an administrative agency before going to court?
Some disputes must be taken first to an administrative agency to let an expert agency try to deal with the problem first and to conserve the court's time.

32. What is the difference between an adjudicatory hearing and a rulemaking hearing?
An adjudicatory hearing is like a trial. A rulemaking hearing is like a legislative hearing.

33. How does an administrative hearing differ from a civil trial?
An administrative hearing is much less formal than a trial. The rules of evidence are not strictly followed, and the participants may represent themselves or be represented by a nonlawyer.

34. What is contained in a typical administrative agency decision?
The following are included in a typical administrative agency decision: an evaluation of the evidence, the findings section, the decision.

35. What are the most common forms of ADR, and how do they differ from each other?
The two most common forms are mediation and arbitration. The main difference is that mediation is usually voluntary (although in some courts, especially family courts, it is increasingly becoming court ordered prior to trial) and the parties do not have to accept the recommendation of the mediator. The mediator's role is principally to act as a neutral third party to help the parties reach a mutually acceptable resolution. Arbitration is often mandated, the arbiter reaches a decision, and the parties must abide by it.

36. What do the proponents of ADR see as the advantages of ADR over traditional litigation?
The proponents of ADR argue that ADR saves time and avoids at least some of the expenses associated with going to court. Also, hopefully the parties will feel better about a solution they helped to work out as opposed to a court imposed remedy.

37. Describe the different styles of mediation and the types of situations for which each style might be most appropriate.
The facilitative model is more nondirective. The facilitative mediator does not give legal advice, provide an opinion as to the relative value of the parties' positions, or make predictions. The facilitative mediator does not propose any particular solution. This approach might be best when the parties will have an ongoing relationship with each other, such as in a case of a dispute over child custody.

The evaluative mediator is more likely to voice both legal and personal opinions and may try to encourage the parties to reach an agreement that the mediator thinks is in their best interests. This style may be more appropriate in meditations between strangers who will have few future dealings with each other, such as in the case of an automobile accident.

Chapter 6

Finding and Interpreting Statutory Law

In the text, we present statutory analysis before case analysis for three reasons. First, it is easier for students to find the elements of a rule when it is in statutory form that it is when it is in a case holding. Second, we want to encourage students to think creatively and critically about rules before turning to the courts for their interpretation. Finally, statutory analysis also offers a more straight-forward deductive model making the teaching of the IRAC method easier than when it is applied to a series of case holdings.

Legal Reasoning Exercise, page 133

1. Before the enactment of the following statute, under the common law a married woman was not allowed to sue in her own name. Instead the lawsuit was brought in her husband's name. Assume you have a client who wishes to sue her spouse for negligence. Read the statute. Do you think she will be able to sue her husband? Why?

> Mass. Gen. Laws ch. 209, § 6
> A married woman may sue and be sued in the same manner as if she were sole; but this section shall not authorize suits between husband and wife.

Under the plain language approach, "shall not authorize" could mean prohibit. Also, this is a statute in derogation of the common law, so it should be narrowly construed and hence not be seen as allowing suits. But the statute also states that "this section" shall not authorize, so perhaps the legislature was simply silent on the issue and will leave it to the courts to resolve it. (Or students may suggest that although this section does not authorize it, maybe another does.) It is also remedial in purpose, and so should be broadly construed, thereby allowing suits.

Legal Reasoning Exercises, pages 136-37

2. Assume John shipped obscene phonograph records from Massachusetts to California. He has been charged with violating a federal criminal statute that prohibits interstate shipment of any obscene "book, pamphlet, picture, motion-picture film, paper, letter, writing, print or other matter of indecent character." Has he violated the statute?

Following the canon of ejusdem generis, you could argue that the items should be limited to matters of the same class. Here everything in the statute relates to visual media, not sound and so phonograph records should not be included. Also, following the canon of

strictly construing criminal statutes, you would not include it. However, when looking at a list, another rule of statutory construction states that the members of that list are only examples and are not meant to be exclusive. Following that canon would mean that you could include phonograph records.

3. Assume Gary knowingly transported a stolen airplane from Illinois to Oklahoma. He is charged with violating the following federal statute:

National Motor Vehicle Theft Act, 18 U.S.C. § 408

> Sec. 2. That when used in this Act: (a) The term "motor vehicle" shall include an automobile, automobile truck, automobile wagon, motor cycle, or any other self-propelled vehicle not designed for running on rails;
>
> Sec. 3. That whoever shall transport or cause to be transported in interstate or foreign commerce a motor vehicle, knowing the same to have been stolen, shall be punished by a fine of not more than $5,000, or by imprisonment of no more than five years, or both.

Do you think Gary should be found guilty? Why?

First break the statute into its elements:

1: Section 3 - Transport or cause to be transported

2:   in interstate or foreign commerce

3:   a motor vehicle

4:   knowing the same to have been stolen

Section 2 - says "motor vehicle" includes "any other self-propelled vehicle not designed for running on rails."

The plain meaning approach suggests something running on the ground, and because it is a criminal statute, we should strictly construe it. Therefore, the conviction should be reversed. However, if the intent of Congress was to have the statute apply to any means of transportation, then the conviction should stand.

4. On the basis of the U.S. Supreme Court's decision in the *Caminetti* case, which, if any of the following situations would be found to be in violation of the Mann Act?

> a. A man drives a woman, whom he knows to be a prostitute, from Los Angeles to Las Vegas. The man receives no compensation for his providing this transportation, nor does he receive any share of any money she makes as a prostitute. He took her as a favor to a friend and to have someone to talk to on the trip.
> **No, because he is not transporting her for an "immoral purpose."**

> b. A man drives his girlfriend from Newark, New Jersey, to New York City so that she can perform a striptease number at a stag party.
> **Yes, if a striptease act is an "immoral purpose."**

> c. A man picks up his girlfriend in Sacramento, California, and drives her to Seattle, Washington, where they cohabit without getting married.
> **Yes, this is basically the same facts as *Caminetti*.**

5. For Sarah's case develop a chart, listing each element and the arguments you could make under each for Sarah and the restaurant. For each issue, reach a conclusion. Finally, decide whether you think the restaurant would have a valid defense to detaining Sarah.

Whether statute applies to restaurants

Yes - Merchant could mean anyone in the business of selling; here food is for sale.

No -   **Unlike a grocery store, it is hard to conceal food in a restaurant.**
   The statute's purpose probably is to protect stores where it is difficult for clerks to watch what is happening everywhere.

Detained in a reasonable manner

Yes - Needed to physically restrain her as she was leaving restaurant.
   Held on to her only momentarily.

No - Grabbed her with such force as to break her purse strap.
   Done in front of customers.
   Accused her of stealing.

Reasonable length of time

Yes - Only detained her for five minutes.
   Even allowing for picking up purse contents, was there for less than 1/2 hour.

No - Because she had to search for purse contents, stayed for twenty-five minutes.

Reasonable grounds to believe was attempting to commit larceny

Yes - Money was hidden by napkin.
   Was headed for the door.
   Had not yet received bill.

No - Friend was still at the table.

6. Assume Carl Clay has been charged with burglary. Briefly the facts are as follows:
     Last Friday Carl was watching As the Word Turns, his favorite soap opera, when suddenly the TV screen went blank. Nothing he could do would cause it to work. Unfortunately Carl did not have enough money to buy a new set. He decided to help himself to someone else's.
     He drove to the nearby Sleep Well Motel because he knew that they had recently purchased new 19" TVs. When he got to the motel around 5:00 P.M., he waited in his car until he saw a lady leave her room, ice bucket in hand. She had left the door to her room slightly ajar. Carl quickly ran to the door, opened it, and saw the TV. He went over to the TV, unplugged it, and picked it up. He was about to leave when the woman unexpectedly returned. Knowing karate, she felled him on the spot and then called the office manager, who, in turn, called the police. The TV, which was purchased for $600

and had a resale price of approximately $400, was returned to its rightful place in the room.

Carl has been charged with violating the following statutes:

> General Laws, ch. 228, § 1
> Burglary is defined as the breaking and entering of a dwelling at nighttime with the intent to commit a felony therein.

> General Laws, ch. 228, § 2
> Theft of personal property over the value of $500 is a felony. Theft of personal property of a value less than $500 is a misdemeanor.

a. Develop a chart listing the elements of each statute.
b. For each element, determine whether the facts raise an issue.
c. For each issue, list arguments that both Carl's attorney and the prosecution would raise. Reach a conclusion on each issue.
d. Do you think Carl can be convicted of burglary?

There are two issues: first, was there a burglary which depends partly on second, whether there was intent to commit a theft of personal property over the value of $500. There are four sub-issues to the first issue: breaking; dwelling; nighttime; and theft.

First discuss with the students whether there was an intent to commit a theft, because if there was not, then there can be no burglary. Explain to the students that you do not necessarily discuss statutes or sections in the order they are listed in the statute. I find that it is very helpful to put the following outline on the board as it is developed through classroom discussion. Start off with just the elements listed. Then as you go along, fill in the facts that they think support either side of the argument, and then have them reach a conclusion on each issue.

Breaking - Door Ajar   **Entering = an element but not an issue**
Yes - illegal entry
No - no force used
Conclusion - ?

Dwelling - Motel
Yes - people live there
No - Not permanent residence; not same privacy interest as in a home
Conclusion - ?

Nighttime - 5:00 P.M.
Yes - Evening; people likely to be home
No - Not sleeping; maybe not dark
Conclusion - ?

<u>Intent to Commit a Felony - Value of T.V. must be $500 or more</u>
Yes - original cost $600; would be replacement cost
No - resale value of $400 equals its real value
Conclusion - ?

Personal property is an element but not an issue. (Students may think is was not "personal property" as it was located in a type of business, i.e., a motel room. Because we have only briefly talked about the categories of property, I reassure them that such an assumption on their part is not stupid and learning that "personal property" is a term of art is part of what studying law is all about.)

Legal Reasoning Exercises, p. 151

7. Use the IRAC approach to write an analysis of one of the issues you outlined for Exercise 5 regarding Sarah and the defenses to her possible false imprisonment claim.

8. Apply the principles we have been discussing to Carl's situation, described in Exercise 6, and write an IRAC analysis of his problem.
For both of these exercises, students should start off with an introductory paragraph that briefly states the facts and outlines the issues. That should be following by a series of IRAC paragraphs, one on each issue. Finally, the paper should end with a concluding paragraph that summarizes the result based on the conclusions reached in the preceding discussion.

REVIEW QUESTIONS, page 155-55

1. Why do statutes often contain ambiguous language?
The scope of statutes is general because they are meant to apply to future situations. Also, ambiguity can be due to sloppy writing, or just unanticipated circumstances. Sometimes drafters purposely write the ambiguity into the statute in order to provide a basis for compromise by glossing over conflicts among the legislators.

2. What is meant by looking for the plain meaning of a statute?
The plain meaning approach is the method of statutory interpretation used to try and give the words their ordinary meaning.

3. What are canons of construction? How do courts use them in interpreting statutes?
They are guidelines for interpreting statutes. The courts use them as a starting point to try and interpret ambiguous language.

4. What types of statutes are courts most likely to strictly construe? To liberally construe?
Courts usually strictly construe criminal statutes and statutes in derogation of the common law. They liberally construe remedial statutes.

5. What types of documents could make up a statute's legislative history?
A statute's legislative history includes different versions of the bill, rejected amendments, committee reports, floor debates, statements by the bill's author.

6. What are the dangers in relying on legislative history?

Legislative history only represents what a few said, not why they all voted as they did. There is no way of knowing whether what was said influenced the vote. You can usually find legislative history to support both sides.

7. What type of judge would be more likely to interpret Title VII's prohibition against employment discrimination based on sex to include discrimination based on sexual preference: one who believes in judicial restraint or judicial activism? Why?

A judge who believes in judicial activism would be more willing to see the coverage of the statute changing as the needs of society change.

8. What are the main steps in analyzing a statutory problem?

The main steps in analyzing a statutory problem are as follows:
- **Get the facts**
- **Find a statute**
   Does it apply?
   Check effective date
- **Divide it into its elements**
- **Determine the issues**
- **Analyze the problem: apply law to facts**
   Common sense meaning
   Likely purpose
- **Conclude**
   On each issue
   On problem as a whole

9. What is a statutory element?

A statutory element is a separable part of a statute that must be satisfied for the statute to apply.

10. How does an issue differ from an element?

An issue is a problem created when the element (law) is applied to the client's facts.

11. When reading a statute, why is it important to pay attention to the use of "and" and "or"?

"And" implies a mandatory approach while "or" suggests options.

12. What does IRAC stand for, and why does it provide a useful structure for your legal writing?

IRAC stands for: Issue, Rule, Analysis, and Conclusion. It provides a useful structure because it reminds you of the four basic points that your reader wants to know.

13. What is the function of a road map paragraph? Of a concluding paragraph?

A road map gives the main issue and sub-issues that will be discussed, and the order in which they will be discussed. A concluding paragraph summarizes the discussion and gives the final answer as to the client's problem.

14. Why is it important to use transitions?

Transitions help the reader follow your line of argument.

15. We asked you this question at the end of Chapter 1, but we want to ask it again. Why does the study of law involve more than the mere memorization of rules?

The study of law involves more than the mere memorization of rules because there are too many to memorize, the law is always changing, and you need to apply the law to specific facts to reach a result in any individual case.

Chapter 7

Finding and Interpreting Court Opinions

In this chapter we suggest to students that they will be reading four types of cases:
1. those interpreting and applying enacted law, such as statutes;
2. those deciding the constitutionality of enacted law;
3. those applying established common law principles; and
4. those creating new common law principles.

We think categorizing cases in this way helps students see that they have to "read" cases differently depending on their purpose. For example, in a case that is creating new common law, they will have to be on the alert for broad policy reasons that the court will advance in support of the change in the law. These types of cases often reach the appellate level from a summary judgment or motion to dismiss. Therefore, there are frequently very few facts reported in the appellate decision. On the other hand, in cases applying established common law principles, they will have to be especially cognizant that the specific facts of the case may be controlling, and that even a minor change in the facts could have changed the outcome of the case. Therefore, when briefing the later type of case, the students must be careful to report those very specific facts.

 **Teaching Tip**

Page 160: In the discussion of explicitly versus implicitly overruling prior court decisions, you may need to help the students remember the series of "separate but equal" cases discussed in Chapter 2.

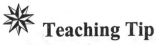 **Teaching Tip**

Page 168: In the text we emphasize that there are many correct ways to brief a case and that students should first determine the purpose for the brief. The method that we have included in the text was developed for the specific purpose of helping students understand the importance of both substantive and procedural facts, the difference between the law as it existed prior to the case (the rule) and the law as it now exists (the holding), the difference between procedural facts (the disposition) and the new rule (the holding), the importance of the reasoning for prediction of how courts will act in the future, and the necessity for critical thinking (the criticism).

DISCUSSION QUESTIONS, page 180

1. Do you agree with the court's reasoning and holding in *McBoyle*? Why?.
This depends on whether the students are more willing to extend the meaning to what the students think the legislature purpose was or feel constrained to give a narrow definition.

2. Did you notice the similarities between the court's approach to analyzing a statute and those discussed in Chapter 6? List the methods of statutory interpretation that the *McBoyle* court used. **(See those listed in the reasoning section of the sample brief for *McBoyle* on page 183 of the text.)**

3. Why would each of the following not be a correct issue for *McBoyle*?
   a. Whether the defendant knew the airplane was stolen
   A factual question can never be the basis for an appeal.

   b. Whether the defendant stole the airplane
   He was not charged with violating a theft statute; also this is a factual question.

   c. Whether the defendant was guilty
   This is too broad as this is the issue in every criminal case.

   d. Whether or not the trial court erred
   That is always the question on appeal and therefore, is so broad as to be useless.

Teaching Tip

The following is a sample brief for *Texas v. Johnson*, page 185.

Texas v. Johnson, 491 U.S. 397 (1989)

FACTS:	Mr. Johnson publicly burned an American flag during a political demonstration. Convicted of violating a Texas penal code prohibiting the desecration of "a venerated object"; Texas Court of Appeals affirmed; Texas Court of Criminal Appeals reversed; cert. granted; U.S. Supreme Court affirmed Texas Court of Criminal Appeals.
RULE:	The First and Fourteenth Amendments prohibit the states from abridging freedom of speech.
ISSUE:	Whether the First Amendment, which protects freedom of speech, is violated when a person is convicted for burning an American flag during a political demonstration.

HOLDING:	The First Amendment, which protects freedom of speech, is violated when a person is convicted for burning an American flag during a political demonstration.
REASONING:	While the First Amendment literally forbids the abridgment only of "speech," the Court has previously held that it also protects conduct when conduct is "sufficiently imbued with elements of communication." Here Johnson's flag burning was part of a political demonstration and so was the type of conduct meant to be protected as speech.
	The Court also rejected the state's two arguments. First, there was no evidence on the record that Johnson's conviction was necessary to prevent a breach of the peace. No breach of the peace actually occurred, and his conduct did not fall into "fighting words" exception. Second, the state claimed that it has an interest in preserving the flag as a symbol of national unity. But if that means prohibiting the type of expression that occurred in this case, then the government is enforcing its own political preferences, something the First Amendment prohibits. In dicta, the Court suggested that its holding will strength and not weaken our loyalty to the flag.
CRITICISM:	In a concurring opinion, Justice Kennedy expressed distaste for the result but stated that it was required because the Constitution compelled it. In dissent, Rehnquist pointed out that there are limits to freedom of speech when the value of the speech is outweighed by society's interest in "order and morality," such as in this case. Also he stated that the act had a tendency to incite a breach of the peace. Finally, Rehnquist thought that it should be left to a democratic legislature to decide whether or not to outlaw flag burning.
	The dissent's argument that Johnson was convicted for the use of "this particular symbol, and not the idea that he sought to convey by it" seems specious at best. Johnson used a flag to make his point. It would not have been as dramatic without it. Therefore, I agree with the majority that this conduct was the equivalent of political speech and should be protected.

DISCUSSION QUESTIONS, page 189

4. Did you notice that more and slightly different facts were brought out by the dissenting justices? This frequently happens. Why do you think the majority did not include all of the facts?

A cynical answer would be that some of the facts do not help the majority argument, and so they are left out.

5. Were you surprised by the tone of the opinion, especially the way in which the dissent was written? Do you think it is appropriate for Supreme Court justices to criticize each other? Each other's opinions?

Students are often surprised at how emotional the justices' writing sometimes is. This will probably also evoke a general discussion about a system that gives such power to nine people, who like everyone have their own set of beliefs and predispositions.

6. In the past few years, many Supreme Court decisions have been decided by a divided court. It is not uncommon to find five/four splits. What do you think this does to the public's perception of the power and role of the Court?

Obviously a divided court does not present as strong a front as does a more nearly unanimous one. Remind the students that the court does not have its own army to back it up. It must rely on all of us simply agreeing to listen to it. Arguably, the more divided the court is, the less moral authority its decisions will have with the public.

✴ **Teaching Tip**

The following is a sample brief for *Keller v. Delong*, page 191. NOTE: In the facts and issue section, remind the students that they should list facts and not conclusions. Under the rule, the second example is better as it more precisely defines the rule at stake in this case. When discussing this case in class, after the students have given the facts and the rule, stop them and make sure they understand that both the trial court and appellate court agreed on this rule. Ask them then, why was this case in court? Their answer is the issue. Finally, make sure the students do not phrase the issue as: Whether the defendant should be found negligent when he fell asleep while driving, thereby killing the defendant. Help them see that this biased statement leaves only one conclusion, and an issue should show the reader both sides of the argument.

<u>Keller v. Delong</u>, 108 N.H. 212, 231 A.2d 633 (1967)

FACTS: The plaintiff passenger was killed when the defendant driver dozed off to sleep and hit a utility pole. The defendant driver had dozed a couple of times before starting to drive and was drowsy just before taking wheel, but had taken no precautions taken: the windows were closed; the heater was on; he did not walk around the car before taking over. J. for D. rev'd.

RULE: Negligence is the failure under all of the circumstances to act as an ordinary person of prudence.

<u>OR BETTER</u>

Negligence occurs if a driver experiences warning symptoms of drowsiness and continues to drive without taking reasonable precautions.

ISSUE:	Whether the defendant driver was negligent, which occurs when a driver experiences warning symptoms of drowsiness and yet continues to drive without taking reasonable precautions, when the defendant felt drowsy as a passenger and took no precautions such as opening a window before taking the wheel.
HOLDING:	Yes, the defendant's failure to use precautions after being warned of drowsiness as a passenger constituted negligence, a failure to be prudent.
REASONING:	Because there had been warning symptoms of drowsiness as a passenger and because the defendant took no precautions to prevent further drowsiness, the court thought that the defendant's falling asleep at the wheel was a foreseeable occurrence. The plaintiff was entitled to have the def's care determined based on what he did as a passenger as well as on what happened once he took over driving.
CRITICISM:	The trial court had the better argument: it thought that dozing as a passenger did not mean that a person could not stay awake when given the responsibility of driving. Therefore, it was not foreseeable that the defendant would fall asleep, and he should not be charged with negligence.

Legal Reasoning Exercise, page 192-93

1. Analyze whether, based on the same reasoning used by the *Keller* court, a court would find George negligent. (Note: The question is not, Was Janice contributorily negligent? Think only about George's potential liability.) Recall from Chapter 4 our discussion regarding the importance of distinguishing between a prima facie case and the defenses. Here you are being asked to focus exclusively on the prima facie case of negligence.

Make a chart in which you list all the ways in which you think *Keller* and George's situation are analogous and all the ways in which you think they are distinguishable. (*Hint*: To argue that two situations are analogous, think in general terms. For example, both situations involved a dangerous activity. To argue that two situations are distinguishable, think specifically. For example, *Keller* involved a motor vehicle, while George's case involved a chainsaw.) Then ask yourself whether the similarities or the differences are more important. If you think the similarities are more important, then you will assume the court will find George negligent. If you think the differences are more important, then you will assume the court will not find George negligent.

I first write the words ANALOGOUS and DISTINGUISHABLE on the board. Then as I discuss this problem with the students, we fill in the facts that the students think go under one label or the other.

ANALOGOUS	DISTINGUISHABLE
Dang. activity	*Car/chain saw
*Warned of Danger/tired	Sleepy/Fatigued
*No precautions	Closed windows/didn't stop
Someone harmed	Death/Eye

*Differences that matter.

Then we begin the discussion of why some of these facts are important. I remind them that some differences are more important than others and others are really irrelevant. We discuss how stating that these two situations are analogous or distinguishable is really another way of asking whether they think this accident was foreseeable. They need to see that ultimately that is a policy question and not really a fact that is right or wrong. This is another place to remind them that there are no right nor wrong answers — just better or worse jobs at pointing out analogies and distinctions.

   Note: The students will have a chance to look at legal analysis in more depth when you get to Chapter 8.

 Teaching Tip

The following is a sample case brief for *Callow v. Thomas*, page 194. Do not be surprised if all of the students see *Callow* as being decided correctly. Then when they get to *Lewis* be prepared to see an about face. These cases are an excellent way of demonstrating how the court's opinion is designed to convince the reader of its correctness. They also demonstrate how even under stare decisis the courts are able to respond to change. In the facts section, help them see that the chronology of events is more important than the specifics such as the exact dates. The page references in parentheses are to the N.E.2d Reporter page numbers.

<u>Callow v. Thomas</u>, 322 Mass. 550, 78 N.E.2d 637 (1948)

FACTS: Plaintiff was injured while riding in car owned and negligently operated by her husband, the defendant. Seven months later the plaintiff petitioned to annul the marriage. The court declared the marriage annulled. The plaintiff then brought this tort action against the husband to recover damages for injuries received in the accident. The case reported to the S.J.C. without decision. Judg. for D.

RULE: Spouses cannot sue each other for torts that occur while they are married. (page 638)

ISSUE: Whether the doctrine of spousal immunity, which prevents spouses from suing each other for torts that arise during coverture, continues to bar a suit when the marriage has been annulled before suit is filed? (page 638)

HOLDING:	Yes, a spouse cannot sue for torts committed during a voidable marriage even though the marriage was later annulled.
REASONING:	Although the annulment decree made the marriage void <u>ab</u> <u>initio</u> (from the beginning), public policy and reality dictate some limits to retroactive effects of the decree of annulment. In the case of a voidable marriage (one valid until nullified by court decree) those transactions concluded and things done during marriage are final and cannot be undone. As a result, no cause of action arises out of acts performed during a voidable marriage even after the marriage is annulled.
CRITICISM:	It seems unfair that an injured plaintiff cannot be compensated if the injury was caused by a spouse, but an injured plaintiff injured by someone else can seek compensation. Unfortunately, the court did not given any reason for why spouses shouldn't be able to sue each other. The court simply said on page 638 "[t]hat no cause of action arises in favor of either husband or wife for a tort committed by the other during coverture is too well settled to require citation of authority." By distinguishing between void and voidable marriage, the court also left open the question of what would happen if in the next case the marriage was void.

7. In Chapter 6 (Legal Reasoning Exercise 1) we looked at the following statute that would seem to govern Janice's case. What dos the *Callow* court say about it?

> A married woman may sue and be sued in the same manner as if she were sole;
> but this section shall not authorize suits between husband and wife.

The court says "[t]here is nothing in our statutes enlarging the rights of married women that can be construed as altering this rule." (page 638.)

8. What is the difference between a void and a voidable marriage? Do you think the court would have ruled the same way if the marriage had been void? Should such technicalities matter?
A void marriage is one that never existed, for example, because of bigamy. A voidable marriage is one that a court has declared void, for example, in a case of a contagious disease. By distinguishing between the two, and talking about legal fictions, the court leaves open the door for allowing suits in a void marriage. Have the students discuss the concept of legal fictions.

9. The result here was the finding that Muriel Callow could not sue her ex-husband. This does not mean that the court thought he was not negligent. Because the court said that she could not sue, the court never heard any evidence regarding his behavior that caused his car to run into a tree. Do you think that there should be such absolute bars to even having a case heard? If so, can you think of other situations where the courts should not allow potential litigants to sue each other?
This is an opportunity to discuss other privileges such as judicial immunity. Make sure the students understand that if immunity is invoked, that the court never gets to the question of liability.

Legal Reasoning Exercise, page 199

2. Based on *Callow*, analyze whether you think the doctrine of spousal immunity will bar Janice's claim.
Normally, if cases are distinguishable, the result will be different. However, in comparing our case to *Callow*, the students should see that the differences actually make for a stronger case against liability.

 **Teaching Tip**

The following is a sample brief for *Lewis v. Lewis*, page 200. The page references in parentheses are to the N.E.2d Reporter page numbers. In the holding section be sure the students understand the importance of including the limitation to motor vehicle accidents.

<u>Lewis v. Lewis</u>, 370 Mass. 619, 351 N.E.2d 526 (1976)

FACTS: The plaintiff wife was injured while a passenger in the car negligently driven by her husband, the defendant. The plaintiff sued her husband for injuries received in the accident. The husband's motion for summary judgment was allowed. The plaintiff was granted direct appellate review. Judgment vacated.

RULE: Under the common law, spouses may not sue each other for torts committed during coverture. Mass. Gen. Laws ch. 209, § 6 provides that a married woman may sue but does not authorize suits between husband and wife.

ISSUE: Whether interspousal immunity, which generally prohibits spouses from suing each other, bars a wife from suing her husband in tort for personal injuries received in an uninsured car accident.

HOLDING: No. Interspousal immunity does not bar claims between spouses, but the holding is limited to accidents arising out of motor vehicle accidents.

REASONING: The realities and principles of today's society have antiquated the interspousal immunity doctrine. Any public policy arguments relating to the doctrine's prevention of collusion and marital discord are insufficient grounds to continue the doctrine. The court interpreted the state statute as neither abolishing nor mandating the continuance of the doctrine. Therefore, the court retained the power to abrogate the doctrine. Because the courts stated that tortious injuries should have a remedy, it abrogated the doctrine in this case, an automobile accident situation, but said that further abolition of the doctrine must await future cases. "Conduct, tortious between two strangers, may not be tortious between spouses. . . ." (page 532)

CRITICISM: The court seemingly stretches the language of the statute to fit its desired result. The future is very unclear as to the viability of other types of tort claims.

---

10. Compare the court's view in *Lewis* regarding the need to defer to the legislative branch with that of the court in *McBoyle*. Those cases, as well as the dissent in *Johnson*, illustrate a constant tension in our system between the elected legislature and the appointed judiciary. While the court will often defer to the legislative branch, there are times when it will not, especially in areas of law not yet touched by legislation. It is then that you will probably see a phrase similar to the one used by the *Lewis* court: "[T]he court not only has the authority but also the duty to reexamine its precedents." Do you think it is appropriate in a democratic society for a court to wield such power?

Obviously, there is no right answer here, but it does raise serious concerns about our judicial system. This is a good time to remind students that when a constitutional issue is not involved the legislature retains the right to enact legislation to counter the court's actions.

11. What exactly did Mrs. Lewis win?

Mrs. Lewis won the right to a trial. Make sure they understand that no one has yet found Mr. Lewis negligent; that he was assumed to be negligent for purposes of deciding the summary judgment motion only. This is a difficult concept for students to grasp. It just doesn't seem fair to them that he can admit his negligence and then later get to take it back.

12. On page 529 of the opinion, the court cites *Sorensen v. Sorensen*, a case in which a child wanted to sue his father for negligent driving. By citing this case, the court seems to suggest that the same principles that apply to children suing their parents should apply to spouses suing each other. Do you agree?

You may want to discuss the case of *Stamboulis v. Stamboulis*, 401 Mass. 762, 519 N.E.2d 1299 (1988) in which the Massachusetts Supreme Judicial Court extended *Sorensen* to hold that a child could sue its parents, even in situations not involving automobile accidents. In that case the mother had taken her three-year-old daughter to work with her at a pizza shop. While she was answering the phone, her daughter tried to put dough through an electronic dough rolling machine. One of her hands was caught in the machine and injured. The court allowed the child to sue, abolishing parental immunity. The court did note that "the fact of parenthood is relevant to the standard of care." This was the first case in the line of Massachusetts cases regarding family immunity in which there was a dissent. The dissent argued that allowance of such a suit "tends to undermine parental authority and discipline by substituting for parents' discretion in the care and rearing of minor children that of the court."

Legal Reasoning Exercise, page 208

3. Based on *Lewis* analyze whether you think the doctrine of spousal immunity will bar Janice's claim.

The students need to focus first on the factual differences between *Lewis* and their case — this is not an automobile accident, and so the strict holding of *Lewis* would bar the claim. In addition, the reasoning that "[c]onduct, tortious between two strangers, may not be tortious between spouses because of the mutual concessions implied in the marital relationship" [page 532] would support a finding for the defendant. However, the court

also indicated in its reasoning that "if there is a tortious injury there should be recovery." [page 532] In addition, in footnote 4, the court in effect, waved a red flag, encouraging future litigants to test the limits of spousal immunity. There is an example analysis of this issue on pages 236-37 of the text.

REVIEW QUESTIONS, pages 210-11

1. What are the four basic categories of court opinions?
The four basic categories are:
1.   **those interpreting and applying enacted law, such as statutes;**
2.   **those deciding the constitutionality of enacted law;**
3.   **those applying established common law principles; and**
4.   **those creating new common law principles.**

2. What is the difference between mandatory and persuasive authority? Why does it matter?
A decision is mandatory authority when it comes from a higher court in the same jurisdiction. Persuasive authority consists of the decisions of courts that do not constitute mandatory authority and the writings of legal scholars. It may therefore include primary authority, such as decisions of other state courts, and secondary authority, such as legal treatises or law review articles. It matters because courts must follow mandatory authority. They may chose to follow or disregard persuasive authority.

Listed below are the possible answers for questions 3 through 8.
a.   U.S. Supreme Court
b.   U.S. Court of Appeals for the First Circuit
c.   U.S. Court of Appeals for the Second Circuit
d.   U.S. District Court for the District of Massachusetts
e.   Massachusetts Supreme Judicial Court
f.   New Hampshire Supreme Court
g.   Massachusetts Appeals Court
h.   Massachusetts Superior Court
i.   New Hampshire trial court

3. If the U.S. District Court for the District of Massachusetts heard a case regarding a federal statutory issue, which of the courts listed above could issue decisions that the district court would have to follow? Why?
a. U.S. Supreme Court and b. First Circuit because the District of Massachusetts court is a federal court located within the First Circuit, the First Circuit Court of Appeals and the U.S. Supreme Court are above it, within the same jurisdiction.

4. If the U.S. Court of Appeals for the First Circuit heard a case regarding a federal statutory issue, which of the courts listed above could issue decisions that the court of appeals would have to follow? Why?
a. U.S. Supreme Court, as the Court of Appeals is a federal court and the United States Supreme Court is the only court above it.

5. If the U.S. Supreme Court heard a case regarding a federal statutory issue, which of the courts listed above could issue decisions that the U.S. Supreme Court would have to follow? Why?

None because there is no federal court above the U.S. Supreme Court. It is always free to overrule its own prior decisions.

6. If a Massachusetts superior court (a trial court) heard a case regarding a Massachusetts state law issue, which of the courts listed above could issue decisions that the superior court would have to follow? Why?

e. Massachusetts Supreme Judicial Court and g. Massachusetts Appeals Court as they are both state courts ranked above the trial courts.

7. If the Massachusetts Appeals Court (an intermediate-level appellate court) heard a case regarding a Massachusetts state law issue, which of the courts listed above could issue decisions that the appeals court would have to follow? Why?

e. Massachusetts Supreme Judicial Court as it is the only state court higher than the Appeals Court.

8. If the Massachusetts Supreme Judicial Court (the highest appellate court in Massachusetts) heard a case regarding a Massachusetts state law issue, which of the courts listed above could issue decisions that the Massachusetts Judicial Supreme Court would have to follow? Why?

None because there is no court higher than the Massachusetts Supreme Judicial Court in Massachusetts and state supreme courts have the final say on state issues

9. For each of these situations listed in questions 3-8, indicate which of the following would be seen as mandatory authority by the court hearing the case. Give a short explanation for each of your answers. (Assume all constitutional provisions and statutes deal with the same issue that the court is facing.)

a.   U.S. constitutional provision
b.   U.S. statute
c.   Massachusetts statute
d.   Massachusetts constitutional provision
e.   New Hampshire constitutional provision
f.   New Hampshire statute

3. a. U.S. Constitution; b. U.S. statute
4. a. U.S. Constitution; b. U.S. statute
5. a. U.S. Constitution; b. U.S. statute
6. a. U.S. Constitution; c. Massachusetts statute; d. Massachusetts Constitution
7. a. U.S. Constitution; c. Massachusetts statute; d. Massachusetts Constitution
8. a. U.S. Constitution; c. Massachusetts statute; d. Massachusetts Constitution
The U.S. Constitution applies to all situations as it is the "supreme law of the land." The first three situations deal with federal law and the last three with state law.

10. What is the difference between analogizing a case and distinguishing a case?
Analogizing is the process of finding similar rules of law and facts in two or more cases. Distinguishing is finding differences.

11. Give an example of when a court decided to overrule precedent and thereby dramatically change the current law.
In the text we gave the example of the 1968 landmark decision of *Dillon v. Legg*. Prior to that decision bystanders could not recover for the emotional distress they suffered when witnessing an accident. Then in *Dillon v. Legg* the California Supreme Court created new law. The court stated that a mother could recover for the emotional injury she suffered when she saw her child injured. Your students will probably be able to think of many other examples, such as *Miranda* or *Roe v. Wade*.

12. Why does court made law generally evolve slowly?
Because we follow the doctrine of stare decisis, normally courts follow the way decisions have been decided in the past.

13. Explain the difference between overruling a decision and reversing a decision.
An appellate court reverses a decision when it concludes that a lower court failed to properly apply the law. An appellate court overrules a prior appellate court decision when it determines that the law needs to be changed.

14. List each part of a brief and describe the function of each.
See Exhibit 7-2, page 176 of the text.

15. Look at each of the following potential case holdings for the *Blair* case. Which one do you think best represents a holding as it should appear in a case brief? Why? What is wrong with the others? Which is the broadest holding? The narrowest?
    a. Yes.
    Too broad.

    b. Yes, burglary is committed when someone enters a partially enclosed carwash. **The definition of the rule is missing.**

    c. Yes, it is unlawful to enter a partially enclosed carwash.
    The rule is missing.

    d. Yes, the defendant should be found guilty.
    It does not give you the new rule.

    e. Yes, burglary, which requires the entering of a building or housetrailer, is committed when someone enters any partially enclosed building designed to protect people or property.
    May be too broad.

f. Yes, burglary, which requires the entering of a building or house trailer, is committed when someone enters a partially enclosed carwash.

Good; this has all of the elements of a good holding. It gives a definitive answer, then states the rule with the broad label first (burglary), followed by the definition, and then the specific facts of the case.

g. Reversed.

These are just the procedural facts.

h. The trial court's decision was correct.

Because this is true fifty percent of the time, it is not helpful.

16. Why is it sometimes important to include the reasoning of concurring or dissenting opinions in a case brief?

While only the majority opinion represents the court's view, what individual concurring and dissenting judges have to say can influence later courts.

Chapter 8

Applying the Law

You may find that you do not have time to go into logic in any great depth. However, I have found that some students better understand the IRAC approach after they study the deductive model. The most difficult concept in this chapter is that of case synthesis. Students naturally want to present a legal analysis as a series of mini-case briefs. It is much more work to instead present the cases as they relate to specific issues. While this is more work, I remind the students that it is their job to do most of the work so that their boss can read their analysis without having to do the students' work for them.

Legal Reasoning Exercise, pages 224-25

1. Read the following article that appeared in the Boston Globe shortly after the Massachusetts Supreme Court decided *Brown v. Brown*. What do you think of the author's comments? Why is the statement "the Superior Court agreed, more or less, with defendant Bill that the wife could have hauled ashes" misleading?

Because the case was dismissed on the basis of spousal immunity, there never was any discussion of the facts that would determine negligence. Make sure that the students understand that given the limited holding in *Lewis*, the trial court had no choice but to dismiss the case. Therefore, it did not agree "more or less, with defendant Bill that the wife could have hauled ashes to sprinkle on the ice that infamous morning." This is not a case about who should sprinkle ashes, but rather a case about whether spouses should be allowed to sue each other so that a trial court can determine those types of factual questions.

Legal Reasoning Exercise, pages 229-30

2. In this first problem you need to argue for a change in the law.

Your firm represents Amanda and Sam Baker, grandparents of two year old Brian Baker. Brian was recently injured in a home accident. The two year old stuck a hairpin into an electrical outlet and was severely burned. The parents had not installed safety plugs in the outlets because they felt the plugs gave a false sense of security. The plugs are easily removed and were not present in many of their friends' homes. The grandparents want to bring a negligence suit on the child's behalf against the parents.

Assume that the Massachusetts Supreme Judicial Court has decided the following cases:

- *Sorenson v. Sorenson* (1975) - A child was injured when his father negligently caused an automobile accident. The court held that children could sue their parents but limited the holding to motor vehicle cases and limited the recovery to the amount of available insurance. For its reasoning the court stated that neither the argument that such suits would disrupt the peace and harmony of the family nor the argument that such actions would tend to promote fraud and collusion was valid.

- *Lewis v. Lewis* (1976) - A wife was injured when her husband negligently caused an automobile accident. The court held that the wife could sue her husband but limited the holding to motor vehicle cases. The court did not limit the recovery to the amount of insurance, stating: "In the present case there is nothing in the record concerning the availability or the amount of the defendant's liability insurance, and we do not refer to insurance as a limiting factor in our holding. We do not interpret the logic (as opposed to the precise holding) of *Sorensen* as turning on the availability of insurance in each case, and we decline to limit liability in interspousal tort actions in such a fashion." The court cited *Sorenson* with approval as standing for the proposition that such suits would not disrupt the peace and harmony of the family or tend to promote fraud and collusion. Finally, while acknowledging that some actions that would constitute torts between strangers might not constitute torts if committed between spouses, the court based its decision on the general principle that normally there should be recovery for tortious injury.

- *Brown v. Brown* (1980) - A wife was injured when she slipped on the front steps that her husband had forgotten to salt. The court held that the wife could sue her husband. The court reasoned that while certain behavior between spouses might not be tortious, that was for a trial court to determine at trial and the case should not be dismissed as a matter of immunity.

Based on the prior case law develop arguments both for and against the child's being able to sue his parents for negligence.

The issues in this problem have already been raised briefly in Discussion Question 12 of Chapter 7, on page 208 of the text. [Discussed above in this Teacher's Manual.] The basic argument against allowing the suit is that the narrow holding of *Sorensen* was that children could sue their parents, but only in motor vehicle accidents and limited to the amount of the liability insurance. Even though the court has since eliminated the concept of immunity as a defense for lawsuits between spouses, the court might still leave this limitation as to parental immunity. The relationship between children and parents is fundamentally different from that between spouses. Allowing lawsuits in cases such as this one could undermine parental authority and discipline by substituting the court's judgment for that of the parents.

The argument for allowing the suit is that following *Sorensen* the court did go on in *Lewis* to allow suits between spouses in motor vehicle accidents with no limitation as to liability insurance. In *Lewis*, 351 N.E.2d 533 (Mass. 1976), the court noted "[w]e do not interpret the logic (as opposed to the precise holding) of *Sorensen* as turning on the

availability of insurance." Id. at 202, n. 4. If the court was to continue this trend of relying more on the logic than the holdings of past cases, then it may decide to eliminate parental immunity just as it did spousal immunity in *Brown*. Both situations involve family immunities and both involve tortious injury. In *Lewis* the court stated that "tortious injury there should be recovery." Id. at 532. It is likely that the policy argument in favor of furthering that goal will prevail over any concerns about disrupting the parent-child relationship.

Note: In *Stamboulis v. Stamboulis*, 519 N.E.2d 1299 (Mass. 1988), the Massachusetts Supreme Judicial Court held that parental immunity would no longer bar negligence suits. In that case, the defendant mother took her three-year-old daughter with her to the family owned pizza shop. The mother left the daughter alone for a few moments while she went to answer the phone. While she was gone the daughter tried to put dough through an electric dough rolling machine and injured her hand. While a divided court did abrogate parental immunity, the dissent was concerned that the court was stepping into areas that would best be left to parental discretion.

3. In this problem you need to show how your case fits with established law.

   Your firm represents the Gilberts. Last week the Gilberts went out to dinner at a fashionable lakeshore restaurant. After dinner they decided to take a stroll down a boardwalk that leads from the restaurant out onto a pier. The walkway was not lighted. About half-way down the pier Ms. Gilbert stepped on a board that gave way due to dry rot. She fell and was seriously injured. About five years ago the restaurant, which owns the pier, decided it was too expensive to keep up with the necessary repairs and had done nothing to maintain the pier since. The restaurant owners posted a sign near the entry to the pier that said: "Danger."

   Assume the Nebraska Supreme Court decided the following case:

   ■ *Weiss v. Autumn Hills* (1986)
   One night the plaintiff, a tenant in the defendant landlord's apartment building, was walking across the unlighted grassy area adjoining the patio of her street-level apartment. Although there was a sidewalk leading to the parking lot, taking the sidewalk took longer than cutting across the grass, and many people chose this shorter route. The area was eroded due to water falling from a defective rain gutter. The plaintiff stepped in a rut covered by weeds and fell. The landlord was found negligent.

   Based on the *Weiss* decision, will your client be able to show that the restaurant was negligent? List all the factual similarities that make you think the restaurant might be negligent. Then list all the factual differences that make you think the restaurant might not be negligent. Decide which of the factual differences or similarities are the most important and why.

Arguments for finding liability include the absence of lights and repairs. Because the walkway lead right from the restaurant to the pier it was foreseeable that restaurant patrons would use it. Finally, the sign was inadequate, especially in the dark with no lights. However, the case is distinguishable from *Weiss* in that *Weiss* involved a landlord. Arguably, landlords owe a higher duty of care to their tenants than do restaurants to their patrons. Also, in *Weiss* it was clear that the route was used by many persons; here there is a question as to whether the walkway was commonly used. Finally, in *Weiss* there was no sign at all. Here there was a sign that clearly said "Danger."

4. This last problem is of the type where you need to base your analysis on a statute and a case interpreting that statute.

Assume you have a client, Jack Brilliant, who has been charged with violating the National Motor Vehicle Theft Act. Last weekend a friend of his, Sam Slick, told your client he had just acquired a new motor boat, but that he did not know how to run it. He asked your client if he would go out for a ride with him on the Connecticut River and show him how to drive the boat. Your client agreed. They left from a marina in Massachusetts and headed south with your client at the wheel. Soon after they crossed the Connecticut boarder, they were flagged down by the marine patrol and arrested. Apparently, Sam had stolen the motor boat.

Based on the language of the statute and the *McBoyle* decision (page 180), what are the arguments that your client should be convicted of violating the National Motor Vehicle Theft Act? What are the arguments that he should not be convicted?

If the students look to the policy behind the statute and question why trains were exempted (by running on tracks, they are hard to hide), then they might see a boat as analogous to a train in that a boat is limited to moving on water, just as a train is limited to moving on railroad tracks. Also, if the students were to adopt the same "plain meaning" approach as was used by the *McBoyle* court, then a boat would not be included under the statute. Of course, most boats can also be transported by placing them on a trailer which would tend to make them like any other motor vehicle, and therefore to be included within the statute.

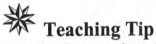 **Teaching Tip**

Page 231: In many introductory courses there is not enough time to have the students write a full-blown law office memorandum. However, we have included a sample memorandum in this chapter for reference and for yet another example of how to include citations in a legal analysis.

REVIEW QUESTIONS, p. 237-38

1. Why is it important to find both analogies and distinctions between your client's facts and the facts of prior cases?
Based on stare decisis, generally if you can find analogies, the cases will be decided the same. If you find distinctions, they will be decided differently, unless the distinctions do not matter.

2. Why is it not enough simply to list the similarities and differences between your client's facts and the facts of prior cases?
You must explain *why* the similarities and differences matter.

3. What factors help to determine whether you should use a particular case in support of your client's position?

You should prefer:

    1.   **a case from the highest appellate court in your jurisdiction;**

    2.   **that was decided recently;**

    3.   **with facts similar to your own;**

    4.   **decided by a unanimous court; and**

    5.   **written by a well known and respected judge.**

4. Assume you have been asked to write an analysis of whether a client is guilty of murder. The case occurred and will be tried in California. List the following in order from most to least authoritative. Explain your choices.

a. A 1995 Illinois Supreme Court decision, with facts similar to your client's facts, in which the defendant was found not guilty of murder.
4th (persuasive, not your jurisdiction)

b. A 1989 law review article that surveys all of the murder statutes in the 50 states.
5th (secondary authority)

c. A 1980 California Supreme Court decision, with facts similar to your client's facts, in which the defendant was found guilty of murder.
2nd (mandatory authority)

d. A 1990 intermediate California Supreme Court decision, with facts similar to your client's facts, in which the defendant was found guilty of manslaughter.
3rd (mandatory authority for the trial court but behind the Supreme Court)

e. A California state statute defining murder and manslaughter.
1st (statutes control over the common law)

f. An article from American Jurisprudence, Second explaining the differences between murder and manslaughter.
6th (secondary authority; only rely on encyclopedias if you have nothing else)

g. A 1995 California Supreme Court decision on breach of warranty in automobile sales.
7th (irrelevant; not our issue)

5. What does it mean to say a case is on all fours?
When a case is on all fours, it is identical.

6. What is the relationship between deductive reasoning and legal reasoning?
Most legal arguments are presented in the form of deductive reasoning: major premise (the law), minor premise (the facts), and conclusion.

Chapter 9

Ethical Dilemmas Facing Attorneys

Many texts place the ethics chapter at the end. We have chosen to include it as the first chapter in the substantive section of the book. While there are ethics alerts throughout all chapters, this chapter gives you the opportunity for an in-depth look at ethical dilemmas that raise basic issues about the nature of our adversary system and the role attorneys play in it.

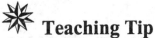 **Teaching Tip**

Of course, throughout the book you should point out to students how ethical dilemmas permeate many legal issues, not just those that are the focus of this chapter. By encouraging them see that there can be more than one "ethically correct" answer to any particular dilemma, you help students develop their ability to argue both sides of a case. You can also help them increase their tolerance of differing points of view.

DISCUSSION QUESTIONS, page 243

1. Approximately 90 percent of all criminal cases scheduled for trial are instead resolved through plea bargaining. In a plea bargain, the two sides work together to reach a compromise. Does this undermine the very notion that ours is an adversarial system?

Even though the goal is to reach a compromise, even in a plea bargaining situation, the client is represented by his or her advocate, who presumably is working to get the "best deal" for the client. The end result is also a process whereby the plea is entered in open court. Arguably, plea bargaining does not threaten the adversarial process as much as do some of the ethical rules, discussed later in the chapter, such as the mandate to return inadvertently received confidential information.

2. It is often said that the function of the adversarial system is to find the truth. How is it then that courts frequently block access to information that would assist in that search for truth? For example, courts routinely exclude evidence if the police officers used unconstitutional means to acquire it, and they do not require spouses to testify against each other.

This should lead to a good discussion about the need to balance the desire to find the truth with other societal goals, such as the protection of individual liberties or the sanctity of marriage.

3. On a basic level, do you think attorneys have to face ethical dilemmas that are fundamentally different from those faced by other professionals, such as physicians or accountants?

All professionals face ethical dilemmas. For example, a doctor may wish to tell a dying patient that he does not have long to live but face a determined spouse who feels she knows her husband best and that he should not be told. Accountants who work for large corporations may feel conflicted between a sense of duty to their employers and to the shareholders in the corporation. Fundamentally, however, a lawyer's ethical responsibilities are different, especially in the context of representing criminal clients. The lawyer must sometimes choose not simply between loyalty to the client versus protecting others, but between safeguarding constitutional protections versus protecting others.

4. In the popular media, attorneys are often referred to as "hired guns." We have also all heard the lawyer jokes: "How do you know when a lawyer is lying? His lips are moving." Why do you think there is this negative perception of lawyers and what they do? Do you think it is a fair characterization?

Many argue that lawyers get a "bad rap" because the public comes to associate them with the clients they represent. For example, if an attorney represents the Klu Klux Klan for its right to march in a parade, the public is likely to see the attorney as supportive of the beliefs of the Ku Klux Klan, rather than as an advocate for freedom of speech and association.

5. What do you think of the statement: "At times following the rules may not lead to the best moral response and indeed may produce an amoral or even immoral response"?

Rules can only be written to provide the right answer most of the time. There will always be exceptional circumstances that test the limits of the rule. In those situations, blindly following the rule may lead to at best an amoral and at worst an immoral response.

6. As you can see, there is substantial disagreement as to when an attorney should be required or even allowed to report a client's future crime. Do you think there are any instances when such reporting should be required instead of merely permitted? Classify each of the following according to whether you think an attorney should be required to report the future crime, allowed to do so at his or her discretion, or prohibited from disclosing it at all. You should also consider whether the test should be a subjective one, based on what the attorney actually thought was likely to happen, or an objective test, based on what a reasonable person would think would happen.

a. A deliberately wrongful act

b. Harm to a financial or property interest

c. Substantial harm to a financial or property interest

d. Any crime

e. A serious violent crime

f. Bodily harm

g. Substantial bodily harm

h. Death

i. Imminent death

Before they begin their study of ethics, students have a hard time understanding why knowing what is "ethical" should be such a problem. Trying to decide when and if an attorney should ever breach a client confidence engages them in a discussion that quickly shows them how there can be intense disagreement as to what is or is not "ethical" behavior. It also illustrates how attorneys can be placed in the bind of doing what is considered to be "ethical" under one of the codes or of doing what they consider to be more justified in a moral or religious sense.

7. Take a look at Figure 9-3. Given your answers to number 6, which rule or combination of rules do you prefer?

Answers will vary, but should make for a good discussion.

8. Do you think that clients will seriously be dissuaded from revealing confidences if they know that their attorney may be allowed to reveal that information after the client's death?

Many argue that there are already so many exceptions to client confidentiality that adding one more will not have any measurable effect. Also, if attorneys explain the need for full information in order to provide proper representation, it is unlikely that clients will choose to remain silent simply because something may be revealed after their death.

CASE DISCUSSION QUESTIONS, page 254 for *New York v. Belge*

1. What do you think the court meant when it said that a "trial is in part a search for truth, but it is only partly a search for truth?"

Because ours in an adversarial system, the interests of the government in finding out the "truth" are not paramount. Individual rights, including the right to an attorney, to a trial by jury, due process, and the privilege against self-incrimination, are all important as well. Therefore, our system is a balance between the rights of the individual and the rights of society.

2. Ultimately, why did the court find that the indictment against attorney Belge should be dismissed?

Although the court talked about needing to balance the rights of the indivudual against the rights of society as a whole (and the emotional harm to the victim's family), in the end the court balanced the constitutional right against self-incrimination against the "trivia of a pseudo-criminal statute." The right against self-incrimination won.

3. Do you think the result would have been the same if attorney Belge had been charged with obstruction of justice?

Possibly, yes. The court said that there was no question that the attorneys' failure to tell the authorities about the victim's body prevented Garrow from being immediately charged with her murder. Therefore, the court noted that if the attorneys had been charged with obstruction of justice "the work of this court would have been much more difficult."

DISCUSSION QUESTIONS, page 254

9. The common justification for having such strict limits on when an attorney can reveal client confidences is because without such restrictions, clients would be afraid to give their attorneys the complete story. Do you think this is really true? Given the complexities of the legal system and hence the need for an attorney to help others through it, do you think a client would risk not getting adequate representation by not being forthcoming to the attorney?

Many commentators have argued that clients are really between a rock and a hard place, in that they have no choice but to reveal confidences if they expect to be adequately represented.

10. What do you make of the fact that in every jurisdiction the confidentiality rules do not apply where the litigation is between a lawyer and the client and the issue is the attorney's fees?

Many see this as evidence that client representation is more about gaining a fee than performing a public service. You might want to ask students, however, how attorneys could prove they had performed a certain legal service without revealing client confidences.

CASE DISCUSSION QUESTIONS, pages 257-58 for *Spaulding v. Zimmerman*

1. Why did the Minnesota Supreme Court agree that the trial court could set aside the settlement? Do you think the result would have been the same if the settlement had involved an adult plaintiff rather than a child? Should it matter?

The Minnesota Supreme Court agree that the trial court could set aside the settlement because the defendants knew about the condition at the time of the settlement and did not inform the court. This fraud on the court gave the trial judge discretion to set aside the settlement. Arguably, the only reason the court had this discretion was because a minor was involved. If the parties had simply made an out-of-court settlement involving an adult, there might not have been the same basis for setting aside the settlement.

2. Did the court view the attorney's decision not to reveal the extent of David's injury as a violation of an ethical obligation or rather as a strategic move that in this case simply did not work out?

The court clearly stated that no ethical canons had been violated and that there was no doubt but that the defendants' attorneys were acting in good faith. The court saw the attorneys' actions as a strategic move that in this particular case simply did not work out.

3. Do you think the court should have tackled head on the ethical and moral issues involved in choosing to keep a client's confidence over saving a child's life?

This case is frustrating for students because the court did not deal directly with the ethical and moral issues involved.

4. David Spaulding was represented by a young, inexperienced lawyer. Perhaps he was not aware that he was entitled to ask for a copy of the defendant doctor's examination. Or perhaps

he just thought it would duplicate the information his own doctors had found. Or perhaps in the rush to settle the case, he simply forgot to ask for a copy. No matter the answer, should the system develop better protections for clients against the inexperience or incompetence of their attorneys?

This is one of the fundamental issues raised by the adversarial system. That is, if we are to have a system whereby clients have to rely on champions to advance their cause, then the system will only work poorly at best if both sides are not adequately represented. You might want to ask students if they think judges should take a more active role if they suspect an attorney is doing an inadequate job.

5. It appears in this case that the defendants' attorneys never even consulted with the defendants about what they wanted to do but just assumed they would not want the information revealed. Should the attorneys have made such an assumption?

You should impress on the students that this was not the attorneys' decision to make. They should have consulted with their clients.

6. Assuming the attorneys had discussed with their clients the decision as to whether the reveal this information, and the clients had said they did not wish to have the information revealed, what options would the attorneys have had?

Under the current rules there is no recourse other than for the attorney to breach the confidence or keep silent. The exceptions do not apply as they only relate to harm from future criminal activity.

7. Consider whether you think your answer to number 6. would change under the newly revised Model Rules. Do you think the defense attorney would have an ethical obligation to reveal the injury? Would you change your answer if David had been suffering from an inoperable tumor rather than a correctable, but life threatening condition?

Under the new rules, an attorney may reveal information to "prevent reasonably certain death or substantial bodily harm." Therefore, the attorney could but would not be required to reveal the existence of the aneurysm. The answer would probably be different if there were an inoperable tumor as the rule only talks about "preventing" harm.

 Teaching Tip

For an interesting review of the *Spaulding* case, read Roger C. Cramton and Lori P. Knowles, Professional Secrecy and Its Exceptions: Spaulding v. Zimmerman Revisited, 83 Minn. L. Rev. 63 (Nov. 1998): "[A] macabre dance in which the real issues in the case – how human beings should behave toward one another when human life is at stake – were skirted by technical legal arguments about a trial court's discretion to reopen a minor's settlement and whether a petition to approve a settlement was a joint petition or merely that of the party submitting it." Id. at 126.

Legal Reasoning Exercises, pages 258-59

1. In Belge, the principal harm had already been done. The client had committed the crime of murder and the girl was dead. Nothing the attorney could do would change that. In Spaulding the harm had also been done, but revealing it would serve to save a life and would not lead to the client's trial for murder. Suppose, however, that a case arose in which the attorney had a chance to still "save the girl," but that his actions would lead to the criminal conviction of his client. Consider the following. On December 17 Gary Krist went to the motel room of Barbara Mackle. He told her he was a detective and that there had been an accident involving a young man driving a white Ford. The young man was in the hospital and asking for her. As her boy friend owned a white Ford, she believed him and opened the door. Krist entered brandishing a knife and forced her into the backseat of his car where he then tied her up. After driving her out into the country, he ordered her into a coffin-like box, equipped with a method for getting air, and buried her alive. He then called her father, told him he had kidnapped his daughter, and demanded $500,000 in ransom. Arrangements were made for Krist to receive the money. On December 19 following Krist's instructions, the father left the money in a suitcase. Krist retrieved the money and left without revealing the whereabouts of Barbara. Two days later on December 21 Krist was arrested when he tried to spend part of the money in order to rent a boat and motor at a local marina.

Assume that Krist meets with his court appointed attorney and reveals where Barbara is located. He thinks she is still alive, but does not know. He said that he left her with a limited amount of food and water, but does not know how long it will last. The attorney encourages Krist to tell the police where Barbara is buried. Krist refuses to do so, feeling that so long as they do not find Barbara, the police have no direct proof that he was the kidnapper. What should the attorney do? What are his options under the Model Code, the Model Rules, and the recently proposed changes to the Model Rules?

This hypothetical is based on the facts of *Krist v. State*, 237 G. 85, 179 S.E.2d 56 (1970). Changing the facts to create this ethical dilemma was suggested in the following law review article: Harry I. Subin, The Lawyer as Superego: Disclosure of Client Confidences to Prevent Harm, 70 Iowa L. Rev. 1091, 1103 (1985). In this situation, the attorney has no right to reveal the information under either the Model Code or Model Rules as the crime has already been committed. Under the proposed 2003 Model Rules the attorney could reveal the information to "prevent reasonably certain death or substantial bodily harm."

2. Consider the case of Leo Frank. Although innocent, he had been convicted of the rape and murder of a fourteen-year-old girl. While he was waiting to be executed, an attorney, who was not involved in the *Frank* case, found out from a prospective client the name of the true murderer. The attorney never revealed the information and Frank was killed when a mob kidnaped him from prison and lynched him. Later in his memoirs, the attorney wrote: "I am one of the few people who know that Leo Frank was innocent of the crime for which he was convicted and lynched. . . . [B]ut the information came to me in such a way that, though I wish I could do so, I can never reveal it so. . . . We lawyers . . . take an oath never to reveal the communications made to us by our clients; and this includes facts revealed in an attempt to employ the lawyer, though he refuses the employment." Consider this attorney's behavior under the Model Code, the Model Rules, the recently proposed changes to the Model Rules, and the

Massachusetts Rule that you can find in footnote 8.

Under both the Model Code and the Model Rules, the attorney may not reveal the information. Massachusetts is the only state that currently provides that an attorney may reveal confidential information to "prevent the wrongful execution or incarceration of another."

3. William Macumber was on trial for first-degree murder. His attorney wanted to call attorney Brown to the stand. Attorney Brown had been the attorney for James Smith in a different murder trial. During his representation of Smith, Smith had confessed to attorney Brown that he was the murderer and had acted alone in the case for which Macumber was on trial. Sometime prior to the Macumber trial, Smith died. After his death, attorney Brown approached Macumber's attorney and volunteered to testify as to what Brown had told him. Should the court allow this testimony?

This is essentially the same scenario as #2 except now the client has died. In most states this would not change the need for the attorneys to keep the information confidential. See *State v. Macumber*, **544 P.2d 1084 (Ariz. 1976) in which the court disallowed the testimony.**

CASE DISCUSSION QUESTIONS, page 262 for *In Re Original Grand Jury Investigation*
1. On what basis did the court decide that the attorney should turn over the client's letter?
The court argued that this case was distinguishable from *Purcell* **in that** *Purcell* **involved a direct communication from the client to the attorney and this case involved a piece of physical evidence. That seems a bit disingenuous, however. The physical evidence was not a gun or other instrumentality of the crime, but rather a letter the client had written. Arguably, it should not matter whether the client's confidential information is conveyed in written or oral form. A more important distinction may be that in** *Purcell* **the information was conveyed directly to the attorney. In this case, an investigator discovered the letter. The court also thought it important that the attorney was not being asked to testify against his client.**

2. The dissent argued that the reasoning in *Purcell* should have been followed and that the court's failure to do so will mean "attorneys and their clients will be less likely to discuss potential crimes, which will decrease the likelihood that the crimes can be prevented." Do you agree? Why or why not?
Of course answers can differ, but it does appear that this approach would have a chilling effect on attorney disclosure.

CASE DISCUSSION QUESTIONS, page 266 for *Nix v. Whiteseide*
1. The court assumes, without really discussing, that Robinson "knew" Whiteside was going to commit perjury. Given the nature of memory and how a person's recollections can change over time, is it fair to say that Robinson "knew" that Whiteside was lying when he said he had seen something metallic?
As Justice Steven points out in his concurrence, "a word is but a the skin of a living thought." With hindsight, it seems clear that Whiteside changed his story based on a belief that otherwise he would be convicted, but how is an attorney ever really to "know" that a client is lying?

2. What guidance does this case provide for other attorneys confronted with a client who recalls events one way shortly after first meeting with the attorney and then differently right before trial? **The court states that first the lawyer should seek to persuade the client not to commit perjury. If that is not successful, withdrawal is an appropriate response.**

3. Why did Justice Steven's concur? **Justice Steven's opinion is a cautionary note, reminding us that a change in a client's memory does not necessarily mean the client is planning on committing perjury. Rather, even the most honest witness may recall or believe he or she recalls events differently than as first remembered.**

DISCUSSION QUESTIONS, page 268

11. Under the Model Rules an attorney has an obligation not to present false evidence, but there is no affirmative obligation to reveal truthful material *facts* unless asked to do so by the other side. However, attorneys are under an obligation to disclose to the court *legal authority* in the controlling jurisdiction that is directly adverse to their clients' position if it has not already been disclosed by the opposing counsel. While there can be arguments as to why the obligation only runs to law from the "controlling jurisdiction" (the state or federal district in which the case is being tried) and what it means for the law to be "directly" adverse, this raises an even more fundamental question: If the goal of a trial is the search for truth, why is there an affirmative obligation to reveal law but not facts?
The lack of obligation to reveal facts is a fundamental aspect of our adversary system. Each side is expected to ask the right questions to gather the facts from the other side. Conversely, the system could not work if the whole proceeding was based on inaccurate law. Also, if the court were to rely on "wrong law" that would have an impact not just on the parties to that litigation but also on others with whom the court has similar dealings.

12. Former Supreme Court Justice Byron White said that if a defense attorney "can confuse a witness, even a truthful one, or make him appear at a disadvantage, unsure or indecisive, that will be his normal course." But is it ethical for an attorney to impeach the credibility of a witness when the attorney knows that the testimony given was in fact truthful? In essence, how is that different from putting on the stand a client the attorney knows is going to lie?
Some might argue that trying to impeach a witness the attonrey knows is truthful is even worse than allowing a witness to testify falsely. At least in the latter case, the attorney is generally passive, while it is the witness who is actively deceiving the court. In the case of trying to impeach the truthful witness, however, attorneys use their professional skills and education to attack the witness and themselves actively mislead the court. Conversely, some would argue that while attorneys should not suborn perjury, it is their duty to "poke holes" in the other side's arguments and testimony.

CASE DISCUSSION QUESTIONS, page 271 for *ABA Standing Committee On Ethics and Professional Responsibility, Formal Opinion 92-368*

1. The American Bar Association concluded that an attorney should not read inadvertently received confidential documents. Instead, the attorney should notify the other lawyer and comply with any request such as to return the unread documents. Do you agree?

Obviously, there is no right answer here and various ethics committees have disagreed. The arguments for returning the document unread are first to protect the other side's client confidences and second to encourage good relations among attorneys. The main argument against is that it would not be in the client's best interests.

2. The Committee discussed the need for protecting client confidentiality, but generally that right is seen as running from the client to the client's attorney, not from the client to the opposing attorney. How does that factor into your thinking about the Committee's conclusion?

This is a sticky point often overlooked by the ethics committees.

3. If attorneys are not to follow the "narrow, literalistic reading" of the Model Rules but rather, as the committee suggests, are to be governed by "basic principles," is there any value in having a set of specific rules?

The rules still serve the purpose of answering most of the questions most of the time. However, in the difficult case, the strict rules may have to be interpreted in light of more basic principles.

4. Many attorneys see a move towards "professionalism" as a misguided attempt to subvert the adversarial system. What do you suppose is the basis of their argument?

Attorneys must be careful that in their desire to do a favor for another attorney (and hopefully get one in return) they are not putting this desire to "get along" ahead of the client's needs. For example, assume attorney Black's client is in jail waiting a bail hearing and the attorney for the prosecution calls with a personal emergency asking for a few hours delay. Should attorney Black grant the request with the result that his client will have to remain in jail even a moment longer than originally contemplated when the time for the hearing was set?

DISCUSSION QUESTIONS, page 271

13. In the ABA Opinion, the committee raised the following hypotheticals to bolster its position that it would be unethical for an attorney to use missent information. Example 1: During a lunch break in a deposition, lawyer B left notes in a conference room either in an unlocked briefcase or on the conference room table. Lawyer A, arriving back from lunch early, could not ethically review the materials to which he now has easy access. Example 2: After a closing at lawyer A's office, lawyer B accidentally leaves a file or a briefcase behind. Lawyer A could not ethically take advantage of this inadvertence and rifle the file or inspect the briefcase before returning it. Example 3: In positioning an overhead projector on a shared counsel table in a courtroom during a recess, court personnel inadvertently moves the prosecutor's notes into a position in front of the defense counsel's place at the table. Again, ethically the defendant's attorney could not take a quick peak at those notes. If an attorney were to take advantage of any of the above situations

and read the confidential information, do you think that presents a different situation than the one presented in the Ethics Opinion? Why?

In each of these hypotheticals, the attorney would have to positively act in order to read the information. This is different from the inadvertent disclosure scenarios in which the attorney innocently read or received the information before realizing it was not meant to be shared. As the court noted in *Aerojet General Corporation v. Transport Indemnity Insurance*, 22 Cal. Rptr.2d 862, 866 (Cal. App.1993), "[t]he attorney-client privilege is a shield against deliberate intrusion; it is not an insurer against inadvertent disclosure."

14. In this day of fax machines and e-mails, it is all too easy to pick the wrong fax number off of a list or the wrong address from a computerized address book. Is it fair to penalize attorneys when they mistakenly dial the wrong number?

Attorneys are penalized all the time for making errors. Arguably, this type of error should be treated no differently.

Case Discussion Questions, page 273 for *Professional Ethics Commission of the Board of Overseers of the Bar, Opinion No. 146*

1. The majority opinion seems to be that an attorney should not be responsible for correcting the mistakes of the opposing attorney. Even the dissent stated "After all, Attorney Z should not be expected to rectify every mistake made by opposing counsel in the course of litigation." Do you agree? Are there some mistakes that so fundamentally alter the adversarial process that an attorney should be required to rectify opposing counsel's errors?

Under the rules, attorneys are required to correct mistakes directly related to notifying the court of any controlling law. However, other than in the area of inadvertent disclosure of information, there is no area of the practice of law where attorneys are required to correct or even point out mistakes made by their opponents.

2. Why should the lawyer be required to notify the sending lawyer of the document's receipt? See, *Aerojet General Corporation v. Transport Indemnity Insurance*, 22 Cal. Rptr.2d 862 (Cal. App.1993) in which the court stated that the attorney had not violated any ethical rules by not notifying the opposing attorneys immediately after he inadvertently received documents originating from them, including a memorandum that revealed the existence of a witness about whom he had not known and whom he subsequently deposed.

Arguably notification is just another part of the courtesy attorneys should show their opponents, but the rules do not mandate it. Note that the Maine opinion only states that the attorney "should" notify the opposing attorney, not that she must do so.

3. Do you think a different result should occur if an attorney left a file folder behind during a break in a deposition and while out of the room, the attorney took the folder and surreptitiously copied it? What if a disgruntled staff member working in the opposing attorney's firm had sent the document to the attorney?

In the first hypothetical, the attorney would be actively involved in "stealing" information from the other side. Under none of the existing ethics opinions would this be seen as appropriate. The second scenario is more troubling. Here the release of the information is not inadvertent, but it is also not through anything that the receiving attorney has done.

15. When an attorney receives information that the opposing side has sent accidentally, that attorney has four options:

■　　　To refrain from reading the information, and then to contact the opposing attorney and return the document unread.

■　　　To read the information, contact the opposing attorney, and return the document.

■　　　To read the information, contact the opposing attorney, and refuse to return the document.

■　　　To read the information and use it.

Given our adversarial system and your own sense of justice, which approach do you think is best?

This should encourage a debate about courtesy and "doing unto others as you would hope they would do unto you" versus being the client's champion within the adversarial process.

16. Attorney White represents the plaintiff who was injured in an automobile accident. She and her client have decided to settle the case if they can obtain at least $200,000. The settlement talks are set to begin tomorrow and her strategy is to start by asking for $300,000, hoping to end up at $200,000. As attorney White is reviewing the files in preparation for the settlement talks, she discovers a one page fax that she had not noticed before. It is from the defendant's insurer and was obviously intended to reach the defendant's attorney. It contains just one line: "Offer $100,000, but you have authority to settle for up to $500,000."

a. What should attorney White do?

Once she has read the information, there is little the attorney can do to undo the harm to the other side. (How can she ignore the information she now has?) As a zealous advocate, she could remain silent about what she knows and use the information in her negotiations for her client. See, for example, *Aerojet-General Corp. v. Transport Indemnity Ins.*, 22 Cal. Rptr 2d 862, 867 (Cal. App. 1993) in which the court stated "[o]nce he acquired the information in a manner that was not due to his own fault or wrongdoing, he cannot purge it from his mind. Indeed, his professional obligation demands that he utilize his knowledge about the case on his client's behalf." Therefore, the duty of zealous advocacy may even <u>require</u> the attorney to use the information. Some students may feel, however, that she should at least notify the other side of what she has learned. You might want to ask them how then they think the negotiations are likely to proceed if she does so.

b. Do you think that it should matter if that the fax was intermixed with other documents?

This scenario presumes that the attorney was not on notice that she was reading confidential information from the other side until she had already read it. This is different from the situation where the attorney receives, for example, a misdirected fax but realizes she is looking at confidential information before reading it.

c. What if attorney White was wandering by the fax machine as it came in? As she pulled it out, she saw the cover sheet that contained the following language:

Privileged and Confidential-All information transmitted hereby is intended only
for the use of the addressee(s) name above. If the reader of this message is not the

intended recipient or the employee or agent responsible for delivering the message to the intended recipient(s), please note that any distribution or copying of this communication is strictly prohibited. Anyone who receives this communication in error should notify us immediately by telephone and return the original to us at the above address via the U.S. mail

The cover sheet showed that the fax was to be sent to the opposing attorney but the fax number was for Ms. White's office. What should she do?

Such warnings are now so ubiquitous that it is questionable whether such warnings have any effect whatsoever. In addition, how is an attorney to know if the information is not intended for her receipt unless she first reads it?

CASE DISCUSSION QUESTIONS, page 279 for *Commonwealth v. Croken*

1. What is the danger to a client when his or her attorney is having a personal relationship with another attorney who works for the same organization that is prosecuting the client?
The court talks of the danger of "inadvertent breaches of confidentiality." For example, a "spouse may have knowledge of out-of-town investigative trips at or around the time of preparation for a particular case; clients and witnesses may contact the lawyer at home or leave messages on the home answering machine," etc.

2. Do you think this case would have been decided differently if Jane Doe had been the prosecuting attorney instead of simply being an attorney working in the office?
If Jane Doe had been the prosecuting attorney, it is likely the court would have found an actual as opposed to a merely a potential conflict or would have found that the potential conflict created a situation of ineffective assistance of counsel.

3. The defendant stated that he would never have retained Attorney LaLiberte as his attorney had he known of LaLiberte's and Ms. Doe's relationship. Why is this statement and the attorney's total failure to reveal the potential conflict not enough to form the basis for a new trial?
The problem is that the court was forced into assessing the situation after the representation had been completed. The court determined there was no actual conflict as Jane Doe did not work on the case. The question then became whether there was a potential conflict that interfered with the attorney's effective assistance. The court found that there was nothing that impaired the attorney's independent professional judgment.

4. How is a client ever truly to know whether confidences and secrets were shared if the majority of the evidentiary hearing is based on the testimony of the two individuals who have the alleged conflict?
Clearly this is difficult. The court held an evidentiary hearing at which both the attorney and Jane Doe stated that they had never discussed the case. As they are the only two people who know the truth, there is little that the defendant can do. You may want to ask the students whether in such situations the court should presume a conflict and then put the burden of proof on the attorneys to prove otherwise.

DISCUSSION QUESTIONS, page 280

17. Why should Mr. Brown's partner be penalized in his choice of attorney just because attorney Smith happened to represent Mr. Brown years ago in an unrelated matter?

The notion of attorney-client loyalty assumes that the attorney will remain faithful to keeping client confidences forever. Therefore, an attorney can never use knowledge gained from a client to later work against that client's best interests.

18. Model Rule 1.7 states that "notwithstanding the existence of a concurrent conflict of interest . . . a lawyer may represent a client if the lawyer reasonably believes that the lawyer will be able to provide competent and diligent representation." Is that a bit like asking the fox to guard the hen house?

The rule states the lawyer must "reasonably" believe. Therefore, the rule encompasses both a subjective and an objective element. The attorney must him or herself actually believe that he or she will not be affected by the conflict plus a reasonable outsider looking at the situation must agree with that assessment.

DISCUSSION QUESTION, page 281

19. Attorney Judith Nathanson is an attorney who earned her law degree with the purpose of helping to advance the status of women in the legal system. In her divorce practice, she only represents wives. As she only has a certain amount of time and energy to devote to her clients, she feels it essential to use her resources to redress social and legal wrongs done to women. Therefore, when Mr. Stropnicky asked her to represent him in his divorce, she refused. Should she be required to represent him? Should it matter that in his marriage he had assumed the role of homemaker and childcare giver? Is this analogous to an attorney with white supremacist views arguing the she should be able to decline to represent non-white clients?

This is based on a trial court decision: _Nathanson v. Commonwealth_, 16 Mass. L. Rep. 761 (Superior Ct. 2003). In that case Mr. Stropnicky filed a complaint against attorney Nathanson with the Massachusetts Commission Against Discrimination, arguing that she was practicing gender discrimination in a place of public accommodation. The court agreed, holding that "it is not permissible for an attorney to assert a discriminatory agenda as grounds that she is unable to advocate zealously for a client."

CASE DISCUSSION QUESTIONS, page 286 for _Gagnon v. Shoblom_

1. Why did the Massachusetts Supreme Judicial Court think the trial court had erred in disapproving the agreed upon fee?

The court noted that in the appropriate case it could disapprove a fee which exceeds the percentage in the fee agreement, a fee to which the client never agreed, or one that was plainly unreasonable, but that none of these factors were in play here. In fact no one had challenged the fee. Therefore, the trial court had acted on its own and its determination should be reversed.

2. Mr. Gagnon received a structured settlement in this case. How do you think that might have affected his ability to pay his attorney's fees?

You may need to explain to the students the specifics of how structured settlements work. Here the client only received an initial payment of $800,000 and yet he owed almost $3 million in attorney's fees.

3. Do you agree with the trial court judge that the percentage an attorney earns should decrease as the size of the client's award increases? Why or why not?

On the one hand, such a limitation might work to discourage attorneys from working their hardest to get the largest awards for their clients. On the other, at some point 1/3 of a very large award will far exceed the time and expenses that the attorney will have expended in the case.

4. Specifically, how do you answer the trial judge's assertion that "[a]ny fee that the attorney exacts from the client under a contingent fee agreement must therefore reduce the client's compensation of his injury below what is fair and reasonable"?

That is, of course, the nature of a contingency fee agreement. Whether the attorney takes 1/3 or 1/4 of the compensation, that fee is always going to reduce the amount available to the client. Proponents of the contingency fee model would argue, however, the alternative is many clients going without representation and therefore receiving nothing by way of compensation.

5. What do you think of the contingency fee agreement in this particular case? Given the facts outlined before the case, it seems apparent that when Goodman had his client sign the contingent fee agreement, he knew that the liability aspect of Gagnon's case would not be difficult to prove, that his client's injuries were catastrophic, and as Shoblom was employed as a driver for a large corporate employer, that it was likely Gagnon would receive a very substantial judgment or settlement from that corporate employer.

Other evidence that attorney Goodman thought that the case would settle quickly can be found in the changes made to the contingency fee agreement, so that 33.3% was the only percentage option. (Options relating to a possible trial and appeal had been crossed out.) However, it would be very difficult to fashion a rule based on attorneys being penalized for taking "easy" cases and winning them quickly versus attorneys taking more difficult cases in which they are required to spend more time. Indeed, the contingency fee model assumes that some cases will be "easy" wins to compensate the attorney for the difficult wins and those cases in which the attorney loses and is paid nothing.

6. In addition to representing Donald Gagnon, attorney Goodman had also been retained to represent the administrator of the dead woman's estate in her claim for wrongful death and the dead woman's mother for her claim of negligent infliction of emotional distress. Clearly, Goodman could make use of much of the work he had already done on the *Gagnon* case in

preparing those additional cases, for which he was also charging a fee. Do you think those clients should receive some sort of a discount for work that had already been done and paid for?

This problem is not unique to contingency fee situations. For example, assume attorney Smith charges a flat fee of $500 for a simple will. The first time she drafts such a will, it might take her ten hours. By the time she is doing her fiftieth will, it may be taking her only one hour. Should she start charging less or is it ethical for her to continue to charge $500 per will?

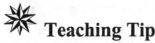 **Teaching Tip**

Page 285: We included the copy of the contingency fee agreement in this case so that the students could see what one actually looks like and to show how a "boiler plate" agreement can be edited by the parties.

CASE DISCUSSION QUESTIONS, page 291 for *In re Arons*

1. The court seems to be stating that it is better for parents to have no representation at all than non-lawyer representation. Do you agree?

The court essentially stated that the need to regulate nonlawyer practice outweighed any benefit individual parents and children would receive from the services of lay advocates.

2. The court conceded that Ms. Arons was a specialist in education law. Why did they refuse to allow her to advocate on behalf of the parents at due process hearings?

The court was structuring a rule to govern all nonlawyer advocates, not just Ms. Arons. The court's concern was that lay advocates are unregulated and are not answerable to a code of ethics. In addition, they lack formal legal training.

3. Ms. Arons and her colleague prevailed in all five of the Delaware cases in which they appeared on behalf of the families. In an interview with the Wall Street Journal, Ms. Arons was quoted as saying that she never felt at a disadvantage in court, "I found it a piece of cake." Contrast that statement with the court's declaration that "they admittedly lack the training and skills that lawyers are expected to exhibit in matters of evidence and procedure."

It is hard to argue with Ms. Arons' rate of success. A cynic might argue that the bar went after her precisely because she was so successful.

REVIEW QUESTIONS, pages 335-36

1. Describe the adversarial system. How does it vary from a system based on the inquisitional model?

In an adversarial system, lawyers for each side present all of the relevant facts and arguments to a neutral decision maker. In contract, with the "inquisitorial system" used in many European nations, judges are active participants in the search for truth rather than neutral arbitrators. It is judges, rather than lawyers, who determine who will be called as

witnesses, and it is the judges who ask most of the questions of the witnesses. Lawyers are present in the courtroom to assist the judge and the lawyers' duty to the litigants is clearly secondary to their duty to the court.

2. Explain the relationship between the rights contained in the Fourth, Fifth, and Sixth amendments and our adversarial system.
The Fourth Amendment prohibition against unreasonable searches and seizures puts limits on the government's power to search for evidence. The Fifth Amendment privilege against self-incrimination demonstrates that due process rights take precedence over the search for truth. Finally, the Sixth amendment guarantee of the right to counsel recognizes the importance placed on the role of lawyers in our adversarial legal system.

3. Some have described litigation as a battleground. Why is that?
Litigation is often described as a battleground because the attorneys are seen as unwavering advocates for their clients. It is their role to represent their clients' interests against the opposing side.

4. Attorneys are governed either by the Code of Professional Responsibility or the Rules of Professional Conduct. Who originally drafted these documents, and how is it that they govern the behavior of attorneys in a particular state?
They were drafted by the American Bar Association. To govern attorney behavior, a state, usually through its supreme court, must have adopted them.

5. Are attorneys in your state bound by the Code of Professional Responsibility or the Rules of Professional Conduct.
The answer will vary by state. However, most states now follow the Rules.

6. What can happen to attorneys who violate the ethical rules in effect in their state?
Attorneys can receive a private or public reprimand, be suspended, or even disbarred.

7. Why does our legal system place such a high value on attorneys maintaining their client's confidences?
It is believed that for attorneys to adequately represent their clients, they must have complete knowledge of the facts. It is also believed that unless clients are convinced that attorneys will keep that information confidential, they will not be fully candid with their attorneys.

8. How does the attorney-client privilege differ from the ethical rules regarding confidentiality?
The attorney-client privilege does not cover as many situations as do the ethical rules regarding confidentiality. The ethical rules generally cover any confidence regarding the client no matter the source. Therefore, an attorney cannot voluntarily repeat that information without the client's consent. However, a court could require the attorney to testify regarding that information unless it also meets the four part test for satisfying the attorney-client privilege:
> **1. The *client* made a statement**
> **2. to the attorney**

3. while seeking legal advice and
4. while no unnecessary persons were present.

Therefore, the attorney-client privilege is a subset of all confidential information. See Figures 9-1 and 9-2 on page 247 of the text.

9. Mrs. Smith, who is seeking a divorce, entered attorney Black's office for her first interview. Because she was very disturbed over the prospect of a divorce, Mrs. Smith brought her best friend along with her to the interview. Should attorney Black let Mrs. Smith's best friend sit in on the interview? Why?

She should not let the best friend sit in on the interview as it will destroy the attorney-client privilege. Only those with a "need to know" should be part of the conversation.

10. At a cocktail party attorney Sims sees one of his firm's clients kissing someone not the client's wife. At the client's divorce hearing could attorney Sims be required to testify about what he saw at the party? Could attorney Sims ethically tell his wife about what he saw at the party? Why?

Attorney Sims could be required to testify about what he saw as it does not qualify for the attorney-client privilege. It was not a statement made to the attorney in confidence while the client was seeking advice. However, it would be a breach of the ethical rules regarding confidentiality for Sims to tell his wife about what he saw. The ethical rules are broader than the client-attorney privilege and protect any client secrets learned from any source.

11. For each of the follow discuss whether the attorney can reveal the information. Be sure to indicate if your answer would vary depending on whether the state in which this occurred had adopted the Model Code, the Model Rules, or the recently revised 2003 Model Rules.

a. A client tells her attorney that she murdered her husband.
Cannot be revealed.

b. A client tells her attorney that she is planning to murder her husband.
Model Code - may reveal the intent to commit a crime.
Model Rules - may reveal if the lawyer believes the possibility of death is imminent.
2003 Model Rules - may reveal if the lawyer reasonably believes death is reasonably certain.

c. A client tells her attorney that at the end of the week she is planning on stealing all of her employer's cash receipts as she has access to his safe.
Model Code - may reveal the intent to commit a crime.
Model Rules - may not reveal as there is to threat of "imminent death or substantial bodily harm.
2003 Model Rules - may not reveal unless the client is using the attorney's services to commit the crime.

d. A client tells her attorney that her husband is so upset with how the litigation is going that he is planning on killing the opposing attorney.
Model Code and Rules - May not reveal as the person planning on committing the crime is not the client.
2003 Model Rules - may reveal to "prevent reasonably certain death."

e. A client tells her attorney that it was she, and not the woman who is on trial for murder, who killed the victim.
May not reveal. Note: Massachusetts is the only state in which the attorney could reveal this information.

12. What are the major differences and similarities between the Model Rules and the Model Code's approach to allowing attorneys to reveal planned criminal behavior?
The Model Code simply speaks of an intended crime. The Model Rules are more restrictive in that the crime must be one "likely to result in imminent death or substantial bodily harm."

13. If a client tells an attorney she is going to commit perjury, what are the attorney's options?
First, the attorney should try to dissuade the client, pointing out the dangers of testifying falsely. If the persuasion is not effective, the attorney may refuse to continue representation. If the attorney continues to represent the client, the attorney may not offer the false evidence. In some jurisdictions, this rule is modified for criminal defendants who may in a narrative statement.

14. If an attorney suspects but does not know that a client is going to commit perjury, what should the attorney do? Does it matter if the client is the defendant in a criminal case?
As above, the attorney should try to dissuade the client from testifying falsely. Under the rules the attorney at his or her option may refuse to offer the client's testimony if the attorney reasonable believes it is false. This is not allowed, however, in the case of the criminal defendant.

15. What should attorneys do when they inadvertently receive confidential information from the other side?
They should first consult the ethics opinions in their individual state. The ABA has opined that the attorney should notify the opposing counsel, return the information, and not rely on it. Some states, however, have limited the attorney's obligation to notification, and in others, there is a suggestion that it would be unethical to fail to use the information.

16. Give some examples of when an attorney might find her duty of loyalty to her client conflicting with other values she holds.
The text raises many examples of when an attorney may feel that her personal values are being challenged by her need for client loyalty. The most poignant examples involve harm to others, such as the boy with the unknown aneurysm or the kidnaped woman, trapped in a box in an unknown location. Less traumatic, but still difficult situations include how to handle the client whom the attorney suspects of lying and deciding how to handle the "smoking gun" type of evidence found through inadvertent disclosure.

17. What are the two major causes of conflict of interest?

Conflicts of interest can generally be divided into two categories. The first involves situations in which lawyers have a personal or business interest that suggests they cannot give their undivided loyalty to a client, such as being related to the opposing counsel or having a financial interest in a client's business. The second involves either present or past client representation that presents a conflict with the representation of a new client, such as having represented the opposing side in a previous lawsuit.

18. In each of the following situations determine whether you see any potential conflict of interest problems.

    a. Sam was injured in an automobile accident when the car he was riding in was struck in an intersection by a pickup truck. Both Sam and the driver of the car want Attorney Black to represent them against the driver of the pickup truck.

    This is a potential conflict of interest as at some point in the litigation, Sam and the driver may have different interests.

    b Sara and Emily were arrested for the attempted robbery of United Bank. They would like attorney Jones to represent both of them.

    This is a potential conflict of interest as it may be in the best interest of either Sara or Emily to testify against the other.

    c. Attorney Lacy is the prosecuting attorney for the murder trial of Tom Black. Jim White represents the defendant. Halfway through the murder trial, attorney Lacy and attorney White start dating.

    This is a potential conflict. Attorney White should immediately notify his client of the potential conflict and obtain his informed consent.

19. What reasons do attorneys usually give for why they are willing to represent guilty or unpopular clients?

Some rely on the notion that guilt is a legal concept that is determined by a judge or a jury and not by the lawyer.   A person is not considered guilty until after the trial has been completed. A second possible response is that in representing a guilty client, the attorney is just playing a role, similar to the actor who plays the part of the villain in a movie. Third, some believe that the very legitimacy of our adversary system depends on having lawyers willing to represent the "guilty" as well as the innocent. If criminal defendants cannot find attorneys willing to represent them, "the foundation of the judicial system is eroded and the lawyers become the judges of guilt or innocence by their very decision to accept or reject those criminal clients." The importance of attorneys being willing to accept court appointments is stated in Model Rule 6.2: "A lawyer shall not seek to avoid appointment by a tribunal to represent a person except for good cause."

20. What are the three most common methods that attorneys use for charging clients?

The three most common methods are flat fee, hourly rate, and contingency.

21. What is a contingency fee and how does it arguably increase access to justice?

When attorneys charge a contingency fee, they agree to accept a certain percentage of the plaintiff's recovery. This allows clients who would not have enough money to pay an

attorney up front to hire an attorney on the understanding that a fee will be due only if the client recovers compensation.

22. What is the major justification for enforcing unauthorized practice of law statutes?
The major justification for enforcing unauthorized practice of law statutes has been to protect the public from unregulated and untrained lay advocates.

# Chapter 10

Torts

This is one of the longer chapters in the book. However, many tort concepts, especially those relating to intentional torts and negligence, have already been discussed in earlier chapters. Therefore, you may want to assign only parts of this chapter for classroom discussion.

CASE DISCUSSION QUESTIONS, page 300 for *Knight v. Jewett*
1. Did the court think that a battery had occurred? Why?
No. The defendant did not intend to step on the plaintiff's finger.

2. What role do you think Ms. Knight's deposition played in the court's reasoning?
Ms. Knight admitted that she did not think the defendant intended to step on her (no intent) nor to hurt her (motive). While the second is not relevant, the first is. [Note: one of the reasons we included this case was to illustrate to students the importance of pretiral discovery work.]

3. Do you think the result would have been different if Ms. Knight had never watched football nor played touch football prior to her accident?
The result might have been different if the court had found intent. Then the defendant might have raised Ms. Knight's knowing consent as a defense.

CASE DISCUSSION QUESTIONS, pages 302-03 for *Katko v. Briney*
1. Why did the court uphold the jury's verdict in favor of the defendant trespasser?
The court stated that a property owner cannot use deadly force to protect property.

2. The dissent stated: "When such a windfall comes to a criminal as a result of his indulgence in serious criminal conduct, the result is intolerable and indeed shocks the conscience. If we find the law upholds such a result, the criminal would be permitted by operation of law to profit from his own crime." What do you think?
This is a difficult question. The students should think about whether they see any limits to allowing trespassers to recover for injuries caused by their having trespassed.

3. Because the defendant did not raise the issue, this court did not deal directly with whether punitive damages were appropriate. What facts would support such a finding; which facts would argue against such a finding? Do you think punitive damages were appropriate in this case? Why?

For punitive damages there must be an intentional battery with a dangerous weapon. The defendant testified the gun was pointed to hit someone in the legs and that it was loaded. There was no sign posted warning of the gun, and because the windows were covered, it could not be seen from outside. The argument against punitives is that this was merely a case of negligence. The defendant stated he did not intend to injure anyone, but should have realized the likely result of his actions.

4. Should a landowner who sets a trap such as in this case also be found criminally liable if an intruder is seriously injured? Why?

Yes, he should be found criminally liable if he intended to cause serious bodily injury.

5. Do you think the result in this case would have been different if the house had been occupied? Why?

Perhaps the result would have been different if the house had been occupied. Protection of life is seen as a greater value than merely protecting property. However, a problem for the landowner still would be that a spring gun is indiscriminate. There would be no way of knowing ahead of time if it would be the use of appropriate force. For example, what if the trespasser had been an unarmed ten-year-old child?

6. At trial Mr. Briney testified that "[p]rior to this time . . . he had locked the doors, posted seven no trespassing signs on the premises, and complained to the sheriffs of two counties on numerous occasions. . . .[A]ll these efforts were futile and the vandalism continued." What else could the defendant have done to protect his property?

This is a growing problem. See if the students can come up with any solutions, such as posted warnings regarding watch dogs.

 **Teaching Tip**

Page 303: As you discuss the *Coblyn* case make sure the students see the difference between what the plaintiff has to show for a prima facia case and what the merchant has to show to prove a valid defense.

CASE DISCUSSION QUESTIONS, pages 305-06 for *Coblyn v. Kennedy's, Inc.*

1. Why did the court think that there was sufficient evidence of unlawful restraint? Do you agree?

The court noted that the employee stopped him, grabbed his arm, told him he better go with him; another employee was at his side, the plaintiff was an elderly man, and other people were present.

2. Did the court think that the detention had taken place in a reasonable manner? Why?
No, the court did not think the detention had taken place in a reasonable manner. The employee didn't identify himself as an employee nor disclose the reasons for stopping the plaintiff; there was physical restraint in a public place on an elderly man.

3. Did the court think that finding reasonable grounds to detain someone should be based on an objective or a subjective standard? Why? Do you agree?
The court thought it should be an objective standard — probable cause must be based on facts and not on an "inarticulate hunch."

Legal Reasoning Exercise, page 306

1. Martha Smith went to a K-Mart store at about 7:30 p.m. on September 8 to purchase some diapers and several cans of motor oil. She took her small child along to enable her to purchase the correct size diapers, carrying the child in an infant seat which she had purchased at K-Mart two or three weeks previously. A large K-Mart price tag was still attached to the infant seat.

Martha purchased the diapers and oil and some children's clothes. She was in a hurry to leave because it was then 8:00 P.M., her child's feeding time, and she hurried through the checkout lane. She paid for the diapers, oil, and clothing. Just after leaving the store, she heard someone ask her to stop. She turned around and saw a K-Mart security guard, who asked, "Would you please come back into the store?" Martha replied, "What for"? The security guard pulled out a store badge, showed it to her, and said that if she would just come back into the store, he would like to talk to her about it.

When Martha hesitated, the security guard grabbed her by the arm and led her back into the store, stopping just inside the doors. The guard then told Martha that one of the K-Mart employees had informed him that she saw Martha steal the car seat. Martha denied that she had stolen the seat, and explained that she had purchased the seat previously. She demanded to see the person who accused her of stealing the seat. The security guard said that it would take awhile to find the employee. Martha asked if they could wait in a more private place, but the guard said that they could not.

After approximately 20 minutes, the employee was found. The employee stated that she saw plaintiff steal the infant seat by taking it off a table and putting her baby in it. Martha pointed out to the security guard that the seat had cat hairs, food crumbs, and milk stains on it. The guard then said, "I'm really sorry, there's been a terrible mistake. You can go." Martha looked at the clock as she left. The time was 8:30 P.M.

Assume that Martha has sued K-Mart for false imprisonment. Your firm represents K-Mart, and your boss wants to know if the store has a valid defense. Research revealed the following statute:

> ch. 203, § 99
> A merchant or merchant's adult employee who has probable cause for believing that a person has stolen store merchandise may detain such person in a reasonable manner for a reasonable length of time.

Using the IRAC method, write an analysis of the issues in this case. Include arguments that will be raised by both the Martha's attorney and the store's attorney. (Remember, if there are not two sides, you have not selected an issue.)

NOTE: This legal reasoning exercise is based on *Johnson v. K-Mart Enterprises, Inc.*, 297 N.W.2d 74 (Wis. 1980). The court in that case granted the defendant's motion for summary judgment. The following is an outline of possible arguments on either side.

Issue/Rule — probable cause
Argument for — tag on seat; employee thought she saw theft
Argument against — paid for other items; obvious (not trying to conceal it); cat hairs, etc.
Conclusion

Issue/Rule — reasonable manner
Argument for — showed badge; found employee to verify story
Argument against — grabbed arm; done in public although asked to go to a more private place
Conclusion

Issue/Rule — reasonable time
Argument for — got employee as fast as could; 30 min. total not unreasonable.
Argument against — 20 minutes is too long to track down employee; no need for other 10 minutes
Conclusion

DISCUSSION QUESTION, page 307
1. Many argue that shoplifting is a major cause of increased costs. Do you think shopkeepers should be given more or less leeway in deciding when to detain suspected shoplifters?
The common standard is that shopkeepers may detain someone when there is probable cause to suspect shoplifting and the detention is done in a reasonable manner for a reasonable time. Students may argue that probable cause is too high a standard, and something like reasonable suspicion should be enough. You might ask them if they think shopkeepers should be held to the same or to a higher or lower standard than the police.

DISCUSSION QUESTION, pages 309-10
2. In the case against the National Enquirer, Carol Burnett testified that the statements were particularly offensive to her because of her nationally known work against alcoholism.
　　a. Do you think that should affect the amount of the damage award?
　　It could as it might harm her ability to remain a national spokesperson.

　　b. During the trial Johnny Carson on his program The Tonight Show denounced the National Enquirer. How do you think the trial judge should have handled that situation?
　　In the actual trial, the trial judge examined "each juror concerning the effect of the tirade on the juror's ability to participate in a fair and impartial trial and being satisfied in the premises, the trial court excused two of the triers of fact, seated the only available alternate, and proceeded with a panel of eleven, from which it was agreed nine could determine the cause." The appellate court thought that was sufficient protection against juror bias.

c. Do you agree with the dissent that a large punitive award was justified in this case? Why?

This will depend on whether they think the standard should be based on a certain percentage relationship to the compensatory damages or whether they think other factors are more important.

CASE DISCUSSION QUESTIONS, page 313 for *Agis v. Howard Johnson Company*

1. The court stated that "for purposes of ruling on the motion dismissing plaintiff's complaint" it was accepting as true the allegations in the plaintiff's complaint. Why?

Make sure the students understand that in order to rule on a motion to dismiss, the court must accept the facts as presented by the plaintiff. In essence, the defendant is arguing that even if the facts are true, they do not support a claim.

2. What is the most common reason given for refusing to allow a claim for intentional infliction of emotional distress when there is no physical injury? What was the court's response?

The most common reasons given are the difficulty of proof and the danger of fraudulent or frivolous claims. The court responded that the job of judges and juries is to ferret out the truth, and the required elements for the tort of intentional infliction of emotional distress will tend to prevent fraudulent or frivolous claims.

3. What four elements does the court require for a successful claim for intentional infliction of emotional distress?

The elements of intentional inflection of emotional distress are

1. an intentional act

2. that is extreme and outrageous

3. and causes

4. severe emotional distress.

4. Procedurally, what had to happen next in this case for the plaintiff to recover?

The case had to now go back for discovery and/or trial.

DISCUSSION QUESTIONS, page 313

3. What constitutes "extreme and outrageous" conduct is obviously a troubling issue, as is how debilitating the emotional distress must be to be seen as "severe." Consider the facts of *Harris v. Jones*, 380 A.2d 611 (Md. 1977). The plaintiff sued his employer (General Motors) and one of his supervisors, H. Robert Jones. Jones knew that the plaintiff suffered from a speech impediment that caused him to stutter. Jones also knew that the plaintiff was very sensitive about his disability. "Jones approached Harris over 30 times at work and verbally and physically mimicked his stuttering disability.... As a result of Jones' conduct Harris was 'shaken up' and felt 'like going into a hole and hide.'" However, the court concluded that Harris' humiliation was not so intense as to meet the requirement of being severe. Do you agree?

This will depend on how strongly the students feel the court should be involved in protecting a person's sensibilities. It will also depend on whether they think the plaintiff suffered sufficient emotional distress.

4. The March 1984 issue of Hustler magazine ran a parody of an advertisement for Campari Liqueur that featured various celebrities describing the first time they tasted Campari. Hustler's version presented a supposed interview with the Reverend Jerry Falwell, a nationally prominent Protestant minister, conservative political figure, and head of the now defunct "Moral Majority." The "advertisement" claimed that Falwell's first experience with Campari was part of an incestuous sexual encounter with his mother in an outhouse. Shortly after the issue hit the newsstands, Falwell sued the magazine for libel, invasion of privacy, and intentional infliction of emotional distress. If you were the judge, how would you rule on each of these issues?

This is based on the case of *Hustler Magazine v. Falwell*, 485 U.S. 46 (1988).

Libel — Since this was a parody, this could not "reasonably be understood as describing actual facts." Therefore, there would be no libel.

Invasion of privacy — The trial court had granted a directed verdict on this claim. Under the Virginia statute, there was a required showing that the plaintiff's name or likeness be used for advertising or trade purposes and there was no such showing.

Intentional Infliction of emotional distress — The court held that becuase of First Amendment concerns, public figures and public officials may not recover damages for the tort of intentional infliction of emotional distress unless they can also show there was a false statement of fact made with actual malice. Therefore, the plaintiff could not win under intentional infliction of emotional distress.

Note: The trial court's slip opinion makes interesting reading. The judge gives a good summary of the requisite elements of the tort of intentional infliction of emotional distress, and illustrates each element with the plaintiff and defendant's testimony. Here are some excerpts:

"Defendant Flynt correctly states that, for plaintiff to recover on his claim of intentional infliction of emotional distress, he must first show that Flynt 'had the specific purpose of inflicting emotional distress or [that] he intended his specific conduct and knew or should have known that emotional distress would likely result.' Id. This specific purpose is abundantly clear from Flynt's own depositive [sic].

Q. Did you want to upset Reverend Falwell?
A. Yes.
Flynt Deposition at 149.
Q. Do you recognize that in having published what you did in this ad, you were attempting to convey to the people who read it that Reverend Falwell was just as you characterized him, a liar?
A. He's a glutton.
Q. How about a liar?
A. Yeah. He's a liar, too.
Q. How about a hypocrite.
A. Yeah.
Q. That's what you wanted to convey?
A. Yeah.
Q. And didn't it occur to you that if it wasn't true, you were attacking a man in his profession?
A. Yes.

Q. Did you appreciate, at the time that you wrote "okay," or approved this publication, that for Reverend Falwell to function in his livelihood, and in his commitment and career, he has to have an integrity that people believe in? Did you not appreciate that?
A. Yeah.
Q. And wasn't one of your objectives to destroy that integrity, or harm it, if you could?
A. To assassinate it.

Id. at 155-56. . . . With such evidence before it, the jury certainly could reasonably conclude that Flynt bore the requisite tortious intent toward plaintiff.

To be actionable, defendant's conduct must have been outrageous and intolerable in that it offend[ed] against the generally accepted standards of decency and morality. . . . Flynt's personal attack took the form of a graphic mischaracterization of plaintiff's relationship with his own mother and of his personal moral practices. The question of outrageousness in this case was properly before the jury, since reasonable men could disagree about the offensiveness of Flynt's conduct.

Whether plaintiff did, in fact, suffer severe emotional distress is the final consideration. . . . He testified on that point:
Q. Would you tell His Honor and the members of this jury what your personal reaction was when you read this ad in [the November 1983 issue of Hustler] over for the first time?
A. I think I have never been as angry as I was at that moment . . . . My anger became a more rational and deep hurt. I somehow felt that in all of my life I had never believed that human beings could do something like this. I really felt like weeping. I am not a deeply emotional person; I don't show it. I think I felt like weeping.
Q. How long did this sense of anger last?
A. To this present moment.
Falwell Testimony at 36.
Q. You say that it almost brought you to tears. In your whole life, Mr. Falwell, had you ever had a personal experience of such intensity that could compare with the feeling that you had when you saw this ad?
A. Never had. Since I have been a Christian I don't think I have ever intentionally hurt anybody. I am sure I have hurt people but not with intent. I certainly have never physically attacked anyone in my life. I really think that at that moment if Larry Flynt had been nearby I might have physically reacted."

Legal Reasoning Exercise, page 316

2. Review the situation of Mrs. Day presented at the beginning of the chapter. Using the IRAC method, write an analysis of the issues in the case. Include arguments that will be raised by both Mrs. Day's attorney and Mr. Day's attorney. For example, if you represented Mrs. Day, what torts would you argue Mr. Day committed? If you were representing Mr. Day, how would you respond?
Mrs. Day's attorney would argue that the following torts had occurred:

Defamation — Her husband published a false fact, that she had been skimming money, and this resulted in her losing her job.

Intentional Infliction of Emotional Distress — If Mrs. Day can show that she has suffered severe emotional distress, it could be argued that Mr. Day telling her that her mother had a massive heart attack was done intentionally to cause her emotional upset and was the type of statement that is outrageous.

Assault — This would be difficult to prove as Mrs. Day did not feel any apprehension as she did not think Mr. Day would hit her. When he did hit her, her back was turned.

Battery — She will have to prove that Mr. Day's hitting her in the back was intentional.

Conversion — She will have to prove that Mr. Day stole her purse with the intention of permanently depriving her of it.

DISCUSSION QUESTION, page 319

5. In the *Weirum* case the defendants argued that finding them liable would lead to situations in which "entrepreneurs will henceforth be burdened with an avalanche of obligations: an athletic department will owe a duty to an ardent sports fan injured while hastening to purchase one of a limited number of tickets; a department store will be liable for injuries incurred in response to a 'while-they-last' sale." How do you think the court responded?

The court responded that this case was different in that it created an extraordinary risk given the facts. The court stated: "This argument, however, suffers from a myopic view of the facts presented here. The giveaway contest was no commonplace invitation to an attraction available on a limited basis. It was a competitive scramble in which the thrill of the chase to be the one and only victor was intensified by the live broadcasts which accompanied the pursuit. In the assertedly analogous situations described by defendant, any haste involved in the purchase of the commodity is an incidental and unavoidable result of the scarcity of the commodity itself. In such situations there is no attempt, as here, to generate a competitive pursuit on public streets, accelerated by repeated importuning by radio to be the very first to arrive at a particular destination. Manifestly the 'spectacular' bears little resemblance to daily commercial activities."

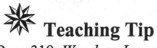 Teaching Tip

Page 319, *Woods v. Lancet*

Point out to the students why the court's statement of the issue : "The precise question for us on this appeal is: shall we follow *Drobner v. Peters*, or shall we bring the common law of this State, on this question, into accord with justice?" (p. 320) is not correct, as least as to how we have defined issue for the purposes of case briefing. Ask the students if they agree with the court's statement that there are differences between "rules of law on which men rely in their business dealings [which] should not be changed in the middle of the game" and the case of a tort-feasor. (page 320) Finally, this case presents an excellent example of a court that follows the philosophy of judicial activism. Prime examples include the court's statement that courts have "not only the right, but the duty to re-examine a question where justice demands it," the court's pointing out the need for the common law to change so that we do not stay "in the Plantagenet period;" and the courts argument that change in this area should come from it and not the legislature. (Page 321 of the text.)

Because *Woods* presents such an excellent example of how an activist court is willing to change the common law, I often have the students brief this case. The following is a sample case brief.

<u>Woods v. Lancet</u>, 303 N.Y. 349, 102 N.E.2d 691 (1951)

Facts: The plaintiff was a nine month old fetus when he was severely injured by the defendant's negligence. Defendant's motion to dismiss granted; affirmed; reversed.

Rule: There can be no recovery for negligently caused fetal injury.

Issue: Whether the defendant can be found liable for negligence despite the rule that denies recovery for injury negligently caused to a fetus when a nine month old fetus was injured through defendant's negligence.

Holding: Yes, recovery is possible for harm negligently caused to a fetus, but the right is limited to injury to a viable fetus.

Reasoning: 1) There no longer is a lack of precedent.
                  2) The court is not bound to follow its own past rules; rather it has a duty to change the law.
                  3) The court does not have to wait for the legislature
                  4) Proof problem is irrelevant; these types of problems occur in every type of negligence case.
                  5) That the fetus does not have a separate existence is not a problem because they limited their holding to a viable fetus.

Criticism: The dissent stated that this problem should be left to legislature to determine issues such as when does viability occur.
                  (Other possible criticism) First, this rule will be constantly changing as medical science changes what viability means. Second, the holding should not have been limited to a viable fetus. For example, shouldn't a fetus harmed in the third month but born with a disability be able to recover? Third, will this lead to kids suing their moms for activities such as smoking or taking drugs while pregnant that may have caused them harm as a fetus.

CASE DISCUSSION QUESTIONS, page 322 for *Woods v. Lancet*

1. Reading this case we learned almost nothing about the facts that gave rise to this lawsuit. What procedural reason explains why we do not know very many of the facts?

This case was decided on a motion to dismiss. Therefore, the court had to accept the facts as true. Becuase the defendant's negligence was assumed for the purposes of this motion, there was no need to go into the facts. [Instructor's note: the defendant was a landlord. The plaintiff's pregnant mother had fallen down a poorly maintained common stairway.]

2. Why did the court decide to overrule *Drobner v. Peters*?

The court overruled *Drobner* for three reasons. First, the lack of precedent is not an absolute bar when justice requires that the common law be changed. Second, the court did not think the proof problems were any different than for other types of cases. Finally, the court did not have to tackle the larger philosophical question of when life occurs, because it limited its holding to a viable fetus.

3. What limitations did the court put on its holding? Why difficulties can you foresee this creating for future litigants?

The court limited its holding to a viable fetus. This creates at least two problems. First, when does viability occur? Second, why should a fetus harmed before viability, but born alive and injured, not be able to recover?

4. Do you agree with the court that this issue was a matter for judicial as opposed to legislative change? Why?

This depends on whether the students want to see an activist court. Make sure they remember that if the legislature does not like the court's approach, the legislature can change it through statute.

LEGAL REASONING EXERCISES, page 322

3. Prosenjit Poddar killed Tatiana Tarasoff. Two months earlier, Poddar had told Dr. Lawrence Moore, a psychologist, that he intended to kill Tatiana. Dr. Moore did not warn Tatiana nor her parents of Poddar's intention. What policy considerations would argue against finding the psychologist liable? If you represented Tatiana's parents, how would you reply to those arguments?

This question is based on *Tarasoff v. The Regents of the University of California*, 551 P.2d 334 (Calif. 1976). The court held that "[w]hen a therapist determines, or pursuant to the standards of his profession should determine, that his patient presents a serious danger of violence to another, he incurs an obligation to use reasonable care to protect the intended victim against such danger. The discharge of this duty may require the therapist to take one or more of various steps, depending on the nature of the case. Thus it may call for him to warn the intended victim or others likely to apprise the victim of the danger, to notify the police, or to take whatever other steps are reasonably necessary under the circumstances."

Arguments against finding liability that the court found unpersuasive included that "imposition of a duty to exercise reasonable care to protect third persons is unworkable because therapists cannot accurately predict whether or not a patient will resort to violence." The court stated that the therapist need not render a perfect performance of prediction, but only the reasonable degree of care of similar professionals. Also, on the facts of the case it was

clear that Poddar presented a serious danger of violence. The risk of unnecessary warnings is a reasonable price to pay to save the lives of possible victims. The defendants had argued that open communication is essential to psychotherapy. The court recognized the public interest in supporting effective treatment of mental illness and in protecting the rights of patients to privacy, however, in balancing that interest against "the public interest in safety from violent assault," the court determined that the latter was more important.

4. The defendant company entered a float in a parade. As the float traveled down the street, employees threw candy to the crowd. Children running to collect the candy injured a spectator. Develop an argument for why the spectator should be allowed to sue the company.
This scenario was analyzed by the court in *Weirum v. RKO General, Inc.*, discussed on pages 318-19 of the text. The court noted that in that case the defendant was liable because the defendant, in throwing the candy, induced the response of the children which resulted in the plaintiff's injuries. Also, the defendant had actual knowledge children were following the float and scrambling for candy.

5. A grocery store customer was mugged on a sidewalk adjacent to the shopping center. The mugging occurred immediately after the customer left the store. The sidewalk was owned not by the grocery store, but by the shopping center. The grocery store knew of numerous similar muggings on the sidewalk. The store employees used the sidewalk to carry bags to customers' cars, and its lease provided that the store could hold sidewalk sales. Analyze whether the grocery store be held liable for the customer's injuries.
These facts are based on the case of *Simpson v. Big Bear Stores Co.*, 652 N.E.2d 702 (Ohio 1995). The majority held that the store was not liable as it did not own the sidewalk. The court stated that "[f]oreseeability alone is insufficient to create liability." The dissent argued that the store should be liable as it used the sidewalk to carry bags to the customers' cars and to hold sidewalk sales.

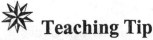 **Teaching Tip**

Page 323, *Sauer* — This is a good case for reminding students that not every case establishes a revolutionary new legal concept. Instead, most are about making refinements to existing law. Here the question was whether the camp should be liable under these very specific circumstances. They should see that even a minor change in the facts might alter the court's conclusion. The following is a sample case brief.

Sauer v. Hebrew Institute, 17 A.D.2d 245, 233 N.Y.S.2d 1008 (1962)

Facts:	A 13 year old at camp was playing a supervised water fight game with other campers of a similar age. He slipped on the wet grass and hit his head on a concrete sidewalk. Judg. for pl.; rev'd.
Rule:	Negligence is the failure to guard against foreseeable danger.
Issue:	Whether the camp should be held liable for negligence, which involves the failure to guard against foreseeable danger when a thirteen-year-old slipped on wet grass during a supervised water fight game.
Holding:	No, the camp should not be found liable for negligence which occurs when there is a failure to guard against foreseeable danger when a 13 year old slipped on wet grass during a supervised water fight game.
Reasoning:	This was an ordinary camp activity that would produce inevitable falls. The only way to eliminate the risk would be to eliminate the game, which would sterilize camping. There was no defect in ground and the camp could not foresee the accident. (The court also opined that the cause might have been the camper's bare feet.)
Criticism:	The camp should have been found negligent for allowing the game to be played so close to the sidewalk. Also, the court did develop a test that can be easily applied in new situations.

CASE DISCUSSION QUESTIONS, page 324 for *Sauer v. Hebrew Institute of Long Island, Inc.*
1. Why did the court find that the camp was not liable for the boy's injury? Do you agree with that decision? Why?
The court had three basic arguments. First, this was a normal camp activity. Second, this type of activity involving water would inevitably cause falls. Finally, the only way to prevent such an injury would be to prohibit normal camp activities, thereby sterilizing camp life. Students who have had children in camp might see this a little differently, assuming that the camp should be liable for this type of accident, especially as apparently it was played near a foreseeably dangerous object, the sidewalk.

2. What facts do you think were most important in helping the court reach its decision?
This was a normal camp activity, played by boys of a similar age, and it was supervised.

6. Most states have statutes prohibiting the sale of alcohol to a minor. Clearly the main purpose of such statutes is to protect minors. If a store sold alcohol to a minor, and the minor while intoxicated drove an automobile that collided with and killed a cyclist, would the liquor store owner be held liable as to the deceased cyclist?

This is based on the case of *Michnik-Zilberman v. Gordon's Liquor, Inc.*, 453 N.E.2d 430 (Mass. 1983). The court found that the store should be held liable. The court noted that the "sale or furnishing of alcoholic beverages to minors is analogous to the general rule that a person may be found negligent for furnishing a dangerous instrumentality to a child who uses it to case harm, since 'the consequences which [follow] ought to have been foreseen and guarded against.'" The court concluded that the statute's intent was not simply to benefit minors, but was intended for the protection of members of the general public as well. Id. at 433.

7. On an icy, snow-covered road the plaintiff lost control of her car, skidded across the center line, and collided with a road grader, driven by the defendant. The defendant did not have the statutorily required class B driver's license. The plaintiff, who was severely injured in the accident, sued the defendant under the theory of negligence per se. How do you think the court ruled and why?

This is based the case of *Hagel v. Schoenbauer*, 532 N.W.2d 255 (Minn. App. 1995). The court stated, "It is well-settled that breach of a statute gives rise to negligence per se if the persons harmed by that violation are within the intended protection of the statute and the harm suffered is of the type the legislation was intended to prevent." Id. at 257. However, because there was no causal connection between the failure to comply with the licensing statute and the accident, the court found that the lack of a driver's license was not even evidence of negligence.

Legal Reasoning Exercise, page 325

7. Every year Camp Good Times holds a hike to the top of Mount Snow or to the top of Barton Hill. Of the two hikes, the one up Mount Snow is a bit more arduous, but either can be accomplished in under an hour. This past year the campers, who ranged in age from seven to twelve, voted to hike up Mount Snow. The fifty campers and two camp counselors made it to the top of the hill in about half an hour with no problems. On the way back down, however, eight-year-old Timmy tripped over a large moss covered log lying across the path. As the result of his fall, he suffered a broken leg. His parents now want to know whether they can successfully sue the camp for Timmy's injury. Please evaluate their claim based upon *Sauer*.

To argue for liability in Timmy's case the students should show how it is distinguishable from *Sauer*. *Sauer* involved a normal camp activity. In Timmy's case, the hike only occurred once a year. The camp could have controlled the risk without eliminating the activity by choosing the easier hike. Also, they were negligent by giving the campers the right to choose the hike, by only having two counselors for fifty campers, and by intermixing campers that ranged in age from seven to twelve. Therefore, just as in *Greaves* the camp add needlessly to the risks inherent in the activity.

To argue against liability, the students should argue this case is analogous to *Sauer*. Even though the hike only occurred once a year, it is the sort of activity that is normal for camps. Like the water game in *Sauer* that naturally makes the ground wet and slippery, logs and tripping are inherent parts of hiking. The only way to eliminate these dangers is to eliminate the activity itself and hence sterilize camp life.

CASE DISCUSSION QUESTIONS, page 328 for *Palsgraf v. The Long Island Railroad Co.*
1. Why did the majority hold that there was no negligence as to Mrs. Palsgraf? Do you agree?
**"Negligence in the air" is not enough. There must be a duty owed to the person complaining.
The plaintiff could not show a wrong to herself, only a wrong to the man who was pushed.**

2. The dissent stated "What we do mean by the word 'proximate' is, that because of convenience, of public policy, of a rough sense of justice, the law arbitrarily declines to trace a series of events beyond a certain point. This is not logic. It is practical politics." Compare that to the quote at the beginning of this chapter.
Although the quote at the beginning feels "logical," the dissent points out that the issue is not one of foreseeability but of setting limits.

3. Part of the dissent that we omitted included the following illustration: "A chauffeur negligently collides with another car which is filled with dynamite, although he could not know it. An explosion follows. A, walking on the sidewalk nearby, is killed. B, sitting in a window of a building opposite, is cut by flying glass. C, likewise sitting in a window a block away, is similarly injured. And a further illustration. A nursemaid, ten blocks away, startled by the noise, involuntarily drops a baby from her arms to the walk." Who out of A, B, C, and the baby should recover from the chauffeur? Why?
The dissent stated that the chauffeur had no reason to believe his conduct involved risk to C or the baby. However he would be liable to A. It is questionable whether he should be liable to B. The issue is whether it should be seen as a question of fact for the jury or of law for the judge.

CASE DISCUSSION QUESTIONS, page 332 for *Anglin v. State Dept. of Transportation*
1. Do you agree with the majority or the dissent? Why?
**This will depend on how far the students think it is fair to carry the chain of causation.
Certainly, but for the pool of water, none of the other events would have occurred.**

2. Two years later, in 1987, this decision was reversed by the Supreme Court of Florida in *Department of Transp. v. Anglin*, 502 So. 2d 896 (Fla. 1987) (or as they so quaintly put it in Florida, "[W]e quash the decision below and remand for proceedings consistent with this opinion.") On what basis do you think the court reached its decision?
The court stated that while "it may be arguable that petitioners, by creating a dangerous situation which caused the respondents to require assistance, could have reasonably foreseen that someone may attempt to provide such assistance, it was not reasonably foreseeable that DuBose would act in such a bizarre and reckless manner. Petitioners' negligent conduct did not set in motion a chain of events resulting in injuries to respondents; it simply provided the occasion for DuBose's gross negligence." The court distinguished a prior case that it said presented a jury question of proximate cause when an intoxicated driver stopped his car in an inner lane of an interstate highway, causing a four car collision. Stopping a "car in a lane of an interstate highway set in motion a chain of events which a reasonable person could have foreseen would create 'a risk that other cars my collide as a result of trying to avoid hitting the stopped vehicle.'"

93

7. Assume you are a legislator and want to draft a statute dealing with social host liability. How would you fashion such a rule? For example, would you limit liability to those cases

   where minors are involved

   where the host knows the guest is intoxicated

   where the host actually serves the alcohol

How would you avoid the concern that finding liability in some cases would potentially lead to unlimited liability for social hosts?

Have the students see if they can set limits on liability by requiring that some or all of these elements be satisfied.

8. An alarm company delayed calling the fire department. By the time the firefighters arrived, the fire had advanced to such a stage that one of the firefighters was killed. The firefighter's widow sued the alarm company, alleging its negligent delay in calling in the fire resulted in her husband's death. How do you think the court decided? Why?

In *Edwards v. Honeywell, Inc.*, 50 F.3d 484 (7th Cir. 1995), the court held that the alarm company was not liable, citing *Palsgraf*. The court stated that the alarm company's duty of care did not extend to firefighters responding to a call. "If 'unforeseeable' is given the practical meaning of too unusual, too uncertain, too unreckonable to make it feasible or worthwhile to take precautions against, then this accident was unforeseeable."

9. Assume you are a legislator and want to draft a statute dealing with social host liability. How would you fashion such a rule? For example, would you limit liability to those cases

   where minors are involved

   where the host knows the guest is intoxicated

   where the host actually serves the alcohol

How would you avoid the concern that finding liability in some cases would potentially lead to unlimited liability for social hosts?

Have the students see if they can set limits on liability by requiring that some or all of these elements be satisfied.

10. Do you think a social host should be liable for accidents caused by drivers who obtained alcohol from the social host? Why? For example, consider the following facts. Margaret Davis gave her daughter, a high school student, permission to hold a party. Davis did not keep alcoholic beverages in her home, and there were none on the night of the party. Before the party began, Davis left. During the unchaperoned party a seventeen-year-old guest obtained beer brought to the party by another guest. While driving home intoxicated, the guest lost control of his car and injured Ruth Langemann. Should Langemann be allowed to sue Davis for her injuries?

This case is based on *Langemann v. Davis*, 495 N.E.2d 847 (Mass. 1986). The court found no liability stating that "[w]e reject the argument that a parent, who neither provides alcoholic beverages nor makes them available, owes a duty to travelers on the highway to supervise a party given by her minor child. We reach this conclusion even if Davis knew or reasonably should have known that alcoholic beverages would be available. The defendant's conduct did not create a risk of injury to the plaintiff for which we are prepared to say the common law should provide a remedy."

8. A woman sees her live-in boyfriend run over by a car and killed. Should she be allowed to sue for emotional distress? Why?

This is based on a Massachusetts superior court case, *Richmond v. Shatford*, in which the court said that she should be allowed to recover. The court did not think there should be a "bright-line" test for who can sue. The argument against such a recovery is that by expanding the allowable plaintiffs beyond the immediate family, this opens the floodgates for future litigation. (Reported in Massachusetts Lawyers Weekly, Aug. 21, 1995, 1, (col. 2)). Note: a Pennsylvania superior court did not allow a cousin to recover for emotional distress when he saw his cousin drown. The court stated that the result might have been different if they had lived together as part of a "family unit." *Blanyar v. Pagnotti Enterprises, Inc.*, 679 A.2d 790 (Pa. Super. 1996).

Legal Reasoning Exercises, pages 336-37

11. Mr. Alack joined a local health club. He signed a two-page, single-spaced contract that included the following language:

> Member assumes full responsibility for any injuries, damages or losses and
> does hereby fully and forever release and discharge [the health club] from
> any and all claims, demands, damages, rights of action, or causes of action,
> present or future . . . resulting from or arising out of the Member's . . . use
> or intended use of said gymnasium or the facilities and equipment thereof.

One day while he was exercising, the handle of a rowing machine disengaged from the weight cable and smashed into Mr. Alack's mouth. It was discovered that the machine's handle was not connected with the necessary clevis pin and that the health club did not require periodic inspections of its equipment. If you were representing Mr. Alack, how would you argue that the release would not bar him from suing the health club for its negligent failure to maintain the rowing machine?

These facts are based on the case of *Alack v. Vic Tanny International*, 923 S.W.2d 330 (Mo. 1996). The court held that "the exculpatory clause was ambiguous and that defendant health club did not insulate itself from liability for future negligence because the exculpatory clause did not use the word 'negligence' or 'fault' or their equivalents so that a clear and unmistakable waiver occurred." Id. at 332. The court also noted that in his testimony Mr. Alack stated that he read the language to mean that he could not sue if he caused himself injury by lifting too much weight or by working out for too long a period. He did not understand the language to absolve the health club for its negligence.

12. Before taking part in a horseback riding tour at the Loon Mountain Equestrian Center, Ms. Wright signed the following release:

> I understand and am aware that horseback riding is a HAZARDOUS ACTIVITY. . . . I therefore release Loon Mountain Recreation Corporation . . . FROM ANY AND ALL LIABILITY FOR DAMAGES AND PERSONAL INJURY TO MYSELF . . . RESULTING FROM THE NEGLIGENCE OF LOON MOUNTAIN RECREATION CORPORATION TO INCLUDE NEGLIGENCE IN SELECTION, ADJUSTMENT OR ANY MAINTENANCE OF ANY HORSE.

While on the tour, the guide's horse kicked Ms. Wright in the leg. Ms. Wright sued for negligence, arguing that the tour guide had failed to control the horse after it had given signs it was about to "act out." If you were representing Ms. Wright, how would you argue that the release should not bar her from suing the tour company?

These facts are based on the case of *Wright v. Loon Mountain Recreation Corp.*, 140 N.H. 166, 663 A.2d 1340 (1995). The court first noted that it would not enforce an exculpatory clause that contravenes public policy, and that such clauses are to be strictly construed against the defendant. The plaintiff did not argue that the clause contravened public policy. Therefore, the court focused solely on the question whether a reasonable person would have understood the clause as releasing the defendant of liability for its own negligence. The court concluded that the clause did not put the plaintiff on clear notice that the intent of the defendant was to avoid liability for its failure to use reasonable care. The language that the court found ambiguous included the following: First, the language emphasizing the inherent hazards of horseback riding followed by the "therefore" clause could lead a reasonable person to understand the language limited to the inherent dangers of horseback riding and not to the negligence of the tour guide in not properly controlling his horse. Second, it was unclear whether the tour guide's failure to control his horse constituted negligent "maintenance of any horse." Finally, the clause was unclear as to whether it related only to injuries caused by the horse the plaintiff was riding.

CASE DISCUSSION QUESTIONS, page 340 for *Irwin v. Town of Ware*
1. Why didn't the court think the police officer's actions fell under the "discretionary functions" exception?
The police officer's actions did not involve making a policy or planning judgment regarding whether to remove intoxicated drivers from the roads. That decision had already been made by the legislature.

2. This case established that the defense of sovereign immunity was not available in these circumstances. However, to recover, the plaintiff still had to establish that the police officer was negligent. What elements of the negligence claim do you think might give the plaintiff problems?
Two issues that may be difficult include resolving whether the officer owed a duty to users of

the highway and whether the driver's negligence was an intervening cause between the officer's negligence and the plaintiff's harm.

3. Many charitable and sovereign immunity claims cap the allowable recovery. In the *Irwin* case, the statute provided that the public employer would not be liable "for any amount in excess of one hundred thousand dollars." There were four plaintiffs in this case. How do you think the parties argued this language should be interpreted?

The plaintiffs argued that the amount should be per claim (some plaintiffs had multiple claims) or at least per plaintiff. The defendant argued that it should be per accident. The court agreed that it should be calculated on a per plaintiff basis.

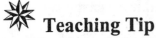 Teaching Tip

Page 343, *Doe v. Miles Labs, Inc.* — This case is longer than some of the others in this chapter, but we included this longer excerpt because of the court's excellent history lesson on the development of tort-based strict products liability.

CASE DISCUSSION QUESTIONS, page 346 for *Doe v. Miles Labs, Inc.*

1. The court discusses a doctrine known as **privity of contract**. What does privity of contract mean, and why did the court see it as limiting the ability of plaintiffs to sue for defective products?

Privity of contract meant that only the original contracting parties were obligated to each other. Therefore, if a consumer were to buy a defective product from a local store, the consumer could not sue the manufacturer as the consumer had no direct contractual relationship with the manufacturer. Similarly, if an employee was injured by defective equipment that the employer had purchased from the manufacturer, the employee could not sue the manufacturer.

2. Why did the court think a tort-based approach to product liability was preferable to one based on contract and warranty law?

The court thought that liability should be established as a matter of law rather than being dependent on the parties voluntary contractual relationship.

3. The court stated: "The argument is often made that strict products liability has the potential to bankrupt manufacturers. Such an argument misses the salutary economic role strict products liability plays. Understood properly, it can be seen that strict liability promotes a rational market place." How so?

The court stated: "Society cannot make rational decisions concerning the allocation of resources unless the price reflects the true costs. When the price rises greatly, reflecting the fact the product produces either substantial direct costs or creates widespread externalities, it is rational to discourage or even abandon consumption of that product. Strict products liability thus allows the marketplace to make better informed decisions." Ask students if they agree.

CASE DISCUSSION QUESTIONS, page 350 for *Giovine v. Giovine*

1. Why couldn't the plaintiff simply have sued for assault and battery?
She couldn't sue for assault and battery because many of the actions happened more than two years (the statute of limitations) before she filed suit.

2. The plaintiff testified that "[d]uring these Friday night incidences he would call me 'bitch' 'C-nt,' 'whore,' 'f-ing son-of-a-bitch' and other vile names." The dissent suggested that the type of emotional distress the defendant caused plaintiff could not be the basis for a claim of intentional infliction of emotional distress because such behavior in a marital context is not "so outrageous in character, and so extreme in degree, as to go beyond all possible bounds of decency, and to be regarded as atrocious, and utterly intolerable in a civilized community." What do you think?
This should evoke a discussion about the changing nature of what society views as acceptable behaviors. Make sure the students see that this is the very reason tort law is constantly evolving.

3. The court did not allow the plaintiff to sue her husband for a battery that occurred in March of 1972, which caused her to suffer a perforated eardrum, resulting in surgery and two weeks in the hospital. The reason the court disallowed this claim is that this was the first time her husband had hit her and the court noted that "the medical condition of battered woman's syndrome does not occur until a woman is battered at least twice." Do you agree with the court's analysis?
If to toll the statute of limitations, you must be able to show that the plaintiff was unable to act on her own behalf, then you probably will have to be able to show more than a single act of battery. The court noted that the plaintiff was not unable to take action after that incident, as she filed a counterclaim for divorce in 1980 that alleged acts of extreme cruelty including the battery. However, the court did say that the evidence of the battery was admissible to help prove the medical condition of battered woman's syndrome.

4. In *Kyle v. Green Acres at Verona, Inc.*, 207 A.2d 513 (N.J. 1965), the defendant's negligence caused the plaintiff to become insane. Insanity was defined as a condition that prevented the "sufferer from understanding his [or her] legal rights." The court held that the statute of limitation would be tolled until a reasonable time after the plaintiff's sanity was restored. In *Jones v. Jones*, 576 A.2d 316 (N.J. App. Div. 1990), the court held that the statute of limitations was tolled for a victim of incest. Should these cases be seen as analogous to *Giovine?* Why or why not?
In each case, the defendant's actions caused the plaintiff to be unable to bring her claim within the standard time set by the statute of limitations. Therefore, it would seem just to toll the statute of limitations until the plaintiff has regained her ability to act independently.

Discussion Questions, page 351

10. Should tort law be an ever expanding concept, or should there be some limits put on liability? If so, what should those limits be?
Possible limits include monetary caps, limitations on punitive damages, or requirements of physical injury or medical evidence.

11. Some argue that there is a litigation explosion; that instead of taking responsibility for their own action, people are resorting in increasing numbers to the legal system for relief. Do you agree?

Why? If you do agree, what should be done about it?

Students may want to argue that each of these new torts go too far and that we have in effect become "litigation crazy." In each case, instead of taking responsibility for their own actions, the plaintiffs are looking for someone to blame.

Discussion Questions, page 354

11. Some argue that the quotation from *State Farm* cited above indicates that the Court will look most favorably on punitive damage awards that are four times that of the compensatory award. Do you agree?

The Court stated that the 4-1 ratio was "instructive" and that "[s]ingle-digit multipliers are more likely to comport with due process." However, the court stopped short of saying that a 9-1 ratio or less is required. It should be noted that there was no physical harm in any of the cases cited in the text. Also, the Court has stated that the degree of defendant's reprehensibility is the strongest indicator of the appropriate punitive damages award. Therefore, no ratio can be seen in isolation from these other factors. Note: On remand the Utah Supreme Court awarded the plaintiff $1 in compensatory and $9 in punitive damages, seemingly taking to heart the Supreme Court's preference for single-digit ratios.

12. Do you think it is fairer to defendants to apply "guideposts" such as the Supreme Court has been using or a simple ratio, such as mandating that in non-personal injury cases punitive damage awards cannot exceed nine times the compensatory award? Would such a rule satisfy society's need to deter future bad conduct?

As noted in the text, if the ratio is set to low, then companies may not be deterred from engaging in certain bad behaviors if they can simply "write it off" as a necessary business expense. On the other hand, a set ratio would certainly help satisfy the constitutional due process concerns regarding notice to the defendant of the severity of the potential punishment. As an interesting side note, an increased emphasis on ratios should encourage plaintiff's attorneys to seek higher compensatory damages so that the denominator will be as large as possible when calculating the ratio for punitive damages.

13. Typically, punitive damages are awarded to the plaintiff because it was the plaintiff who brought the lawsuit. However, punitive damages are designed to punish the defendant rather than compensate the victim. Some have argued, therefore, that punitive damages should be paid to the state (society as a whole) rather than to the individual plaintiff. Indeed, a few states have passed laws that split punitive damage awards between the plaintiff and the state. Alaska, Missouri, and Utah split awards equally between plaintiff and state; Oregon takes 60% of the awards; Georgia, Indiana and Iowa take 75%; and Illinois leaves the allocation up to the discretion of the judge. In Ohio the state Supreme Court on its own initiative recently allocated almost two-thirds of a $30 million punitive damages award to a cancer research fund the court established. What do you think of these various approaches?

This would seem to be a compromise that would allow punitive damage awards to take into account the harm the defendant had done to others besides the plaintiff without giving the plaintiff a windfall. However, this approach might run afoul of the Supreme Court's statement in *State Farm* regarding due process not allowing the parties to adjudicate the merits of other person's claims against the defendant.

REVIEW QUESTIONS, pages 355-56

1. How can the same set of facts result in both a tort and a crime? Will every tort also create criminal liability?

Because both criminal acts and torts can result in harm to a person or property, sometimes the same set of facts will give rise to both a tort and a criminal action. However, every tort will not create criminal liability. Generally, the courts will require a "bad intent" for criminal liability, such as might be found in an intentional tort but not in merely negligent behavior.

2. How can a tort be distinguished from a contract action?

Tort law is based on legal duties established by the courts through the common law or more recently also by statutes. Contract actions are based on the legal duties the parties themselves establish by agreement.

3. What are the elements of assault? Of battery?

Assault: 1. an intentional act, 2. that creates a reasonable apprehension of, 3. an immediate harmful or offensive contact.
Battery: 1. an intentional act, 2. that creates a harmful or offensive physical contact.

4. How can there be an assault and no battery? A battery without an assault?

There can be an assault with no battery when there is apprehension but no contact. There can be a battery without an assault when there is contact without first being aware contact was imminent.

5. Review the situation of Mrs. Day presented at the beginning of the chapter. Do you think she has a valid claim either for assault or battery? Why?

There should be no finding of assault as she didn't think he would hit her and when he did, her back was turned so she didn't see him. Yes, as to battery as there was an intentional, harmful contact.

6. What are the elements of false imprisonment?

The elements of false imprisonment are
1.   an intentional act
2.   that caused confinement or restraint
3.   through force or the threat of force.

7. When does a shopkeeper have a valid defense to a detained person's allegation of false imprisonment?

Statutes usually provide that a shopkeeper may detain a suspected shoplifter only if the shopkeeper can show probable cause to justify the delay. The shopkeeper may detain the suspected shoplifter only for a reasonable time and in a reasonable manner.

8. What are the elements of libel? The defenses?

The elements of libel are publication of a false statement that causes harm to reputation. Defenses to defamation include truth, privilege, and consent.

100

9. In *New York Times v. Sullivan*, what limitations did the Supreme Court put on the ability of public figures to sue the press?
The plaintiff must prove that the defendant acted with malice, that is by either knowing the material was false or by acting with a reckless disregard of the truth. This is to protect freedom of speech.

10. Assume Robin Barker dictates a letter to her secretary. The letter is addressed to Ms. Wanda Jones. In the letter Ms. Barker tells Ms. Jones that she thinks Ms. Jones is a thief. The secretary types and mails the letter to Ms. Jones. Can Ms. Jones sue for defamation? What element is arguably missing?
Ms. Jones would argue that this was a false statement that would hurt her reputation. The question is whether the publication element was satisfied when Ms. Barker dictated the letter to her secretary.

11. A grocery store employee followed a customer to the parking lot and accused her of having meat in her purse. The customer opened her purse and showed that she didn't have any meat, and the employee left. Several passersby heard the remarks, but the plaintiff couldn't identify any them. Should the customer be barred from proceeding with a defamation suit? Why?
"Although a plaintiff must prove that the defamatory remarks were 'published,' it is not necessary to identify any of the people who heard the remarks or have them testify as to what they understood, the court said." *Food Lion, Inc., v. Melton*, **458 S.E.2d 580 (Va. 1995).**

12. How do the torts of defamation and invasion of privacy differ?
Defamation requires that the statement be false. For invasion of privacy the statement may be true.

13. What must a plaintiff prove to win a case of intentional infliction of emotional distress?
The elements of intentional infliction of emotional distress are
1. **an intentional act**
2. **that is extreme and outrageous**
3. **and causes**
4. **severe emotional distress (sometimes physical injury).**

14. What are the four basic elements of a negligence claim?
The four elements of negligence are duty, breach, cause, and harm.

15. Do you think the result in the *Cordas* case would have been different if Mrs. Cordas and her two children had been in the taxicab rather than standing on the sidewalk? Why?
The result probably would have been different because then the risk of harm would have been more foreseeable. However, when deciding on what is reasonable under the circumstances, the court would consider the emergency situation and that the driver was trying to save his own life.

16. Explain the doctrine of res ipsa loquitur.

Res ipsa loquitur means the thing speaks for itself. It applies in those situations where the event ordinarily would not have happened unless someone was negligent; the cause of the injury was under the defendant's exclusive control; and the injury was not due to the plaintiff's actions.

17. When might the court find that a defendant was negligent per se?

If the defendant violates a statute and that statute's purpose is to protect the public, the plaintiff belongs to the group of persons the statute was meant to protect, and violation of the statute was a direct cause of the plaintiff's injury, then some states will hold that violation of the statute is negligence per se.

18. What is the difference between "but for" causation and proximate cause?

But for is actual cause. Proximate cause is a policy decision as to when to say an event is no longer foreseeable.

19. Describe the three basic affirmative defenses to negligence. How do they differ from each other?

Contributory negligence was historically a complete bar. It is based on a reasonable person standard. Assumption of the risk was also a complete bar, but was based on a subjective standard: the plaintiff must have knowingly and voluntarily assumed the risk. Comparative negligence is similar to contributory negligence except it reduces the plaintiff's award by the degree of plaintiff's own negligence.

20. A state court judge approved a mother's petition to have her "somewhat retarded" daughter sterilized. The daughter was told she was to have her appendix removed. Later the daughter married and found out that she had been sterilized. She sued the judge. How do you think the court resolved the case?

These facts are based on *Stump v. Sparkman*, 435 U.S. 349 (1978). The court held judges are immune even if the judge's action is in excess of his jurisdiction and even if the acts were done maliciously or corruptly.

21. A public high school required parents to sign a release of liability form before allowing their children to participate in interscholastic athletics. The parents objected to having to sign the form and went to court requesting that the school district be enjoined from requiring the release. How do you think the court decided the issue?

The Washington Supreme Court invalidated the releases for negligence that the public schools required parents to sign before allowing students to participate in interscholastic athletics on the grounds that they violated public policy. The court stated "there are instances where public policy reasons for preserving an obligation of care owed by one person to another outweigh our traditional regard for the freedom to contract." The court noted the unequal bargaining power (the only way the students would be allowed to play was if the releases were signed) and the great duty of care owed to students, especially in a situation a "student athlete usually placed under the coach's considerable degree of control." *Wagenblast v. Odessa School Dist.#1*, 758 P.2d 968 (Wash. 1988).

22. State Building Codes set forth requirements for safe building. If a building inspector fails in his duty to carefully inspect a building, do you think a purchaser of such premises would have a cause of action for buying a building that was developed in violation of the governmental requirements? Why?

No, there would be no cause of action. The purchaser is not someone to whom the inspector owes a duty. This is to be contrasted with the facts of _Irwin_.

23. Describe the three theories that a plaintiff can use to sue a manufacturer when harmed by that manufacturer's product.

Breach of Warranty: This is a contract based theory. The warranties can be either express or implied. The problems with this theory are 1) that warranties can be disclaimed and 2) privity of contract could prevent a user who did not purchase the defective product from suing the manufacturer.

Negligence: Using negligence as the basis for suit, an injured plaintiff could sue for a negligently manufactured product, a negligently designed product, or for a failure to warn. The problem with this theory is that it may be hard to show that the product's defect was caused by the manufacturer's negligence.

Strict liability: The plaintiff must show that the product was defective and that the defect made it unreasonably dangerous. Also, the product must reach the user without substantial change. Defenses to strict liability include assumption of the risk and product misuse.

24. A woman keeps a pit bull dog as a pet. One day the neighbor children accidentally throw a Frisbee into her yard. In attempting to retrieve the Frisbee, one of the children is severely bitten by the dog. Should the dog's owner be held strictly liable? Why or why not?

This will depend on whether the students think the elements for engaging in an ultrahazardous activity are met. While a pit bull dog is not a wild animal, it is widely believed that it has a higher propensity for violence than most domestic pets.

25. Manuel Sanchez began smoking at the age of ten. Over his lifetime he smoked several different brands of cigarettes. At the age of fifty-three he was diagnosed with throat cancer and died within six months. His widow sued nine different cigarette manufacturers on the theory of strict liability. To win her case, what would Mrs. Sanchez have to prove? Do you think she was successful?

Mrs. Sanchez would have to first convince the court to let her proceed on a market share theory of liability. Then to win under strict liability she would have to prove that the cigarettes contained a defect that made them unreasonably dangerous and that the defect was the cause of his injuries. These facts are based on various cases wherein the plaintiffs have been unsuccessful in convincing the courts that cigarettes are defectively designed so as to make them unreasonably dangerous.

26. Five-year-old Daphne took a disposable lighter from her mother's purse that was stored on the top shelf of a closet in a bedroom in her grandparents' home. While playing with the lighter, she started a fire that severely burned her two-year-old brother, Ruben. While the lighter manufacturer produced lighters both with and without child safety mechanisms, this lighter did not have one. The children's mother sued the manufacturer of the lighter. If you represented the mother, how would you argue the manufacturer should be held liable for the boy's injury? How do you think the lawyers for the

manufacturer would respond?

These facts are based on the case of *Hernandez v. Tokai Corp.*, 42 Tex. Sup. J. 1131, 2 S.W.3d 251 (1999). The court held that the plaintiff must be able to prove that a design defect (the lack of a child restraint) made the product unreasonably dangerous and that the defect produced the injury. The manufacturer had argued that the lighters were intended for adult use only and that warnings against access by children were provided with the lighters. However, the court noted that these were not absolute bars to recovery, but rather factors to be taken into account in determining whether a defect-design claim could be maintained. The court also stated that child's misuse of the product could not serve as a bar to liability where the risk of misuse by children was obvious to the manufacturer. For a similar case see *Campbell v. Bic Corp.*, 154 Misc. 2d 976, 586 N.Y.S.2d 871 (N.Y. Supreme Court 1992).

27. What are the three basic types of damages that a plaintiff can recover in a tort action, and what is the purpose of each?

Compensatory: awarded to compensate the plaintiff for the harm done to him or her. In a tort action involving harm to a person, that might mean the cost of medical bills, lost time from work, and pain and suffering.

> **Punitive: designed to punish the defendant for intentional wrongdoing.**
> **Nominal: awarded when a right has been violated but the plaintiff cannot prove any monetary harm.**

28. What is the difference between general and special damages?

General damages are those damages that you would naturally expect to occur given the type of harm suffered. Special damages (sometimes called consequential damages) are those damages that also flow naturally from the injury, but which may vary depending on the special circumstances of the case. They include the cost of repairing or replacing the damaged property, any medical bills, and replacement of plaintiff's income lost while unable to work.

Chapter 13

Contract Law

Unlike most texts that start with the common law of contracts and then later introduce the UCC, we introduce the UCC right at the beginning of this chapter. Then we integrate the discussion of the UCC with the discussion of the common law principles. I always thought it was unfair to students to first have them memorize all of the common law rules, only later to spring on them the news that many of those rules have been modified or even eliminated by the UCC.

A useful exercise for this chapter is to divide the students into teams of two. Give each team a set of facts involving a simple contract situation such as the lease of an apartment. Then pair them off with another team and have them negotiate the terms of a contract.

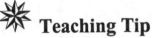 **Teaching Tip**

The chart in Figure 11-2 on page 360 provides a good exercise in reminding them of the step-by-step nature of legal analysis. For example, there is no need to discuss whether a merchant should met the UCC requirements of good faith, it we don't even know if the UCC applies.

DISCUSSION QUESTION, page 362
1. We all enter many contracts every day. Think back over the past week and list all of the contracts that you have entered into.
The students may be surprised to realize how many contracts they have entered into, from buying a newspaper to purchasing a used car.

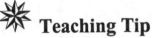 **Teaching Tip**

I have always found that students have a great deal of difficulty in understanding that an executory contract, unlike a gift, is enforceable. The fact scenario with Sally, Jill, Mike and the two watches was designed to help make this difference between gifts and contracts understandable. (Page 363 of the text.)

Legal Reasoning Exercise, pages 365-66

1. Emma Johnson is the owner of two parcels of land. On March 27 Ms. Johnson's son-in-law, Edward Hicks, who was her agent to sell the property, wrote the following letter to James Mellen.

> You will perhaps remember that we spent a pleasant visit on the break water at Nahant last summer. On that occasion either you or your brother-in-law expressed an interest in my Mother's property which is the Johnson cottage. . . . [Mother's] health is such that she will not be able to open the cottage this year. She has, therefore, decided that it will be best to place the property on the market, however, before turning it over to the real estate agents, I am writing the several people, including yourself, who have previously expressed an interest in the property. Our price is $7,500. This property consists of the lot and cottage on the south side of Willow Road, and also a very large plot on which a two car garage is situated running from Willow Road clear through the block to the next street. Just how much property there is in this tract, I cannot tell you at the moment. . . . I will be interested in hearing from you further if you have any interest in this property, for as I said before, I am advising those who have asked for an opportunity to consider it. I might just add that the property would be available for immediate occupancy. By that I mean within such time as the present furnishings could be removed and title transferred.

On March 28 Hicks received a telegram from Mr. Mellon's brother-in-law which read:

> We are interested in your offer. Will look at house tomorrow. Communicate with you first of week.

On the same day shortly after the telegram was received Hicks telegraphed Mr. Mellon:

> Have heard from three interested buyers tonight which means we must accept highest bid for Nahant property. Suggest you wire or phone us Elmsford N. Y. 7292 Saturday your best offer on cash basis.

Before this was received Mr. Mellon telegraphed Hicks:

> I accept your offer on Nahant cottage. Letter in mail.

When Hicks entered into a written contract to sell the property to someone else, Mr. Mellon sued to stop the sale from being completed.

a. Do you think an offer was ever made? Why or why not?

These facts were based on the case of *Mellon v. Johnson*, 322 Mass. 236, 76 N.E.2d 658 (1948). The court stated that "[t]he letter of March 27 was not an offer. It expressed 'a desire to dispose of' the property. It announced that the agent was 'writing the several people, including yourself, who have previously expressed an interest in the property.' Its conclusion, in part, was, 'I will be interested in hearing further from you if you have any interest in this property, for as I said before, I am advising those who have asked for an opportunity to consider it.' The recipient could not reasonably understand this to be more than an attempt at negotiation. It was a mere request or suggestion that an offer be made to the defendant." Also, there is some uncertainty as to how much property is to be included in the sale.

b. Do you think Mr. Mellon's suit was successful? Why or why not?

Because there was no offer, there was no contract. Mr. Mellon lost his suit.

CASE DISCUSSION QUESTIONS, page 368 for *Lefkowitz v. Great Minneapolis Surplus Store, Inc.*

1. Why did the court hold that in this case there was a binding contract for the black lapin stole?
It was a definite offer and left nothing open for negotiation.

2. Why was there no binding contract for the fur coats?
The offer was too indefinite as the value was not known. Therefore, there was no way to craft an appropriate remedy.

3. On the plaintiff's first visit, the store informed him of its "house rule" limiting the offer to women. Why didn't the court find that term to be part of the second offer?
The terms had not been made a part of the published offer.

Legal Reasoning Exercise, pages 370-71

2. UCC, 2-207 provides as follows:

(1) A definite and seasonable expression of acceptance or a written confirmation which is sent within a reasonable time operates as an acceptance even though it states terms additional to or different from those offered or agreed upon, unless acceptance is expressly made conditional on assent to the additional or different terms.

(2) The additional terms are to be construed as proposals for addition to the contract. Between merchants such terms become part of the contract unless:

(a) the offer expressly limits acceptance to the terms of the offer;

(b) they materially alter it; or

(c) notification of objection to them has already been given or is given within a reasonable time after notice of them is received.

Please evaluate each of the following situations and determine first, whether a contract exists and second, if so, what its terms are.

a. Value City, a Georgia retailer, sends an order form to RCV, a Mississippi manufacturer, ordering 100 televisions at $200 each. On the back of the form in fine print is the following:
Seller expressly warrants that the goods are fit for the ordinary purposes for which they are sold. Seller shall assume all costs of shipping.
RCV sends back an acknowledgement form. On the back of the form in small print is the following:
All disputes arising out of the agreement must be submitted to binding arbitration.

b. Value City, a Georgia retailer, sends an order form to RCV, a Mississippi manufacturer, ordering 100 televisions at $200 each. On the back of the form in fine print is the following:
Seller shall assume all costs of shipping.

RCV sends back an acknowledgement form. On the back of the form in small print is the following:
All goods are sold "as is" with no warranties of any kind.

107

c. Value City, a Georgia retailer, sends an order form to RCV, a Mississippi manufacturer, ordering 100 televisions at $200 each. On the back of the form in fine print is the following:

> Seller expressly warrants that the goods are fit for the ordinary purposes for which they are sold. Seller shall assume all costs of shipping.

RCV sends back an acknowledgement form. On the back of the form in small print is the following:

> All goods are sold "as is" with no warranties of any kind.
> Buyer shall assume all costs of shipping.

All three situations deal with merchants. In each case there is a contract. In a. and in b. the issue is whether the additional term materially alters the contract. If it does, it does not become a term. If not, it is part of the contract. In c. the terms are different instead of additional. Some commentators say that 207(2) says nothing about different terms and so they cannot be part of the contract. Others state that the different terms cancel each other out and are not part of the contract. In effect, the use of different terms acts as a silent objection to them and so they cannot become a part of the contract. A third view treats them as additional terms with the question being whether they would materially alter the contract. Clearly the term regarding warranties would. The term regarding shipping might or might not materially alter the contract depending on the added cost.

DISCUSSION QUESTION, page372
2. Much of contract law is based upon the theory of freedom of contract, that is, the parties are free to create their own contract terms as they, and not the court choose. How can you reconcile the courts' equitable power to find a quasi-contract when no contract exists with this notion of freedom of contract?
This question should get the students thinking about what is more important — a bright line rule that courts will only bind parties to agreements that have met all of the requirements for a valid contract or whether the courts should be free to craft an equitable remedy to "do justice" when the parties have perhaps deliberately not fulfilled all of the requirements for a contract, because they do not want to be bound.

Generally people should be left free to contract as they wish. However, there are times when it would be unjust to allow someone to benefit from services or goods received without paying for them, simply because the formal rules of contract law had not been satisfied.

CASE DISCUSSION QUESTIONS, page 374 for *Hamer v. Sidway*
1. Why didn't the court simply view the uncle's offer to pay his nephew $5,000 as a gift?
The court thought there was valid consideration to support a contract. The court stated that consideration is either some right accruing to one party or some detriment suffered by the other. However, the courts will not inquire whether there is actual benefit as this would leave open to controversy in too many cases whether the consideration was factually of benefit to the person who received it. Therefore, the emphasis should not be on whether one party is profiting but rather on whether the other party gave up a legal right.

2. If the court had decided it was a gift instead of a contract situation, how would that have changed the result?
Because there was never any delivery of the money (a requirement for a valid gift to be enforceable), the nephew would not have been entitled to the money.

Note: There was a second issue in the case that you might want to mention to your students. Apparently, there was some dispute as to whether the original agreement was in writing as required by the Statute of Frauds as it was not to be performed within a year. However, there was nothing in the complaint to indicate there was no writing (as obviously it would not have been in the best interests of the plaintiff to raise this issue) and no such defense was put into the answer. Therefore, the court held that the defense was not available.

CASE DISCUSSION QUESTIONS, page 377 for *Alaska Packers' Association v. Domenico*
1. What does this court say is the rule about allowing a modification of a contract with no new consideration? Why does the court think that is the only just result?
There can be no modification of a contract without new consideration. The court stated that any other result would allow one party to take an unjustifiable advantage of the situation. A prime example is this case in which there was no possibility to find replacements and thereby forcing the appellant into agreeing to the sailors demands.

2. How do you reconcile this decision with the notion of freedom of contract? That is, shouldn't the parties be free to change the terms of their contract at any time?
These two concepts are conflicting. Although courts generally state that parties should be able to make any agreement, even a bad one, the courts are also concerned that equity be done and that once a contract is formed one party not be allowed to "hold up" the other party. However, viewed in that light the two concepts are not conflicting. In the "hold up" situation, one of the parties is only agreeing because of coercion and so is not really enjoying the benefits of freedom of contract.

3. Can you think of any circumstances when it would be fair to allow the parties to modify their contract without new consideration?
If truly unforeseen difficulties arose, and the only way the contract could be performed would be to alter the circumstances, then alteration without new consideration might be in the best interests of all parties. For example, if unforeseen circumstances meant that a supplier would have to go bankrupt within six months if forced to fulfill the terms of a twelve month contract, both parties might agree to a change in terms so that the supplier could stay in business and meet at least partial contractual responsibilities for the full twelve month period.

CASE DISCUSSION QUESTIONS, page 381 for *Quality Motors Inc. v. Hays*
1. What does the court say is the general rule about the right of minors to disaffirm contracts?
An infant may disaffirm a contract, except those made for necessaries, without being required to return the consideration received, expect such part as may still exist.

2. What should this dealer have done differently in this case?

The dealer should not have encouraged the minor to use a third party (realizing it was a subterfuge) and should have taken the car back when first requested to do so by the father.

3. In general, how can merchants protect themselves in dealings with minors?

Merchants can protect themselves by not selling to minors.

4. Some states simply require the return of the goods, no matter their condition. Others require that the adult be placed in the same position that he or she was in prior to the contract. Which approach do you think is better?

With more and more minors having the money to buy major items, the students will probably think that the adult should be placed in the same position he or she was prior to the contract.

CASE DISCUSSION QUESTIONS, page 383 for *Lucy v. Zehmer*

1. What did the court think was the appropriate test for determining if there was a serious intent to be bound?

The court applied a reasonable person test. The court stated that "[w]e must look to the outward expression of a person as manifesting his intention rather than to his secret and unexpressed intention. 'The law imputes to a person an intention corresponding to the reasonable meaning of his words and acts.'"

2. Specific performance is not an absolute right but rather a question of equity. Do you think it was "fair" to enforce this contract?

The problem with sales of land is that usually the land is unique and so money damages are not adequate. In this case it looks like both sides may have been less than serious, but unfortunately for Mr. Zehmer, the court held him to what any reasonable outsider would have thought his intention to be.

3. The court stated: "Seven or eight years ago [Lucy] had offered Zehmer $20,000 for the farm which Zehmer had accepted, but the agreement was verbal and Zehmer backed out." Why was Zehmer able to back out of that agreement but not this one?

Contracts for land must be in writing to be enforceable.

CASE DISCUSSION QUESTIONS, page 387 for *Vokes v. Arthur Murray, Inc.*

1. Why did the court categorize the dance studio's statements as "fact" rather than "opinion"?

The court cited a number of situations when an "opinion" can be seen as "fact," including 1) where there is a fiduciary relationship between the parties; 2) where some trick was employed by the representor; 3) where the parties do not in general deal at "arm's length;" 4) when the representee does not have equal opportunity to be appraised of the truth or a falsity of the facts represented; or 5) the statement is made by one with superior knowledge.

2. Which facts do you think the court found particularly relevant in reaching that decision?

The plaintiff was a widow without a family; she was sold fourteen dance courses in less than sixteen months totally $31,0000; the techniques went beyond sales puffing and

intruded into area of undue influence; they made false representations that she was improving in her dancing ability when actually she had no dance aptitude.

3. What do you think would have kept the statements of the dance studio in the realm of mere "sales puffing"?
This is obviously a question of degree and the students (as do the courts) may well disagree as to how hard the sell can be before it goes beyond puffing and intrudes on false representations.

CASE DISCUSSION QUESTIONS, page 392 for *Webster v. Blue Ship Tea Room, Inc.*
1. Why did the court think Ms. Webster failed in her claim for breach of an implied warranty?
The presence of fish bones in fresh fish chowder is to be expected and does not impair its fitness. The chief should not be forced to reduce the pieces of fish in the chowder to minuscule size in order to determine if they contain any pieces of bone. This would destroy the essential nature of the dish.

2. Why did it matter that the plaintiff was brought up in New England? Would the result have been different if she lived in the Midwest and this was her first trip to the East Coast?
It might matter as the court did take the time to point out that the plaintiff was born and brought up in New England and stated that it was a fact of "some consequence." However, the court also cited a case from Ohio dealing with a piece of oyster shell in fried oysters in which the court also did not find any liability.

3. Do you agree with the court that this is a different case from one in which the food is contaminated? Why?
Yes, this is a different case. In a sense, a bowl of fish chowder is not "defective" if it has a natural substance, such as fish bones in it. Such items are foreseeable. However, there is no justification for contaminated products.

Legal Reasoning Exercise, page 392
3. Janice Jones, along with her family, visited a Big Bill's Family Restaurant, a national chain. She was eating a piece of fried chicken when she bit into something that she thought was a worm. Naturally she became quite upset and has been unable to eat chicken since. Expert witnesses are likely to state that, instead of a worm, the object was actually either the chicken's aorta or its trachea, both of which would appear wormlike. Ms. Jones wants to know whether she can successfully sue the restaurant for breach of warranty. Please evaluate her claim based on *Webster v. Blue Ship Tea Room, Inc.*
This legal reasoning exercise is based on *Hong v. Marriott Corp.*, 656 F. Supp. 445 (D. Md. 1987). Comparing the facts to *Webster*, the court noted that "[u]nlike New England Fish Chowder, a well-known regional specialty, fried chicken (though of Southern origin) is a ubiquitous American dish." The court distinguished prior cases where no liability was found based on the substance being a natural though inedible part of the edible item consumed. In those cases, such as oyster shells in fried oysters, the natural item was reasonably to be expected in the dish. Based on the "reasonable expectation" test, however, the court could not "conclude that the presence of a trachea or an aorta in a fast food fried chicken wing is so reasonably to be expected as to render it merchantable."

111

1. Why did the court find for the plaintiff contractor?

The use of the wrong pipe was not intentional. Also, functionally there is no difference between the type of pipe contracted for and the type of pipe installed. Therefore, because the commission was both trivial and innocent, the commission can be compensated for through payment of any resulting damage. Basically, the court was of the view that it was better to take a flexible approach in these types of cases than to follow a stricter standard that might not equate to justice in an individual case. Therefore, the damages should be the difference in value and not the cost of replacement.

2. The dissent essentially states that people have a right to get what they contract for. The majority does not see things in such black and white terms, saying, "We must weigh the purpose to be served, the desire to be gratified, the excuse for deviation from the letter, the cruelty of enforced adherence." Which view to you think best serves the needs of the contracting parties?

You will find students become surprisingly outraged by this case. Many will think that the whole point of forming a contract is to get what you bargained for, and they will insist that the defaulting party should have to make changes no matter the cost.

3. What could the owner have done to ensure that there would be no deviations from his specifications?

In the contract, the owner should have used language to clearly indicate that performance of every terms was a condition of recovery.

4. Would this case have had a different outcome if the contractor had deliberately substituted the pipe in order to save money? Why?

This case might well have had a different outcome if the contractor had deliberately substituted the pipe. The court pointed out that the substitution in this case was accidental. If the owner could have shown, however, that the contractor deliberately substituted pipe, for example to save money, then the owner would have a valid claim not only for breach of contract but also for fraud.

 Teaching Tip

Students always have difficulty grasping the concepts behind third-party rights. I have found that putting Figures 11-6 through 1-8 (pages 398-99 of the text) on the board or overhead helps the students to visualize the differences between assignment and delegation on the one hand and third-party beneficiaries on the other.

 Teaching Tip

If you would like your students to see how mistakes can slip into a boilerplate contract when it is reused for a new client and is not carefully proofread, let them read the following Employment Contract and ask them to spot as many mistakes as they can and suggest revisions

Employment Contract

An agreement dated June 1, 1998, between Grimshaw, Stewart, and Bigley, PC., a law firm specializing in environmental law, and Sandra Baker.

WHEREAS the FIRM wishes to avail itself of the services of Ms. Baker; and WHEREAS Ms. Baker is willing to perform services for the FIRM, all in accordance with the following terms and conditions,
NOW THEREFORE, it is agreed as follows:

1. EMPLOYMENT
The FIRM agrees to hire Ms. Baker, and he agrees to serve the FIRM as a paralegal, with overall responsibility in the area of environmental litigation.

2. TERM
This contract shall endure for three years.

3. COMPENSATION
The FIRM agrees to compensate Ms. Baker $2,000 per month plus such additional bonuses as it shall deem just.

5. CONTINUING EDUCATION
Ms. Baker agrees to attain whatever continuing professional education is necessary. The FIRM agrees to compensate her for such education so far as it is in furtherance of his employment.

6. RESTRICTIVE COVENANT
Due to the confidential nature of the business of the FIRM, Ms. Baker agrees that should she cease employment for any reason whatsoever she will not work for another law firm specializing in environmental law for three years from the date of her termination.

7. TERMINATION BY THE FIRM
At any time during the course of this agreement, the FIRM may terminate the services of Ms. Baker for any reason.

8. TERMINATION BY MS. BAKER
Termination by the employee may be made only by following the provisions outlined in clause five above.

Signed this day, _____   _____

The basic purpose of this exercise is to remind students of the dangers of relying on boilerplate language. They should find the following:

Clause 1.	**"he" should be "she".**
Clause 2.	**It needs to be determined from when the three years begins.**
Clause 3.	**"additional bonuses as it shall deem just" is too vague to be enforceable.**
Clause 4.	**Missing.**
Clause 5.	**"whatever professional education is necessary" is another vague phrase. In the second sentence "his" should be "her".**
Clause 6.	**There is no geographic limitation, and three years is probably too long a time period. Students should be informed that most states will not support anti-competition clauses regarding attorneys as they unduly interfere with the clients' choice of attorney. Ask them if they think the same policy reasons should apply to paralegals.**
Clause 7.	**This clause is inconsistent with clause 2.**
Clause 8.	**Refers to a clause five that clearly is not the clause five included in this form contract.**

REVIEW QUESTIONS, page 402-05

1. How do the courts determine if the UCC governs a contract situation?

The subject matter must involve the (1) sale of (2) goods. Direct the students to Figure 11-2 on page 360.

If the UCC does apply, then you need to decide if either party is a merchant as special rules apply to merchants. Finally, when interpreting the UCC you need to keep the provisions of Article 1 in mind; specifically, the policy to liberally construe its provisions, that parties can normally vary the terms if desired, that unless displaced, the common law still applies, and finally that everyone must act in good faith.

2. Why does it matter under the UCC whether one or both of the parties are merchants? Give at least two examples.

It matters because special rules govern merchants. A merchant is defined as someone who
1.   deals in the goods that are the subject of the contract, or
2.   "holds himself out as having knowledge or skill peculiar to the practices or goods involved" in the contract, or
3.   who employs someone who has such knowledge and skill. Under this last standard the employee's knowledge and skill is then attributed to the employer. UCC § 2-104(1).

Examples of code provisions that differ when a merchant is involved include
   ■   **Good faith**
   ■   **Firm offer**
   ■   **Additional terms**
   ■   **Modification without new consideration**
   ■   **Implied warranties**

3. Describe each of the following contracts according to the categories listed in Figure 11-3.
   a. Carlos says to Mary, "Will you paint my house for $2000"? Mary replies, "Yes, I would be happy to."
      Bilateral; express; informal; executory; valid.

   b. Carlos says to Mary, "I will pay you $2000 if you paint my house next week." The next week Mary begins to paint the house and gets about half-way done when severe weather forces her to wait until the next week to finish the job.
      Unilateral; express; informal; executory; valid.

   c. Janet writes to Jim, "I will give you $600 for your car." Jim sends back a letter that says, "I accept."
      Bilateral; express; informal; executory; valid.

   d. Joan says to Bill, "I will give you $5000 if you kill Robert." Bill kills Robert, but Joan refuses to give him the $5000.
      Unilateral;express;informal;executory;void.

e. Every Saturday Jimmy came to the Booth's home and mowed their lawn for $15. One Saturday Jimmy arrived while Mr. Booth was on the phone. Mr. Booth simply waved at Jimmy, who then mowed the lawn.
Unilateral; implied-in-fact; informal;executory;valid

4. What are the three basic elements of a valid contract claim?
The three elements are offer, acceptance, and consideration.

5. What is the objective view of contract law?
The objective view determines whether a contract has been formed from an objective outsider's point of view, rather than looking at the actual intent of the parties.

6. What are the four basic elements that every offer should contain?
Every offer should contain four basic elements: the parties; the subject matter (quantity); the price; and the time for performance.

7. Juan says to Jim, "I would like to sell my watch to you." Jim replies, "Great. I will be happy to give you a fair price for it." Has a contract been formed? Why?
No, there was no agreement as to price.

8. Sally offers Tom a job as a paralegal, saying she will pay him "what he is worth." Tom accepts. Has a contract been formed? Why?
No, "what he is worth" is too indefinite.

9. Janet says to Joan, "I am eager to sell my antique vase to you." Joan says, "Would you consider $400 for it"? Has a contract been formed? Why?
No, this is just a preliminary negotiation.

10. We Growum, a garden center, places the following advertisement in the Sunday paper.
    Spring Planting Sale
    Lilac bushes $20
Tuesday John goes to the garden center. All of the lilac bushes have been sold. He sues for breach of contract. Will he succeed? Why?
No, there was no indication of the number of bushes available. Students may want to raise the issue of "bait and switch," but that is a matter of consumer protection law, not contract law.

11. Acme Lawn Care receives a call asking them to mow a lawn at 423 Main Street. Unfortunately, the mowers misread the address as 432 Main Street. They arrive at that address, unload their mowers, and begin their work. Mr. Adams, the owner, is home and sees what they are doing. He says nothing and lets them complete the job. When they finish and ask to be paid, he refuses. Would a court require Mr. Adams to pay, and if so, under what theory?
The court might have him pay under a theory of unjust enrichment. Because Mr. Adams saw what they were doing and did not ask them to stop, he unfairly took advantage of their mistake.

12. What are the three ways an offer can be terminated?

An offer can be terminated through the offeror's revocation, the offeree's rejection or counteroffer, or by operation of law.

13. When may an offeror not revoke an offer?

Normally a contract offer can be revoked at any time. However, it may not be revoked if the other party has given consideration for the offer to remain open for a reasonable length of time (option contract) or if a merchant gives a signed writing promising to hold the offer open for a reasonable time (merchant's firm offer).

14. What is the difference between an option contract and a merchant's firm offer?

While an option contract must be supported by consideration, a merchant's firm offer must be in a signed writing but it does not have to be supported by consideration.

15. What is the name of the rule that states that the acceptance must completely agree with the terms of the offer?

It is the mirror image rule.

16. How has the UCC changed the mirror image rule?

If the parties intend to make a contract, then even the use of additional or different terms in the acceptance will not prevent the contract from being formed. Generally, the new terms are viewed as suggestions for addition to the contract. Between merchants they become a part of the contract unless the original offer limited acceptance to its terms, the new terms "materially alter" the contract, or the offeror objects to the terms. However, there will be no contract if the acceptance states that the offeror must agree to the new terms.

17. An uncle offers his nephew $5,000 if the nephew promises not to smoke marijuana or use other illegal drugs during the next four years while he is away at college. Has a binding contract been formed? Why?

No, this situation is distinguishable from that of *Hamer v. Sidway*. In that case, the nephew had the legal right to smoke and drink. There is no legal right to smoke marijuana or use other illegal drugs. Therefore, the nephew in this case is not giving up a legal right and so there is no consideration.

18. John volunteers to take care of Sam's pet rabbit while he is away on vacation. When Sam returns, he is very pleased with the good care John gave his rabbit and tells him that he is going to pay him $50. When John arrives the next day to receive his money, Sam said that he has changed his mind. Is Sam under a contractual obligation to pay John for the care of his rabbit? Why?

Sam is not under a contractual obligation because as John had already done the work before Sam made the offer, his caring for the cat is considered past consideration. Past consideration will not support a contract.

19. Anna Sacks was an employee of the Ajax Company for thirty-seven years. The president of the company told her that (in consideration for her outstanding service) when she retired, the

company would pay her $200 per month for life. Two years later she retired and began receiving the payments. Shortly thereafter, the company was sold, and the new president refused to continue the payments, arguing that there had never been a valid contract between Ms. Sacks and the company. How do you think the court resolved the case?

There is no valid contract because past consideration is not valid consideration. But here the court might find detrimental reliance. She retired because she thought she would be receiving $200/month.

20. Millie requested bids from three different contractors for a price to repair the roof on her house. The bids ranged from $5,000 to $20,000. Naturally, Millie accepted the $5,000 bid from We'gottcha Roofing. On a Monday We'gottcha began work by first removing all of the old shingles. The weather prediction was for rain by the end of the week. We'gottcha told Millie she had a choice. Either she could pay them a "bonus" of $15,000 and they would continue work on her roof, or they would have to take the rest of the week to finish other jobs they had started. Millie, afraid all of her household contents would be ruined if rain hit her "deshingled" roof, agreed to the extra money. Will Millie be required to pay the $15,000 bonus? Why?

Millie will not be required to pay the extra money. The roofers were already under a pre-existing duty to perform their work. You may need to help the students see why this is a "hold-up." I find that they often think that because Millie agreed to the extra money, that she should have to pay. Also, have them take another look at the original bids. It may be that the roofers originally underbid while planning to add on the "bonus" later.

21. Marvin began negotiations with the Big-W food chain to open a franchise store. The Big-W representative said that first Marvin would have to sell his bakery to raise the necessary money. Marvin was hesitant to do so, but based upon Big-W's representations that his selling the bakery was the only thing preventing them from finalizing the contract, Marvin did so. However, once he had sold the bakery, Big-W said they had found someone else and refused to sign a franchise contract with Marvin. If Marvin were to sue Big-W, would he win under a contract action? Why? Is there any alternative?

This hypothetical is similar to *Hoffman v. Red Owl Stores, Inc.*, discussed in the text on pages 377-78. This can lead to a discussion of how under traditional contract law Marvin would have no remedy even though he relied to his detriment on the Big-W promises. Under a more modern view, he may get some relief if he can show that the promises were made with the intent to induce his action, he relied on the promises, and that it would be unjust not to enforce the promises.

22. Name the six major defenses to a contract action.

The six major defenses are as follows:

    (1)   Lack of Contractual Capacity (Examples: being a minor or intoxicated)
    (2)   Illegal Contract
    (3)   Against Public Policy
    (4)   Lack of Genuiness of Assent (Examples: fraud, mistake of mutual fact, undue influence, duress)
    (5)   Breach of Warranty
    (6)   Lack of a Writing

23. Jim, who is sixteen years old, buys a stereo from Circuit Playground. Jim takes the stereo to the beach and ruins it when it becomes filled with sand. Jim takes it back to the store and demands the return of the money he paid for the stereo. Will the store have to refund his payment?

The majority view is that the store will have to refund his payment. The minority view would hold that the store must give a refund, but minus any damage caused to the stereo.

24. Mark and Bill are sitting at a bar drinking. They discuss the possibility of Mark selling Bill his watch for $50. Bill leaves, but Mark remains and continues to drink. Two hours later Bill calls Mark and offers him $5 for the watch. Now very intoxicated, Mark mutters, "Whatever." The next day Mark has no memory of the phone call. Will the court enforce this arrangement? Why?

Although it is difficult to support a defense based on intoxication, Bill would have a good chance here. First, a reasonable person would not expect someone to take $5 for a $50 watch. Second, there is evidence there was no meeting of the minds because Bill was very drunk. The court would look to the period of time he was drinking and his lack of memory of the phone call.

25. Sara offers to sell her car to Janet for $800. Janet thinks Sara means her 1978 VW Beetle and agrees. Sara was thinking of her 1970 VW van. Has a contract been formed? Why?

No, they each were thinking of a different car. Therefore, there was no meeting of the minds.

26. A law firm requires all new attorneys to sign an agreement that states that if they leave the firm for any reason, they will not work for another law firm or open their own practice within a fifty-mile radius for two years. How do you think the court would treat such an agreement? Why?

In determining the validity of covenants not to compete the courts look to the reasonableness of the distance and time. Here fifty miles might be appropriate but two years may be viewed as too long. In addition, the court might view the covenant as against public policy as interfering with a client's right to select the attorney he or she wishes.

27. What is the difference between a warranty of merchantability and an implied warranty of fitness? How do both of those differ from an express warranty?

A warranty of merchantability means that the product is fit for ordinary purposes. An implied warranty of fitness means that the seller understands that the product is being purchased for a specific purpose and the buyer is relying on the seller's knowledge in selecting the product. Both of these warranties are implied. Express warranties must be based on statements, samples, or descriptions and must go to the basis of the bargain.

28. Joan offers to buy Bill's sailboat for $2,000. Bill agrees and asks Joan to put it in writing. Joan leaves an e-mail message for her secretary, stating that she wants him to draft a contract stating that she agrees to buy Bill's sailboat for $2,000. The next day Joan changes her mind. If Bill sues for breach of contract, will he succeed? Why?

This contract must be in writing because the sale is for goods over $500. The question is whether there is a writing. The form does not matter so an e-mail may be viewed as a

writing if the court views an electronic transmission as a writing. The signature can be any authentication so the e-mail header containing the sender's name is probably sufficient.

29. What are the four ways in which the parties' contractual obligations can be discharged?
The four ways to discharge contractual obligations are through performance, agreement, impossibility, or commercial impracticality.

30. How does each of the following differ from the others - complete performance, substantial performance, and material failure to perform?
Complete performance ends both parties' obligations. Substantial performance occurs when the essential terms of the contract have been performed. Because not all terms have been performed, however, substantial performance results in a breach. Normally, the breaching party will still be entitled to the contractual price minus any damages caused by the breach. A material breach occurs when there is a serious failure to fulfill the contractual terms. The nonbreaching party is relieved of all contractual obligations.

31. Jones contracted with Smith to log all the timber from his land between the months of September and December. Jones found he was not able to complete the work in the agreed time because his operations were slowed (1) by a local ordinance prohibiting logging during the hunting season which occurred in September and (2) by unusually heavy rains in the remaining months. Should Jones's lack of performance be excused? Why?
The question would be whether either of the events were foreseeable. If they were, they should have been factored into the original contract terms. The court will not find commercial impracticability and will not excuse the performance. Probably both of these events were foreseeable.

32. The city of Portage contracts with Get Going Builders to demolish a vacant building and replace it with a park. John Jakes is delighted, as his property is right across the street from the intended park. He envisions a significant increase in his property value. At the last minute the city decides to forgo the park in favor of increased pay for its fire fighters. John is dismayed and wants to sue the city. Will he succeed in his suit? Why?
No, John will not succeed as he was an incidental beneficiary.

33. Martha contracts with Sam, a noted concert pianist, to take a series of ten music lessons. After the second lesson Sam is offered the opportunity to go on a world tour. He contacts William, a lesser known pianist, to take over his lessons. Martha is upset. Does she have any grounds to complain?
Yes, because generally you cannot delegate personal duties.

34. What is the difference between an assignment and a delegation?
An assignment involves the transfer of rights. A delegation involves the transfer of duties.

35. What is the difference between assignments and delegations on the one hand and third party beneficiary contracts on the other?
Assignments and delegations are done after the contract is formed; third party beneficiaries are added at the time of the contract formation.

36. When is specific performance an appropriate remedy?

Specific performance is used in situations where there is no alternative comparable product available, such as a particular parcel of land or a rare piece of art.

37. What is cover?

When a seller breaches, the buyer is under a duty to "cover, that is to buy substitute goods.

38. What are consequential damages?

Consequential damages arise out of special circumstances that must be foreseeable to other party.

39. Sara Smith is a struggling young artist. Recently, however, she was "discovered" when an art dealer saw one of her paintings hanging in a local art gallery. The art dealer contracted with Sara to hold a major showing of her work in six months, November 1. Under the contract Sara was to show no less than ten original paintings. In preparation for the show Sara contracted with Paint Masters, Inc., for four cases of her favorite oil paints to be shipped no later than July 1. Sara heard nothing more from Paint Masters, Inc., until September 1 when one case arrived. Sara attempted to find the same paint from other sources but was able to procure one only more case at $200 more than she had contracted to pay Paint Masters. Because of the delay in shipment, Sara was able to complete only six paintings and the show was canceled. Sara would like to sue Paint Masters, Inc., for the lost profits she would have received from her heightened recognition had the show gone as planned, for the money she had to spend on alternate paints, and for punitive damages to teach Paint Masters a lesson. Please evaluate Sara's situation.

Her lost profits are too indefinite to form the basis for consequential damages. Also, she did not alert the other party of the consequences of what would happen if she did not get her paint in time. She will be able to recover the extra money that she had to spend on the alternative paints. Punitive damages are never appropriate in contract actions unless an intentional bad act, such as fraud, can also be proven.

40. Kate contracts with Bennett to buy 100 guitars at $300 each. Kate hopes to resell the guitars for $400 each. When the time for delivery arrives, Bennett refuses to deliver the guitars. Kate then spends $100 in phone calls trying to obtain an alternate supplier. Finally, she finds substitute guitars, but has to pay $350 each for them. She saved $50, however, because in her contract with Bennett she was going to have to pay the shipping. In her new contract, the seller paid the shipping. How much is Kate owed in compensatory damages?

She had to spend an extra $50 for 100 guitars = $500 plus she spent a total of $100 in incidental damages, for a total of $600. However, she also saved $50, so she will be allowed to recover $550.

41. The city of Kalamazoo hired Good Builders, Inc., to build a new courthouse for $560,000. Good Builders had barely broken ground when the city notified them that it would not be able to pay for the building after all and asked Good Builders to stop all work. Good Builders refused, saying, "Hey, you guys signed a contract. We know our rights." At the time the city asked them to stop, Good Builders had expended $5,000 on materials, approximately $3,000 of which could have been returned at no loss to themselves. By completing the project, however, Good Builders expended an additional $400,000. In a breach of contract action by Good Builders against the

city, how much money do you think the court should award Good Builders? Why?

They will recover $2000. That is the amount of money they could not recoup at the time they learned of the other party's breach. At that point they should have stopped all work on the project.

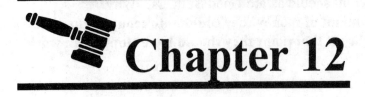

Chapter 12

Property and Estate Law

The law in this chapter is not as "dynamic" as that in the other chapters. However, even in the staid world of property law things are changing, especially in the area of eminent domain. Property and estate law are also very vocabulary laden. I usually try to help my students by telling them they need a basic familiarity with the all of the vocabulary, but then emphasizing for them the concepts I really want them to master, especially the differences between joint tenancy and tenancy in common and the dangers of dying intestate.

DISCUSSION QUESTIONS, page 411

1. Should a condominium association that wishes to appeal to seniors be allowed to prohibit children from living in its units? What are the policy arguments for and against? How would you distinguish between children living in the unit versus those just visiting? Specifically, if you cannot discriminate on the basis of race, why should you be able to discriminate on the basis of age?

Courts have been more willing to allow discrimination in adult housing under the theory that old age, unlike other categories, is one that everyone eventually falls into. The court usually supports the rights of elders to live in "peace and quiet," especially in a ownership situation, such as a condominium as opposed to an apartment complex.

2. Sam and Mary are planning to marry and build a home. With her own money Mary plans on purchasing a piece of property. She wants Sam's name to appear on the deed as a joint tenant. Do you think this is advisable?

No. Right now they are planning to marry. However, if they decide to go their own ways, Mary will be stuck with having given Sam a one-half interest in the land. And because she wants to make him a joint tenant instead of a tenant in common, if she were to die, Sam and not Mary's relatives, would become the sole owner of the property.

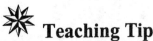 **Teaching Tip**

Page 413, *Baiz v. Hoffius* — We chose *Biaz* to illustrate and review principles of statutory interpretation the students learned in Chapter 6. Note how the court first points out that the role of the court is to determine legislative intent by first looking to the plain meaning of the statute. Then the court notes the need to liberally construe remedial statutes, but also the need to avoid conflicts with other statutes.

1. The court in *Baiz* quoted from *State of Minnesota v. French*, 460 N.W.2d 2 (Minn. 1990), for the general proposition that the state's requesting protection for unmarried couples in acquiring rental housing was the cause for much of society's problems. In that case, the dissent had this to say:

> Religious and moral values include not discriminating against others solely because of their color, sex, or whom they live with, avoiding unnecessary emotional suffering, showing tolerance for nontraditional lifestyles, and treating others as one would wish to be treated. . . . It may be difficult for some individuals to recognize invidious discrimination, but one must not lose sight of the continuing fight of minorities to be protected from a "probable majority" point of view. It was not long ago that blacks and women were widely viewed as second-class citizens. Discrimination usually comes in less obvious forms -- such as against single parents, those with AIDS, homosexuals, the elderly, and those living together -- but no less invidious forms. The majority, in effect, would have us return to the day of "separate but equal" where individuals such as French would be permitted to keep their neighborhoods free of "undesirables" and "nonbelievers."

****

> Discriminating against unmarried individuals living with members of the opposite sex is neither the cause or the solution to societal woes.

Id. at 17, 20. Who do you think presents the better argument, and why?

Obviously there is no right answer here. In *Baiz* the court quotes from *French* for the very broad proposition that our present social order is in disarray and that to allow governmental protection for cohabiting unmarried persons would only add to those problems. No matter what the students' personal beliefs are they should see the dangers of this type of argument.

2. What did the court state was the first step in statutory analysis?
The main goal of statutory interpretation is to give effect to legislative intent. The first step is to look at the specific statutory language. (Plain meaning approach). The court stated that "[j]udicial construction of a statute is not permitted where the plain and ordinary meaning of the language is clear."

3. Why did the court think that the refusal to rent to a unmarried couple did not violate the state's fair housing laws?
The statute was meant to protect status (the status of not being married) but not to protect criminal behavior (unmarried cohabitation). The court stated that the legislature is presumed to know of existing laws, in this case those criminalizing unmarried cohabitation. The court thought its interpretation of status versus conduct was necessary in order to avoid conflict between the statutes. Although recognizing that courts ordinarily are to liberally construe a remedial statute, the court refused to do so in this case.

4. Why did the court refuse to discuss the issue of whether the landlord's religious beliefs justified the discrimination?
Neither trial court addressed that issue so the issue was not reserved for review. Also, the

court refused to reach the constitutional issue, because as a general principle if the question can be resolved as a matter of statutory interpretation, the court will not address the constitutional issues.

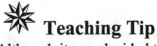 **Teaching Tip**

Although it was decided too late to be included in the text, a case worth watching is *County of Wayne v. Hathcock*, 684 N.W.2d 765 (Mich. 2004). In that case, the Michigan Supreme Court overturned a 1981 case to hold that the government could not use its power of eminent domain to take residential property so that a private developer could build an office complex.

DISCUSSION QUESTION, page 420
3. Why should the government be able to take somebody's property without his or her consent? Give some examples of what you would view as legitimate uses of eminent domain.
At times in order to further goals for the good of all of society, the government must have the power to take private land even over the landowner's objection. (Of course, the government must give just compensation for the land.) For example, if a major highway was planned but would be left with an uncompleted section because of individual landowners refusal to sell their land, then a few could block what is needed for the many.

Legal Reasoning Exercise, pages 426-27
1. For each of the following questions, assume the decedent died without a will and all the decedent's debts have been paid, as have all of his last sickness, funeral, and settlement of estate expenses. Base your answers on the following statutes:

Ch. 190, § 1 Spouse's share of property not disposed of by will
A surviving husband or wife shall be entitled to the following share in the spouse's real and personal property not disposed of by will:
    (1) If the deceased leaves kindred and no issue, and the whole estate does not exceed two hundred thousand dollars in value, the surviving husband or wife shall take the whole thereof; otherwise such survivor shall take two hundred thousand dollars and one half of the remaining personal and one-half of the remaining real property.
    (2) If the deceased leaves issue, the survivor shall take one-half of the personal and one half of the real property.
    (3) If the deceased leaves no issue and no kindred, the survivor shall take the whole.

Ch. 190, § 2 Distribution of personal property
The personal property of the deceased shall be distributed in the proportions hereinafter prescribed for the descent of real property.

Ch. 190, § 3 Descent of real property
When a person dies seized of real property, it shall descend, subject to the rights of the husband or wife of the deceased, as follows:
    (1) In equal shares to his children and to the issue of any deceased child by right of

124

representation; and if there is no surviving child of the intestate then to all his other lineal descendants. If all such descendants are in the same degree of kindred to the intestate, they shall share the estate equally; otherwise, they shall take according to the right of representation.

(2) If he leaves no issue, in equal shares to his father and mother.

(3) If he leaves no issue and no mother, to his father.

(4) If he leaves no issue and no father, to his mother.

(5) If he leaves no issue and no father or mother, to his brothers and sisters and to the issue of any deceased brother or sister by right of representation; and if there is no surviving brother or sister of the intestate, to all the issue of his deceased brothers and sisters. If all such issue are in the same degree of kindred to the intestate, they shall share the estate equally; otherwise, according to the right of representation.

(6) If an intestate leaves no kindred and no widow or husband, his estate shall escheat to the commonwealth.

a. Juan died, leaving a wife, Carmen, whom he adored, and a brother, James, whom he hated and had not seen for the past thirty years. For each of the following determine how much of Juan's estate Carmen will inherit and how much James will inherit.

(1) Juan leaves $180,000.

Wife Carmen: **$180,000 as the decedent did not leave any issue and the entire estate did not exceed $200,000. [ch. 190, § 1(1)]**

Brother James: **$0**

(2) Juan leaves $500,000.

Wife Carmen: **$350,000 as the decedent left no issue but did leave kindred and the estate was over $200,000. Carmen as the surviving wife takes $200,000 plus 1/2 of the remainder ($150,000) for a total of $350,000. [ch. 190, § 1(1)]**

Brother James: **$150,000 because the decedent left no issue and no father or mother; the remainder goes to his brother.**

(3) Juan leaves $500,000. Assume James had predeceased Juan but has a living child, James, Jr., whom Juan has never met.

Wife Carmen: **$350,000 - same as under (2).**

Nephew James, Jr.: **$150,000 as the issue of the deceased brother. [ch. 190, § 3(5)]**

b. William died with an estate of $500,000. He left a wife, June, but no issue and no kindred. How much will June inherit? **$500,000 [ch. 190, § 1(3)]**

c. Mary died with an estate of $500,000. She left a husband, John, and two living children, Rachel and Albert. How will the estate be divided among her husband and children?

Husband John: **$200,000 [ch. 190, § 1(2)]**

Daughter Rachel: **$125,000 [ch. 190, § 3 (1)]**

Son Albert: **$125,000**

d. Roberto died with an estate of $500,000. He left a wife, Maria, and a living child, Bill, who has a child, Jill. His other child, Sam, predeceased him. Sam has two living children, Tracy and Tim. How will the estate be divided among his wife, Maria; his child, Bill; his grandchild Jill; and his grandchildren Tracy and Tim?

Wife Maria:	**$250,000 [ch. 190, § 1(2)]**
Son Bill:	**$125,000 [ch. 190, § 3(1)]**
Grandchild Jill:	**$0**
Grandchild Tracy:	**$75,000 [ch. 190, § 3(1)] - taking by right of representation**
Grandchild Tim:	**$75,000 - same as Tracy**

Note: I find it useful to diagram this problem and the next one on the board.

e. Samantha died with an estate of $500,000. She left no husband and no children. They had all predeceased her. However, she did leave five grandchildren. Two of the grandchildren, Amy and Albert, are the children of her deceased son, Robert. The other three grandchildren, Bonnie, Brad, and Bennett are the children of her deceased daughter, Emily. How will the estate be divided among the five grandchildren?

Grandchild Amy:	**$100,000 [ch. 190, § 3(1)**
Grandchild Albert:	**Same**
Grandchild Bonnie:	**Same**
Grandchild Brad:	**Same**
Grandchild Bennett:	**Same — as all descendants are in the same degree of kindred, they share equally. This distinguishes this problem from the prior example where one of the children was still living.**

CASE DISCUSSION QUESTIONS, page 431 for *In Re Till*

1. The court noted that a presumption of undue influence arises if there was a confidential relationship between the testator and the beneficiary. What factors determine whether there was a confidential relationship? Did the court find such a relationship in this case? Why?
The court looks to factors such as "the amount of time that the beneficiary spent with the testator, whether the beneficiary handled many of the testators personal or business affairs, and also whether the testator had ever sought the advice of the beneficiary." The court said that such a relationship did not exist in this case because Julie spent very little time with Frank, she never handled any of his personal or financial affairs, and while Frank may have listened to some of her suggestions, he never relied on her for advice. This is important because without establishing a confidential relationship there is no presumption of undue influence. Therefore, the court had to go on to independently determine if undue influence had been present.

2. In the absence of proof of a confidential relationship, what are the four elements the court stated are necessary to prove the existence of undue influence?
The four factors for proving a confidential relationship are the "(1) decedent's susceptibility to undue influence; (2) opportunity to exert such influence and effect the

wrongful purpose; (3) a disposition to do so for an improper purpose; and (4) a result clearly showing the effects of undue influence."

3. The court concluded that there was no undue influence. Do you agree?
This will depend on whether the students see Frank as a lonely, but clear-headed man who did what was natural, that is, rewrote his will to benefit the only person who was nice to him or as a case of a young woman taking advantage of a sick, old man.

DISCUSSION QUESTION, page 431
4. Under what circumstances do you think people should be able to withdraw life-support equipment from someone who is in an irreversible coma? Should doctors be allowed to "help" a patient die by giving the patient a lethal dose of morphine or some other drug when the patient has an incurable disease, is in great pain, and wishes to end the misery? What should be done if that person is in a coma and did not have a formal living will but did tell a close relative that he or she did not wish to be kept alive in such a situation?
This question raises many difficult questions including the current controversy over physician assisted suicide. It is another example of how medical science may be outrunning the ability of the court to frame new answers as science forces us to make choices that were not asked of us just a few years ago.

REVIEW QUESTIONS, page 432

1. Define the two basic types of property.
Real property consists of land and whatever is permanently attached. Personal property is everything else.

2. Why is it important to know if property is classified as personal or real?
Determining whether property is real or personal can have important consequences as the courts apply different rules to the different types of property. For example, the UCC only applies to the sale of goods (personal property).

3. Describe the three basic types of freehold estates.
The three types of freehold estates are fee simple absolute (right to title for life or some other indeterminate period of time); conditional fee estate (the owner retains ownership only as long as certain conditions are met); and life estate (ownership for life).

4. Why might it be important to know whether two friends shared ownership in a house as joint tenants or as tenants in common?
If a joint tenant dies, the joint tenant's share of the property automatically passes to the other joint tenant(s). A tenant in common can bequeath his or her share to whomever he or she chooses.

5. Describe two ways in which an owner's right to use his or her property may be limited by private arrangement.

An owner's right to use his or her property may be limited through a restrictive covenant (a provision in a deed that prohibits specified uses of the property) or by easement (a right to use property owned by another for a limited purpose).

6. Describe the four basic types of leasehold estates.

The four types of leasehold estates are tenancy for a term (for a set period of time), periodic tenancy (for set rental periods, such as by the month), tenancy at will (either the landlord or tenant can stop the tenancy at any time), and tenancy at sufferance (the person in possession has no legal right to be there).

7. What is a constructive eviction, and how does it relate to the implied warranty of habitability?

A constructive eviction occurs when the landlord does something to deprive the tenant of quiet enjoyment of the land, such as shutting off the water or changing the locks. If the tenant is forced to abandon the property, then the tenant can rely on the constructive eviction as a defense to any further requirement to pay rent. An implied warranty of habitability is a requirement that property be fit for the purpose for which it is being rented. Therefore, if the landowner fails to maintain the premises in a way that breaches this implied warranty, that could give rise to a constructive eviction.

8. What are a land contracts? Can you envision any problems with their use? For example, do you think the terms of a standard land contract generally favor the buyer or the seller?

In essence a land contract is an installment sales contract. The buyer takes physical possession of the property and begins making monthly payments to the seller which will be applied to the agreed on sale price of the property. The terms generally favor the seller. The seller retains legal title to the property until all the agreed on installment payments have been made. If the buyer for some reason defaults in making the payments, the contract is broken, and the seller gets to keep title to the property, as well as any payments that were made during the course of the contract.

9. How does someone acquire property through adverse possession?

For someone to qualify for ownership by adverse possession, that person's use of someone else's property must be actual, open, adverse, and exclusive for a statutorily determined number of years, usually between five and twenty.

10. According to the dictates of the Fifth Amendment, if a state wants to take private property, what must it do?

If the state wants to take private property, the property must be taken for a public purpose, and the government must provide the owner with just compensation.

11. What is the distinction between lost and mislaid property? Why does it matter?

Property is classified as lost if the owner has involuntarily parted with it and does not know where to find it. On the other hand, if the owner deliberately placed it somewhere and then forgot where it had been placed, it is classified as mislaid rather than lost. It matters because if you find lost property, you acquire title that is good against everyone except the

true owner. But if you find mislaid property, property that was inadvertently left behind, such as a ring next to a sink, then you acquire no ownership rights in it.

12. What does it mean to say someone died intestate?
A person dying without a will is said to have died intestate.

13. Why is it not a good idea to die without a will?
It is not a good idea to die without a will because the state intestacy statute may distribute your assets in ways that you do not want.

14. Define each of the following:
a. formal will   **A formal will is one that has been prepared on a word processor or typewriter and has been properly signed by the testator (the person making the will) and the required witnesses.**

b. holographic will   **A holographic will, or informal will, is one that was handwritten by the testator, without the necessary witness signatures.**

c. nuncupative will   **A nuncupative will is an oral will.**

15. Why is the purpose of a simultaneous death clause? Give an example of when such a clause would be relevant and why it would be important.
A simultaneous death clause states that if a person named as a beneficiary in the will dies within a short period of time after the decedent dies, it will be assumed for purposes of the will that the person in question failed to survive the decedent. Such clauses are normally inserted for tax purposes. Without such a clause the estate of each decedent might be taxed as though each survived the other and hence inherited the property from the other. Therefore, estate taxes would have to be paid twice.

16. What is the purpose of a trust?
A trust is a legal relationship in which one party holds property for the benefit of another. The property is transferred to a trust fund, where it is to be used for the benefit of a designated person or persons rather than passing directly to them as part of the probate process.

17. What types of property do not have to go through the probate process?
Property that does not go through probate include jointly owned property, life insurance proceeds, and a living trust.

Chapter 13

Laws
Affecting Business

In this chapter we depart from the norm by combining various topics of concern to business: business forms, commercial paper, and secured transactions. We then devote the bulk of the chapter to employment discrimination. While unconventional, we think that in today's world employment law is becoming increasingly important. It also gives the students the opportunity to study a series of U.S. Supreme Court cases that involve statutory interpretation, thereby reinforcing the legal analysis skills the students have learned in earlier chapters.

CASE DISCUSSION QUESTIONS, page 439 for *Van Dyke v. Bixby*
1. Why was it crucial to the plaintiff's case to prove that Dr. Alt and the other doctors were working together as a partnership?
This proof was crucial because partners are liable for the negligence of their partners. In order to be able to reach the assets of the other doctors, the plaintiff had to prove they were working together in a partnership.

2. What evidence do you think was particularly relevant in answering that question?
The doctors signed a certificate showing they were conducting a business under the name The Johnson Clinic. The endorsement page of a professional liability insurance policy stated that the doctors were doing business as copartners. A billing statement showed all of the doctors associated with The Johnson Clinic. Also, statements of certain of the defendants in answers to interrogatories and the testimony of two of those defendants that they were partners was admissible. (This was not considered conclusive as one can believe he is a partner when he actually is not.) Taking all of this evidence together, there was sufficient evidence that a partnership existed.

LEGAL REASONING EXERCISES, page 443
1. Write a memorandum analyzing the advantages and disadvantages of each of the four major business forms in light of the needs of Alice and her friends.
The focus of this memorandum should be on the different needs of the partners. For example, Betty is retired and would not want any type of unlimited liability. The main idea of the business is Alice's and she may not be happy sharing ownership control with others.

Issues for Business Forms

		Invest/Savings Left
Alice - 30/baker/single parent	Wants to run business	$0/$50,000
Betty - 62/retired	Wants no part in day to day	100,000/130,000
Claire - 20/student	Wants no part in day to day	invest building
Dan - 25/odd jobs	Wants to manage	5,000/5,000

Sole Proprietorship
    Advantages for all - simple to form
    Disadvantage to all - liability for personal assets
                     dies with owner

Partnership
Advantages -	Fairly easy to form
	Each could have a say in how business is run
	Single taxation
Disadvantages -	Unlimited liability for everyone
	Liable for each other's actions
	& each can bind the company
	Dies with death or withdrawal of partner

Corporation
Advantages -	Limited liability to what invest in the company
Disadvantages -	Costly to form
	Costly to run
	Double taxation

Limited Liability Company
Advantages -	Limited Liability (appealing to all)
	Single Taxation
Disadvantages -	new form

Alice
Wants management control so likes sole proprietorship or partnership
But greater worry as single mom has to be liability, so would prefer corp. or LLC

Betty
As a retiree, her biggest concern is liability, so cannot do a partnership. Sole proprietorship O.K. if really wants no say in business. If wants say or to be part of growth of company, should choose corp. or LLC. Might go for a limited partnership.

Claire
Student with limited liability, and no desire for control but still would probably prefer limited liability of corporation or LLC.

Dan
Wants management control and so would not go for sole proprietorship. Young with earning power so not as concerned as others with liability. Still probably would prefer LLC.

2. Assume Alice and her friends have decided to form a partnership. Draft a partnership agreement that will best satisfy all of the parties' needs.

This makes an excellent group exercise. Have the students form groups of four in which each represents the interests of one of the four friends. After each group has drafted its agreement, have a general class discussion that compares the agreements in light of how well they protected each of the friend's interests and how well they planned for unexpected calamities, such as one of the four friends wanting to leave the business.

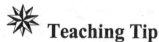 **Teaching Tip**

Obviously a whole chapter could be devoted to each of the topics of commercial paper and secured transactions. However, we have only set aside a few pages for each. Our purpose here is not to teach them a lot of detail that they will likely rapidly forget. Rather our purpose is to help them see the main function of commercial paper — to substitute for money, and the main purpose of secured transactions — to leave the creditor with something if the debtor defaults.

CASE DISCUSSION QUESTIONS, page 453 for *O'Connor v. McDonald's Restaurants of California, Inc.*
1. What factors will be particularly important in determining if an employee is on a "frolic of his or her own"?

The court considered various factors in trying to determine if the employee was pursuing a special errand on behalf of the employer or was pursing a personal objective. Those factors include: Evans's intent; the nature, time and place of Evans's Conduct; what work Evans was hired to do; and the amount of time consumed in personal activity.

2. Why did the court reverse summary judgment in this case? Does this mean the plaintiff will be able to hold McDonald's liable for his injury?

The court thought there was enough evidence to raise a triable issue about the combination of personal entertainment and company business that occurred at Duffer's house. Therefore, it was inappropriate for the court to dismiss the case prior to trial. This does not mean that the plaintiff will necessarily be able to hold McDonald's liable. Before that can happen a jury must determine that Evans had not abandoned his special errand when he went to the gathering at Duffer's.

DISCUSSION QUESTIONS, page 457
1. What do you think Mr. Smith was trying to accomplish by amending the statute to include sex discrimination?

He was probably hoping that so many would be opposed to that amendment that the whole statute would be defeated.

2. In Chapter 6, we said that one way to try to discover the intent of the legislature is to look at legislative history. Having just read an excerpt from legislative history for Title VII, what can you extrapolate about the value of relying on legislative history?

You have to take legislative history with a large grain of salt.

3. In addition to the categories that Congress included in Title VII, can you think of any other categories that should be included to completely protect individuals from employment discrimination?

This should lead to a general discussion of why it is sometimes lawful to discriminate and other times not. Students might want to include the categories of age, physical disability, mental disability, sexual orientation, and obesity.

CASE DISCUSSION QUESTIONS, page 461 for *Diaz v. Pan American World Airways, Inc.*
1. Why did the male plaintiff win his claim of sex discrimination?
This was a case of overt discrimination, and the only defense open to the airlines was a bona fide occupational qualification (BFOQ). The court was concerned that the exception not swallow the rule and narrowly interpreted the exception to require that the court apply a business necessity and not a business convenience test. Discrimination on the basis of sex can only occur "when the essence of the business operation would otherwise be undermined." (Page 460 in the text.) Because the primary function of the airline is to transport passengers safely, creating a pleasant environment does not go to the essence of the business.

2. In the district court trial, Pan Am introduced evidence of a survey that indicated 79 percent of all passengers, both men and women, preferred female stewardesses. What did the circuit court of appeals have to say about an employer using such customer preferences to make hiring decisions?
The court stated that "[w]hile we recognize that the public's expectation of finding one sex in a particular role may cause some initial difficulty, it would be totally anomalous if we were to allow the preferences and prejudices of the customers to determine whether the sex discrimination was valid. Indeed, it was, to a large extent, these very prejudices the Act was meant to overcome." (Page 461 of the text.)

3. During the trial Dr. Eric Berne, author of *Games People Play*, testified, trying to explain in psychological terms why most passengers prefer female stewardesses. "Dr. Berne explained that the cabin of a modern airliner is, for passengers, a special and unique psychological environment ('sealed enclave'), characterized by the confinement of a number of people together in an enclosed and limited space, by their being subjected to the unusual physical experience of being levitated off the ground and transported through the atmosphere at high speed, by their being substantially out of touch with their accustomed world, and by their own inability to control events. That environment . . . creates three typical passenger emotional states . . . a sense of apprehension, . . . a sense of boredom . . . and . . . a feeling of excitement. . . . [F]emale stewardesses . . . would be better able to deal with each of these psychological states. . . . [P]assengers of both sexes would . . . respond better to the presence of females than males. He explained that many male passengers would subconsciously resent a male flight attendant perceived as more masculine than they, but respond negatively to a male flight attendant perceived as less masculine, whereas male passengers would generally feel themselves more masculine and thus more at ease in the presence of a young female attendant. He further explained that female passengers might consider personal overtures by male attendants as intrusive and inappropriate, while at the same time welcoming the attentions and conversation of

another woman."

How do you think this testimony should have factored into the court's decision?

This testimony should not factor into the court's decision as it was just another way of expressing customer preference, something the court has stated is not a valid basis for allowing a BFOQ.

DISCUSSION QUESTION, page 462

4. Johnson Controls, Inc. manufactures batteries. In the process, lead is a primary ingredient. Because the company was afraid that exposure to lead could lead to harm to any fetus carried by a female employee, the company excluded women who were pregnant or "capable of bearing children" from jobs that exposed them to lead. When a group of women challenged this policy, the company argued that it was a BFOQ. How do you think the court resolved this issue?

This hypothetical is based on *U.A.W. v. Johnson*, 499 U.S. 187 (1991). After eight employees had become pregnant with blood lead levels exceeding that set by OSHA, the company had developed its fetal protection policy. To be able to work, a woman had to present medical documentation that she was infertile. The court of appeals supported summary judgement for the employer stating that the fetal protection policy was reasonably necessary to further the industrial safety concern that is part of the essence of respondent's business. The United States Supreme Court disagreed. First, it stated that this is a case of facial discrimination as the company only required female employees to prove they were not capable of reproducing despite evidence that lead exposure is also harmful to male reproductive system. Therefore, as this was a case of overt discrimination, the only defense available was the BFOQ. However, this policy did not present a case for a valid BFOQ as its intent was to protect the fetus, but it did not go to the women's ability to perform the job. There was no evidence that pregnant women could not perform their work adequately. The court disregarded the company's fears that it would be inundated by tort claims from injured fetuses by noting that if the employer fully informed the women and did not act negligently, there would be no basis for a tort suit.

CASE DISCUSSION QUESTIONS, page 464 for *McDonnel Douglas Corp. v. Green*

1. What do you think happened next in this case?

The case was remanded on the issue of pretext. The respondent was given an opportunity to show that petitioner's stated reason for respondent's rejection was in fact pretext. The court suggested that relevant to such as showing would be evidence that white employees involved in similar acts were retained or rehired; petitioner's reaction to respondent's legitimate civil rights activities; and petitioner's general policy and practice with respect to minority employment. Statistics can be used to help show whether petitioner's refusal to rehire Green was part of a general pattern of discrimination against blacks.

2. Why do you think the court established such an elaborate procedure for establishing the plaintiff's prima facie case?

Cases in which the plaintiff is alleging a discriminatory motive but where the employer is arguing it acted for a nondiscriminatory business reason present difficult proof problems. However, given the history of discrimination in our country, the court thought that if the plaintiff could establish that he belonged to a protected category, that he was qualified;

that he was rejected; but that the employer continued to seek applicants, then absent any other evidence, it was fair to assume that the only reason for the rejection was because of unlawful discrimination.

3. How do you think the test proposed in this case could be modified to cover a case of a person denied a promotion?
The court noted in footnote 13 that the facts necessarily will vary and that the prima facie proof required will thus also vary. For example, step four might involve proof that someone other than the plaintiff received the promotion.

CASE DISCUSSION QUESTIONS, page 468 for *Griggs v. Duke Power Co.*
1. What did the U.S. Supreme Court understand to be the objective of Title VII? That is, precisely what does it proscribe, and what does it require?
The objective was to achieve equality of employment opportunities and to remove barriers that had operated in the past to favor white employees over other employees. Policies, even though facially neutral, cannot continue to operate to freeze the status quo of prior discriminatory employment practices. Therefore, the statute "proscribes not only overt discrimination but also practices that are fair in form, but discriminatory in operation. The touchstone is business necessity. If an employment practice which operates to exclude [any protected category] cannot be shown to be related to job performance, the practice is prohibited." [Page 467 in the text.]

2. Do you think the *Griggs* decision is a fair reading of the statute? Should an employer be found in violation of an antidiscrimination statute when there is no proof of prejudice or biased motive?
The answer to this is obviously open to debate. However, the statute does prohibit both overt discrimination (failure to refuse to hire, etc. because of such individual's race, color, religion, sex, or national origin) as well as practices that deprive individuals of employment opportunities. The basic question is whether the emphasis should be on the motives of the employer or the end result no matter the motive — that is, whether members of protected categories have the same opportunity as all others at obtaining employment.

3. What does business necessity mean, and what is its role in the order of proof discussed in this case?
Business necessity means that an employment practice must be related to job performance. For example, any test must measure the "person for the job and not the person in the abstract." [Page 468 in the text.] Therefore, general intelligence tests that have not been shown to be job related cannot be used as a screening device.

4. Did the employer prove business necessity? Why?
No, the employer was not able to prove business necessity. The evidence showed that employees who have not completed high school nor taken the tests performed satisfactorily. Also, both requirements were adopted without any meaningful study as to their relationship to job performance.

5. In footnote 6 the Court noted that "[i]n North Carolina, 1960 census statistics show that, while 34% of white males had completed high school, only 12% of Negro males had done so. . . . Similarly, with respect to standardized tests, the EEOC in one case found that use of a battery of tests, including the Wonderlic and Bennett tests used by the Company in the instant case, resulted in 58% of whites passing the tests, as compared with only 6% of the blacks." What do you make of these statistics?

These statistics show that using either the high school graduation requirement or the tests would have a substantial adverse impact on blacks. While the court stated that there was no need to find any "bad intent" on the part of the employer, these statistics along with the timing of the introduction of the standardized testing requirement (the day Title VII became effect) might lead some to believe that this was also a case of intentional discrimination.

CASE DISCUSSION QUESTIONS, page 474 for *Ellison v. Brady*

1. Why did Ellison wait so long before making a formal complaint against Gray?
She probably waited so long because she had hoped she could work it out herself. This is a common reason, along with embarrassment, that prevents women from reporting these types of cases sooner.

2. Is every utterance of a sexual or racial epithet grounds for a Title VII lawsuit? Why?
Not every utterance is grounds for a Title VII lawsuit. The court noted that "[f]or example, the 'mere utterance of an ethnic or racial epithet which engenders offensive feelings in an employee' is not, by itself, actionable under Title VII. To state a claim under Title VII, sexual harassment 'must be sufficiently severe or pervasive to alter the conditions of the victim's employment and create an abusive working environment.'" [Page 471 in the text.]

3. Why did the majority adopt a reasonable woman standard? Why did the dissent disagree? Who do you think made the better argument and why?
The court stated that it adopted "the perspective of a reasonable woman primarily because we believe that a sex-blind reasonable person standard tends to be male-biased and tends to systematically ignore the experiences of women." [Page 472 in the text.] The court acknowledged that the reasonable woman standard may classify conduct as unlawful even when the harasser does not realize the conduct creates a hostile work environment. The dissent thought that basing the standard on what the victim perceives is analogous to what women have been fighting against in rape trials. The dissent thought it should be the accused and not the victim who should be subjected to scrutiny. The students response as to which standard is better will vary depending on whether they think female victims and male perpetrators do see the world differently or whether there can be a gender neutral standard.

4. Why did the court think it appropriate to classify conduct as unlawful sexual harassment even when the harasser does not realize his conduct creates a hostile working environment?

The court stated that Title VII is not a fault-based tort. Rather Title VII is aimed at the consequences of employment practices, no matter the motive.

DISCUSSION QUESTION, page 474
5. A Fox one day invited a Stork to dinner and, being disposed to divert himself at the expense of this guest, provided nothing for the entertainment but some thin soup in a shallow dish. This the Fox lapped up very readily, while the Stork, unable to gain a mouthful with her long narrow bill, was as hungry at the end of dinner as at the beginning. The Fox meanwhile professed his regret at seeing his guest eat so sparingly and feared that the dish was not seasoned to her liking. The Stork said little but begged that the Fox would do her the honor of returning her visit. Accordingly, he agreed to dine with her on the following day. He arrived true to his appointment, and the dinner was ordered. But when it was served up, he found to his dismay that it was contained in a narrow-necked vessel, down which the Stork readily thrust her long neck and bill, while the Fox was obliged to content himself with licking the neck of the jar.

Is this fable about disparate treatment or disparate impact? Why?
This is an example of disparate impact — a facially neutral practice, providing food in either a shallow disk or in a narrow-necked vessel, that has a disparate impact by preventing form all equally being able to partake of the dinner. In *Griggs v. Duke Power Co.*, the court referred to this fable stating, "Congress has now provided that tests or criteria for employment or promotion may not provide equality of opportunity merely in the sense of the fabled offer of milk to the stork and the fox. On the contrary, Congress has now required that the posture and condition of the job-seeker be taken into account. It has — to resort again to the fable — provided that the vessel in which the milk is proffered be one all seekers can use. The Act proscribes not only overt discrimination but also practices that are fair in form, but discriminatory in operation." [Page 467 in the text.]

Legal Reasoning Exercises, pages 479-80

3. Dianne Rawlinson sought employment with the Alabama Board of Corrections as a prison guard. Alabama had established minimum height and weight requirements for all prison guards of 120 pounds and 5 feet 2 inches. These combined requirements excluded 41.13 percent of the female population and less than 1 percent of the male population. Ms. Rawlinson was refused employment because she failed to meet the minimum 120-pound weight requirement. The prison argued that the requirements were necessary because they have a relationship to strength. Ms. Rawlinson filed a charge of discrimination with the EEOC. While her claim was pending, the Alabama Board of Corrections adopted another regulation prohibiting female guards in any maximum-security institution housing men. In those prisons the inmate living area is divided into large dormitories with communal showers and toilets that are open to the dormitories and hallways. The main duty of prison guards in such a setting is to maintain security. Because of inadequate staff and facilities, no attempt was made in the four maximum-security male prisons to segregate inmates according to their offenses or levels of dangerousness, leading to what some described as a "jungle atmosphere." Ms. Rawlinson

then amended her charge to also challenge this regulation. Write an analysis discussing whether you think Ms. Rawlinson was successful on either claim.

The hypothetical is based on *Dothard v. Rawlinson*, 43 U.S. 321 (1977). The court found that she had presented a case of disparate impact as to the height and weight requirements. The court agreed that the plaintiffs had shown that these requirements had a discriminatory impact on women applicants. The employer was not able to rebut through a showing that the requirements were job related becuase there was no evidence correlating the height and weight requirements with the requisite amount of strength thought essential to job performance. In addition, if strength were a bona fide job requirement, there are other ways to more directly test for strength. (The dissent thought that height and weight were correlated with the appearance of strength which was a job requirement.)

However, the court did not find any unlawful disparate treatment. Although the regulation overtly discriminated against women, sex was a bona fide occupational qualification. While acknowledging that the BFOQ defense provides "only the narrowest of exceptions," under the particular facts of this case, sex was a BFOQ. The court noted that in the usual case an argument that a job is too dangerous for women is answered by allowing the woman to make that choice. However, in this "jungle atmosphere," the court stated that a "woman's relative ability to maintain order in a male, maximum security, unclassified penitentiary of the type Alabama now runs could be directly reduced by her womanhood. . . There would also be a real risk that other inmates, deprived of a normal heterosexual environment, would assault women guards because they were women." The dissent lambasted the majority for perpetuating the myth that women, willingly or not, are seductive sex objects.

In writing their analysis, the students do not have to reach the same results as did the Supreme Court. Rather you should be checking to make sure they see that the height and weight requirements raise issues of disparate impact, that the no women in maximum security male prisons rule raises issues of overt discrimination, and that they properly describe the stages of proof that each side will have to present under each theory.

4. Judith Smith was a unit director at a facility for the mentally retarded. Ms. Smith's six-month rating was "outstanding." She came in conflict, however, with the superintendent over an issue regarding the reorganization of the facility. The superintendent wanted to centralize all power within his office. Ms. Smith and the other unit directors thought it would be in the best interest of the patients and staff to also give them an opportunity to participate in policy decisions. The superintendent refused to consider that option. The unit directors then wrote a letter critical of the superintendent. Shortly thereafter Ms. Smith was fired. Ms. Smith sued, alleging that her dismissal was against public policy. Write an analysis explaining how you think the court resolved this issue.

This hypothetical is based on *Smith-Pfeiffer v. Fernald State School*, 533 N.E.2d 1368 (Mass. 1989). The court stated that how the facility should be organized was a matter of opinion. "Internal policy decisions are a matter of judgment for those entrusted with decision making within the institution." The defendant was entitled to a directed verdict as the court refused to broaden the exception to at-will discharges to those in which discharges were based on employees "performing appropriate, socially desirable duties."

5. A hospital administrator promoted a fifty-two-year-old "fishing buddy" because he wanted to help his friend. A better qualified, younger black woman sued, saying that her rights under Title VII had been violated. Write an analysis of the arguments each side would make.

The plaintiff might bring a claim alleging both overt discrimination based on sex and race or a disparate impact claim, based on the facially neutral policy of selecting people based on who the employer knows as this has a disproportionately disparate impact on racial minorities and women. This hypothetical is based on *Foster v. Dalton*, 71 F.3d 52 (1st Cir. 1995). In that case, the court found that the facts could have supported an inference of discriminatory intent or simple favoritism, with no racial animus. The district court found the later. The court noted that if it could review the facts de novo it might have reached a different result. However, it also noted that "an employer can hire one person instead of another for any reason, fair or unfair, without transgressing Title VII, so long as the hiring decision is not spurred by race, gender, or some other protected characteristic." Thus, the district court's assessment of the evidence was not clearly erroneous. Therefore, the court agreed that no disparate treatment could be found as the administrator was motivated solely by a desire to help his friend and not by dislike for the plaintiff's race or sex. The plaintiff's disparate impact case was also rejected as she introduced no evidence to show that the hospital had a regular practice of using the "old boy network" to hire white males.

REVIEW QUESTIONS, pages 480-82

1. What are the four basic forms of business organizations and what are the main advantages and disadvantages of each?

The four basic business forms are the sole proprietorship, partnership, corporation, and limited liability company.

The main advantages of the sole proprietorship are that it is the simplest form to start and maintain; business profits are taxed as ordinary personal income; and the owner retains complete control over the business operation. The major disadvantage of the sole proprietorship is that all the owner's personal assets, regardless of whether they are related to the operation of the business, are available to satisfy business-incurred debts. In addition, the business dies with the owner and the owner is often limited in funding to his or her own resources.

The main advantages of the partnership are that a number of people can form a partnership and that the partnership assets are only taxed once as personal income to the partners. The main disadvantages to a partnership are that every partner assumes liability for the actions of every other partner and as with a sole proprietorship, personal assets can be taken to pay for business liabilities.

The main advantages of the corporate form are that the investors have the advantage of being owners without having to assume any liability beyond the cost of their individual shares, that the corporate form has perpetual existence, and the shares are transferrable. Unlike a partnership, a corporation has a continuing life of its own that is not affected by the death of a stockholder or the exchange of shares of stock. The major disadvantage of a corporation is the "double taxation" involved. The corporation's profits are taxed at the corporate level before dividends are distributed to shareholders. The shareholders

then are taxed again on the dividends they receive. Also, limited liability may be illusory at least as to business debts as banks and other creditors often require shareholders in small corporations to provide personal guarantees to secure loans.

The main advantages of the limited liability company is that it provides for the limited liability that is afforded by the corporate form and the single taxation that occurs in a partnership. The major disadvantage is that because the statutes authorizing these new forms are of very recent origin (generally the early 1990s) there is very little case law as yet to guide us in understanding how the courts will view these new business forms.

2. What is the most common reason for changing from a sole proprietorship to a partnership or a corporation?

The most common reason is the need for additional capital to finance the business's expansion.

3. Name the ways that a general partnership can be terminated.

A partnership can be formed by a written agreement, by an oral agreement, or by operation of law.

4. What are the essential elements that the court looks for in trying to determine whether a partnership exists?

Most courts have adopted a three-part test to determine if a partnership exists. They will look at the facts of each individual case to see if there is
   1. common ownership,
   2. a sharing of the profits and losses, and
   3. a shared right to management.

5. What types of information are contained in a business's articles of incorporation?

The articles of incorporation must include the legal name of the corporation, the purpose of the corporation, a list of the incorporators and directors, the name and address of a registered agent (the person designated to receive service of legal documents), and the share structure.

6. List the general responsibilities of a corporate board of directors.

The board of directors is responsible for the management of the corporation. The board typically makes major policy and investment decisions, as well as appointing, supervising, and removing corporate officers.

7. Why might forming a limited liability company be preferable to forming either a partnership or a corporation?

It might be preferable to forming a partnership because it provides limited liability to the owners. It might be preferable to forming a corporation because it offers single taxation and because generally it is easier to form and maintain.

8. Name the requirements for an instrument to be negotiable.
To be negotiable, an instrument must
      1. be in writing,
      2. be signed by the maker or drawer,
      3. be an unconditional promise or order to pay,
      4. state a specific sum of money,
      5. be payable on demand or at a definite time, and
      6. be payable to order or to bearer.

9. What must be satisfied for someone to be a holder in due course?
A holder in due course is someone who
      1. gives value,
      2. in good faith (a subjective standard), and
      3. without notice that the instrument is overdue or has been dishonored or has any claims against it or defenses to it (an objective standard).

10. What are the two basic functions of commercial paper?
Commercial paper has two basic functions: as a substitute for money and as a credit device.

11. How does one become a holder of a negotiable instrument?
A person becomes a holder of a negotiable instrument that is bearer paper by proper delivery. If it is order paper, it must be properly delivered *and* have all necessary indorsement.

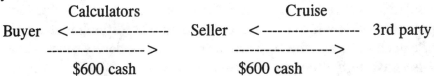 **Teaching Tip**

Students often have trouble understanding that the point of commercial paper is to be as good as cash. To make this point, I often have the students act out these next three problems. I bring in props: a dollar bill (the $600), a toy boat (the cruise), and a calculator (the 1,000 calculators). Then I have students play the role of buyer, seller, and third party and exchange the various items.

12. Buyer pays Seller $600 in cash for 1,000 calculators. Seller then takes the $600 and uses it to pay for a cruise.

```
            Calculators                       Cruise
     Buyer  <--------------------  Seller  <-------------------- 3rd party
            -------------------->          -------------------->
               $600 cash                      $600 cash
```

If the calculators prove to be defective and the seller is insolvent, who loses, the buyer or the third party who accepted $600 from the buyer?
The buyer loses because he has no claim against the third party.

13. Buyer signs a contract with Seller promising to pay $600 for 1,000 calculators on or before 6/6/98 . Seller then assigns the contract to the owner of a travel agency in payment for a cruise.

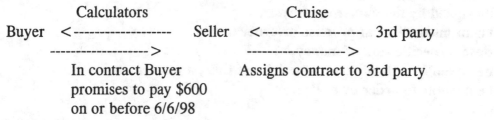

                   Calculators   Cruise

Buyer   <-------------------   Seller   <-------------------   3rd party
        ------------------->   ------------------->

        In contract Buyer   Assigns contract to 3rd party
        promises to pay $600
        on or before 6/6/98

If the calculators prove to be defective and the seller is insolvent, who loses, the buyer or the 3rd Party who accepted the assigned contract rights from the buyer?
The buyer is excused from performance and does not owe any money under the contract to the third party. The third party as an assignee only got the same rights as the seller and also took on the same defenses that would be available against the seller. [Moral: getting an assignment right under a contract is not as good as getting cash.]

14. Buyer signs a note promising to pay Seller $600 for 1,000 calculators on or before 6/6/98. Seller then delivers the note to the owner of a travel agency in payment for a cruise.

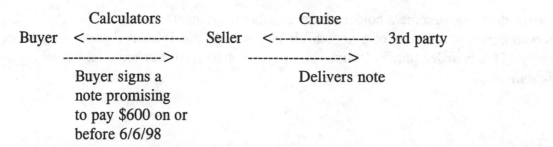

                   Calculators   Cruise
Buyer   <-------------------   Seller   <-------------------   3rd party
        ------------------->   ------------------->
        Buyer signs a   Delivers note
        note promising
        to pay $600 on or
        before 6/6/98

If the calculators prove to be defective and the seller is insolvent, who loses if the note is a negotiable instrument? Who loses if the note is not a negotiable instrument? Why?
If the note is a negotiable instrument, the then buyer must pay. (Moral: receiving negotiable paper is as good as getting cash.) If the note is not negotiable, then the third party stands in the same position as the assignee in the prior problem. (Ask the students what the travel agency needs to know before accepting the note: i.e., is it like money, so that no matter what happens the agency gets paid.)

15. In a secured transaction what is the difference between attachment and perfection?
Attachment is the process whereby if the debtor defaults, the creditor has the rights to the secured collateral. Perfection means that the creditor also has priority over other creditors who may also have rights to the same collateral.

16. Name the requirements that a creditor must meet in order to have an enforceable security interest against a debtor (to have the interest attach).
For a creditor to have an enforceable security interest against the debtor, the following must be true: 1. The creditor must either possess the collateral or have a signed security

agreement, 2. the creditor must have given something of value, and 3. the debtor must have rights in the collateral. [See Figure 13-5, page 447 in the text.]

17. How may a creditor perfect a security interest?
The requirements for perfection are 1. possessing the collateral, 2. filing a financing statement, or 3. giving money to purchase consumer goods. [See Figure 13-5, page 447 in the text.]

18. What are the two main concerns of a creditor if a debtor defaults?
A creditor who has obtained a security interest has two main concerns if a debtor defaults. First, the creditor wants to be able to obtain the secured collateral from the debtor. Second, the creditor wants to have priority over other creditors who may also have rights to the same collateral.

19. Define a *floating lien*, and give an example.
A floating lien is a security interest that can be retained in collateral even when the collateral changes in character or location. Examples include a security interest in proceeds or after-acquired property.

20. Define a *purchase money security interest*.
A purchase money security interest arises when a seller gives credit to a debtor so that the debtor can purchase an item.

21. What is the main benefit of being a holder in due course rather than a mere holder?
A holder in due course has the right not only to enforce the agreement but also to be exempt from some of the defenses that could have been asserted against the original payee.

22. List the following creditors in order of priority, starting with those that have the highest level of priority: general creditors, perfected security interest holders, unperfected security interest holders, buyers in the ordinary course of business, lien creditors, and perfected purchase money security interest holders.
The general order of priorities among creditors and buyers is as follows: 1. buyers in the ordinary course of business, 2. perfected purchase money security interests, 3. perfected security interests, 4. lien creditors (such as a trustee in bankruptcy), 5. unperfected security interests, and 6. general creditors.

23. What are the four basic duties that a principal owes an agent?
The principal must cooperate with the agent, compensate the agent for losses incurred in the course of discharging the assigned duties, and pay the agreed-on fee for the agent's services.

24. What are the basic duties that an agent owes a principal?
Agents owe their principals competent performance, notification of any important information (notice to the agent is considered to be notice to the principal, so the agent

must keep the principal informed), loyalty, obedience, and an accounting of all moneys spent and earned.

25. Name two of the factors a court will look to in trying to determine if an employer-employee or an employer-independent contractor relationship exists.
The courts look to who controls the details of the job, who owns the tools, who sets the hours, how the worker is paid, whether the worker receives training from the employer, whether the worker in engaged in a business different from the employer's, and how long the worker has been employed.

26. Give two examples of why it would matter whether a relationship is one of employer-employee or one of employer-independent contractor.
[See Figure 13-6, page 450 in the text.]

27. When will an employer be held responsible for an employee's act?
To find an employer responsible under the doctrine of respondeat superior, a plaintiff must prove that 1. a true employer-employee relationship existed, 2. the employee was legally responsible for the injury, and 3. at the time of the negligent action the employee was "working within the scope of his or her employment."

28. In a Title VII case alleging discriminatory treatment, how does the plaintiff prove the prima facie case? What must the defendant do in response? What must the plaintiff do to rebut the defendant's response?
To prove the prima facie case for discriminatory treatment, if the plaintiff can show overt discrimination, the defendant's only defense is the BFOQ. If there is no showing of overt discrimination, then the plaintiff can prove her prima facie case by showing that 1. he or she is a member of a protected class, 2. he or she applied and was qualified for the position, 3. his or her application was rejected, and 4. the employer continued to seek other applicants for the same position or filled the position with someone who was not within the protected class. The employer then has to articulate a valid reason for not hiring, for not promoting, or for firing the plaintiff. Finally, the plaintiff has the burden of proving by a preponderance of the evidence that the employer's reason is really just a pretext and that the employer actually acted with a discriminatory intent.

29. After *Griggs* can employers use tests to evaluate people for hiring and promotion purposes? Why?
Yes, they can use tests so long as they are shown to measure job performance. As the Court in *Griggs* noted, Congress did not mandate that the less qualified be preferred, but rather that qualification for the job be the controlling factor.

30. In a Title VII case alleging discriminatory impact, how does the plaintiff prove the prime facia case? What must the defendant do in response? What must the plaintiff do to rebut the defendant's response?
To prove the prima facie case, the plaintiff must prove that the facially neutral practice disproportionately discriminates against a protected class (often demonstrated through

statistics). Then the defendant has an opportunity to prove business necessity — that is, the practice "bears a demonstrable relationship to successful performance of the jobs for which it was used." Finally, the plaintiff can try to prove that an equally useful but less discriminatory alternative exists that could be used by the employer.

31. How does the presentation of an age discrimination case differ from that of one under Title VII?

For a disparate treatment case, employees can use a modified version of the *McDonnell Douglas* four-part analysis:

1. the plaintiff belongs to the protected class of 40 year olds or older,
2. the plaintiff applied for a job for which the plaintiff was qualified,
3. the plaintiff was rejected, and
4. the position remained open or was filled by someone substantially younger or not in the protected class.

The courts disagree as to whether it is possible to bring a case based on disparate impact.

32. Under the ADA who is a qualified individual?

A qualified individual with a disability is an individual with a disability who can perform the essential job functions.

33. What is employment at will?

An employee is considered to be "at will" when the employee has not signed a formal contract with the employer governing the employment relationship, and there is no union to protect the rights of the employee. Therefore, the employee is free to leave work at any time, and likewise the employer is allowed to fire the at will employee at any time so long as the reasons for the dismissal do not violate any federal or state statutes.

34. Name two exceptions to the employment at will doctrine.

When employers have established employee handbooks that spell out various personnel procedures, the courts have generally required those employers to follow their own rules. In addition, a few courts have stated that employers owe employees an implied covenant to act in good faith. Finally, many courts have found a public policy exception that prevents an employer from firing an employee when the employer's actions are seen as harming not only the employee but also society as a whole. Examples include an employer firing an employee for asserting a legally guaranteed right, such as applying for worker's compensation; for doing what the law requires, such as reporting for jury duty; and for refusing to do an unlawful act, such as committing perjury.

Chapter 14

Family Law

Family law is always one of the students' favorite topics. It is also one where you are likely to find a lot of class "experts" who either themselves have just been through a divorce or who have helped a friend or relative through one. In either case, they may want to spend a lot of class time discussing their view of family law. To keep this from becoming too disruptive, and without in any way discounting the value of their feelings, you might want to take some time at the beginning of the discussion to talk about this. You can acknowledge that the topics in this chapter often hit close to home, and therefore, everyone should be especially careful to keep the discussion on a professional level.

DISCUSSION QUESTIONS, page 485

1. The following section from the Illinois Marriage and Dissolution of Marriage Act illustrates the types of prohibitions that appear in many state statutes:

> **750 Ill. Comp. Stat. 5/212**
> (a) The following marriages are prohibited:
>   (1) a marriage entered into prior to the dissolution of an earlier marriage of one of the parties;
>   (2) a marriage between an ancestor and a descendant or between a brother and a sister, whether the relationship is by the half or the whole blood or by adoption;
>   (3) a marriage between an uncle and a niece or between an aunt and a nephew, whether the relationship is by the half or the whole blood;
>   (4) a marriage between cousins of the first degree; however, a marriage between first cousins is not prohibited if:
> > (i) both parties are 50 years of age or older; or
> > (ii) either party, at the time of application for a marriage license, presents for filing with the county clerk of the county in which the marriage is to be solemnized, a certificate signed by a licensed physician stating that the party to the proposed marriage is permanently and irreversibly sterile;
>   (5) a marriage between 2 individuals of the same sex.

What do you think is the legislative purpose behind each of these provisions? With which ones do you agree or disagree?

The likely purpose behind each of these provisions is as follows: (1) to prevent bigamy; (2) this first part could have its roots in trying to prevent genetic problems that can arise from the married couple being too closely related; however, as adoption is also included,

the basis is more likely in the general societal prohibition against relatives intermarrying; (3) same as (2); as (4) allows an exception for cousins who are unable to have children, at least part of the rationale supporting the prior provisions must relate to the fear of breeding children with genetic defects; (5) a desire to prevent marriages between gay men or lesbian women.

2. List as many valid reasons as you can for why states require a marriage license.
The students will probably list reasons that range from the very mundane (for example, as a way to raise revenue for the state) to those with a boarder societal purpose, such as being in a position to control how closely related two people can be and still qualify for marriage.

3. As part of the legal requirements for getting married many states require a waiting period between the time the license is issued and the time the actual marriage can take place. Do you think states should impose these types of waiting periods? If yes, why and how long should they be? If no, why not?
The rationale for such waiting periods relates to the seriousness of the undertaking. By requiring both parties to wait and consider the step they are about to take, hopefully any doubts will be resolved by postponing the marriage. From the viewpoint of societal costs it is a relatively cheap to postpone or call off a wedding but fairly expensive to proceed with a divorce or annulment.

4. As part of the legal requirements for getting a marriage license some states require a blood test for such things as sexually transmitted diseases or AIDS. Would you support such requirements? Why?
Many states had been cutting back on requiring blood tests. Opponents of such tests see them as an example of the state's being too intrusive into the private lives of its citizens. However, with all of the fear that has been generated by the AIDS crisis, many see premarital testing as one way of at least informing infected persons of the disease so that hopefully they can receive help and not transmit it to the partner.

CASE DISCUSSION QUESTIONS, page 491 for *Opinions of the Justices to the Senate*
1. According to the court, what tangible and intangible benefits flow from marriage?
Tangible benefits include "rights in property, probate, tax, and evidnce law." Intangible benefits include "private and social advantages" such as fulfilling "yearnings for security, safe haven, and connection."
What hardships are created by denying same-sex couples the right to marry?
Hardships include "the absence of predictable rules of child support and property division, and even uncertainty concerning whether one will be allowed to visit one's sick child or one's partner in a hospital."

2. How does the Massachusetts Constitution's equal protection provision differ from the U.S. Constitution's Fourteenth Amendment protections?
As noted in footnote 2, unlike the U.S. Constitution, the Massachusetts Constitution explicitly forbids sex discrimination: "Equality under the law shall not be denied or

abridged because of <u>sex</u>, race, color, creed or national origin." **Massachusetts Constitution, Article 1 (emphasis added).**

3.　　In what ways did the statutory proposal for civil unions differ from marriage? **Except for the difference in name, the legislation purported to confer all the "benefits, protections, rights and responsibilities' of marriage."**

4.　　Why do the justices who wrote this opinion think there is more involved than just "a squabble over the name to be used"? **The court stated that prohibiting the use of the word "marriage" by same-sex couples was more than semantic. This choice of language assigned same-sex couples to a second-class status, and as the court stated "[t]he history of our nation has demonstrated that separate is seldom, if ever, equal.**

5.　　Do you agree that the decision to allow same-sex marriages should be only a matter of constitutional interpretation and not a matter of social policy? **It seems a bit disingenuous of the court to state that this is only a matter of constitutional interpretation. However, the court's basic philosophy is that its job is not to bow to public pressure, but rather to reach a decision based on their view of the constitutional requirements.**

6.　　How does the court respond to the argument that Massachusetts's same-sex marriages may not be recognized in other states or by the federal government? **Basically the court responds that how other states and the federal government react is beyond their control and is simply not relevant to their decision making. "That such prejudice exists is not a reason to insist on less than the Constitution requires."**

7.　　Unlike the Massachusetts Supreme Judicial Court, the U.S. Supreme Court does not give advisory opinions. What do your think are the advantages and disadvantages of this type of action? **Advisory opinions are useful because they can forestall much fruitless effort. For example, in Massachusetts, the legislature saved itself from hours of work in drafting and enacting legislation that the Massachusetts Supreme Court would then have invalidated as unconstitutional. On the other hand, the major disadvantage is that advisory opinions are antithetical to our adversary system wherein all concerned parties present their arguments and the court dictates a mandatory resolution. In an advisory opinion, only one sides presents its case and then is not bound by the outcome.**

DISCUSSION QUESTIONS, page 492

5. Until 1967 Virginia had an antimiscegenation law, prohibiting interracial marriage. An interracial couple was convicted of violating the statute and given a one-year jail sentence. The sentence was suspended but only on the condition that the couple leave Virginia and not return for twenty-five years. The couple appealed their conviction. In *Loving v. Virginia*, 388 U.S. 1 (1967), the U.S. Supreme Court held that Virginia's statute violated the due process

clause of the Fourteenth Amendment. Marriage is a fundamental right that states cannot regulate absent a compelling state interest. Should the Supreme Court be asked to decide whether statutes prohibiting same-sex marriages are unconstitutional, the *Loving* decision might form a basis for arguing by analogy that statutes banning same-sex marriages are unconstitutional. Do you think the two situations are analogous? If you were arguing for preserving the statutes prohibiting same-sex marriage, how would you distinguish the *Loving* decision?

The two cases are analogous in that in each it could be argued that marriage is a fundamental right. However, the students might see them as distinguishable. The law in Virginia was based on a classification that is illegal both under the Constitution and by federal statute (the Civil Rights Act of 1964). While sexual orientation is a protected category in some state statutes, it is not universally recognized as such. It could also be argued that allowing such marriages would open the doors to all kinds of marriages, including those involving polygamy.

6.   Every state has laws against polygamy — that is, having more than one husband or wife at a time. What do you think are the arguments for and against allowing a man to have more than one wife at a time or a woman to have more than one husband at a time? Are such laws a form of religious discrimination against Mormons and Islamics, who have traditionally allowed men to have more than one wife?

These laws are a form of religious discrimination. However, the courts have adopted a balancing test and have found that the states' interest in promoting the traditional family outweighs the rights of any religious group to practice polygamy.

7.   M.T., a transsexual, was born a male but had the mental and emotional reactions of a female. She underwent surgery to become female. In a state that bans same-sex marriages do you think she would be able to obtain a marriage license to marry a man? Explain the basis for your answer.

In *M.T. v. J.T.*, 355 A.2d 204 (N.J. Sup. Ct. 1976), the court stated that at the time of the marriage the plaintiff was a female. Other courts have held to the contrary, stating that chromosomal criteria are the determining factor and that an individual's sex is permanently fixed at birth. See, for example, *Kantaras v. Kantaras,* 2004 Fla. App. LEXIS 10997, 29 Fla. L. Weekly D 1699 (Fla. Dist. Ct. App. 2d Dist. July 23, 2004) ("Whether advances in medical science support a change in the meaning commonly attributed to the terms male and female as they are used in the Florida marriage statutes is a question that raises issues of public policy that should be addressed by the legislature.")

DISCUSSION QUESTIONS, page 493

8.   The prenuptial agreement between a Catholic woman and a Jewish man stated that any children born of the marriage would be raised Jewish. After the couple divorced, the wife was given custody of the children. The father went to court, seeking to have the prenuptial agreement enforced. How do you think the court responded?

This hypothetical is based on the case of *In re Weiss*, 49 Cal. Rptr. 339 (Cal. App. 1996).

The husband said he would allow his child to be exposed to his wife's religion (go to church) but not to be indoctrinated (join the child's choir). The court stated that "[g]iven the fine and perhaps illusory line between experience and indoctrination, improper judicial entanglement in religious matters would be inevitable if [the husband's] request was to be accommodated." Judicial involvement would also encroach on the fundamental right of the wife to change religious convictions as she chose and to expose her children to her changed beliefs. Therefore, the court said the agreement was unenforceable under the First Amendment.

9 . A prenuptial agreement stated that the wife could not share in her husband's property. During the early years of their marriage, the couple kept their businesses and bank accounts separate. Eventually, however, the wife left her job to work full-time for no pay in the pro-shop at her husband's golf course. When the golf course was in financial troubles, she cashed in her retirement plan and took out a loan to keep the business going. Now the couple has divorced, and the wife wants "her share" of the husband's golf course. What do you think the court decided?
These facts are based on the case of *In re Marriage of Baxter*, 911 P.2d 343 (Or. App. 1996). The court stated that circumstances had changed and by their conduct the parties had demonstrated a mutual intent to rescind the agreement. The court awarded her 1/3 of the value of the business. It did not consider the remedy of simply returning her money.

CASE DISCUSSION QUESTIONS, pages 495-96 for *Aronow v. Silver*
1. The *Silver* court refused to apply a "fault standard." Do you think it should matter who was at fault for breaking off the engagement? Why?
If this is seen as purely a business contract arrangement, then perhaps "fault" should matter. The party in "breech" should not be rewarded. However, many students may think that this should be treated as a completed gift, and the ring should not have to be returned under any circumstances. The last approach is that the ring would have to be returned if the woman broke the engagement, no matter who's "fault" it was as fault may be an impossible fact to prove.

2. In the cited case of *Albanese v. Indelicato* why did the court treat the diamond ring and the engagement ring differently? The *Silver* court did not apply different standards to the engagement ring and stock. Can you reconcile these seemingly different approaches? Do you think one approach reaches a fairer result?
The *Albanese* court stated that the engagement ring is a symbol of the coming marriage. As the ring is a conditional gift, it the marriage is called off, the ring should be returned. The diamond ring, however, was no different from any other unconditional gift. On delivery, the requirements for a gift were complete. In the *Silver* case the court saw the purchase of the stock as being in anticipation of the marriage. Also factoring into the court's decision could have been the fact that Philip's money was used to purchase the stock with the understanding that it was to be placed in their joint names. The broker, however, issued the stock in Elizabeth's name only. She then sold it without Philip's knowledge after the engagement was broken.

3. Elizabeth's parents also sued, seeking recovery of various wedding expenses paid by them. Do you think they should be able to recover? Why?

The court stated that the parents were not able to produce any legal theory on which their claim could be based, and no evidence was introduced to show that there was any contractual arrangement between the parents and Philip which would make him liable. Therefore, they were not able to recover their costs.

DISCUSSION QUESTIONS, page 497

10. Most statutes require the parties to be "mentally competent" in order to marry, but what does that mean? Should someone who has a mental or genetic disability, such as Down's syndrome, be allowed to marry? Should a court annul a marriage if the parties later allege they were so intoxicated at the time of the ceremony that they did not realize the significance of their actions?

The courts have never been able to clearly define how "mentally competent" a person must be to be able to marry. Theoretically, there should be no prohibition against anyone marrying for mental incompetence so long as they understand the consequences of undertaking marriage vows. A few courts have allowed marriages to be annulled where the person was so intoxicated as to not be able to remember the ceremony.

11. Before the honeymoon was even over, Ashley Jones realized that her new husband had a major drinking problem. When he refused to seek help for his drinking problem or look for a job, she sought to have the marriage annulled. If you were the judge, would you grant her an annulment? Why?

This is based on the case of *In re Marriage of Johnston*, 18 Cal App. 4th 499, 22 Cal. Rptr. 253 (1993). As the court noted, after twenty months of marriage, the prince had turned into a frog. However, the court held that there were not sufficient grounds for an annulment. If she wanted to end her marriage, the appropriate route was through divorce.

Legal Reasoning Exercise, pages 502-04

1.   Brian LeClair lives in Tucson, Arizona. In early 1994 he bought a small home for $50,000, $45,000 of which he financed through a mortgage. Later that year, Brian met Monica, and they married within the week. Brian was later to regret his quick decision.

Shortly after they were married, Brian discovered that Monica liked to shop. In fact, she entered the marriage with approximately $5,000 in credit card bills. During their marriage this pattern persisted, with Monica on average charging $500 per month for clothes and jewelry for herself. Brian and Monica each deposited their earnings in a joint checking account, and each paid half of the monthly mortgage payments.

When Brian's father died in 1995, he left Brian 100 shares of stock, valued at $10 per share. Brian, knowing little about investments, asked Monica to handle his stock for him. She did so, and through careful buying and selling Brian now owns 150 shares of stock, valued at $15 a share. Brian's father also left Brian his mother's wedding ring, which as part of his father's estate was valued at $1,000. A jeweler recently appraised it at $1,500. Finally, his father left him $5,000 which he deposited into his and Monica's joint banking account.

In 1996 Monica stated that she was tired of living in Brian's tiny house and wanted to buy some land so that they could build a new, larger home. Brian was against the purchase both because of the cost and because of the rumors the land was about to be rezoned industrial. Monica went ahead anyway and took out a $20,000 loan from Commercial Savings to purchase the land. Brian did not sign the loan papers. The deed, however, lists them as joint owners. When the rumors proved to be true, the value of the land plummeted to $2,000.

Last week Monica informed Brian that she was tired of being married and that she needed some "space." The next day when Brian got home from work, he found that she was gone. Later that day when he opened the mail, he found a letter from Commercial Savings notifying him that the remaining amount of the loan ($18,000) was due immediately as Monica had not made any payments in the last year. Also, there was a letter from the credit card company showing Monica's total balance of $12,000. As far as Brian could tell, at least $4,000 was money she had charged before they were married.

Brian has come to your firm because he is thinking of initiating divorce proceedings against Monica. He realizes, however, that Arizona is a community property state and is concerned first, that he may be liable for what he considers to be Monica's debts, and second, that she may claim some of his property should be categorized as community property, thereby allowing her to take one-half. Your boss wants you to research 1) whether Brian is liable for either the Commercial Savings loan or Monica's credit card bills, 2) if a court were to find him liable, which assets would qualify as community assets and hence be available to satisfy a community debt, and 3) which remaining assets Monica might be able to claim belong one-half to her as her share of community property.

The contested assets include the stock valued at $2,250, the house (with a mortgage of $40,000 and a resale value of $60,000), the diamond ring valued at $1,500, the land worth $2,000, and $10,000 in their joint checking account. As to the latter, Brian claims that $5,000 is from his inheritance, $4,000 came from money he earned, and the remaining $1,000 came from Monica's earnings.

In doing your research, you found the following Arizona statutes:

Chapter 25-211	All property acquired by either husband or wife during the marriage, except that which is acquired by gift, devise or descent, is the community property of the husband and wife.
Chapter 25-213	All property . . . of each spouse, owned by such spouse before marriage . . . is the separate property of such spouse.
Chapter 25-214	C. Either spouse separately may acquire, manage, control or dispose of community property, or bind the community. . . .
Chapter 25-215	A. The separate property of a spouse shall not be liable for the separate debts or obligations of the other spouse. .

Chapter 25-215

D. [E]ither spouse may contract debts and otherwise act for the benefit of the community. In an action on such a debt or obligation the spouse shall be sued jointly and the debt or obligation shall be satisfied: first, from the community property, and second, from the separate property of the spouse contracting the debt or obligation.

The main purpose of this exercise is to remind students of how to engage in statutory interpretation and to write well-organized IRAC analysis. This is mostly a problem that requires careful organization. The students should understand that when they write their analysis, they should go in the same order as the questions presented to them, that is, it must be established that Brian is liable for at least one of the debts before they need to argue about which of his assets could be used.

Brian would argue that he is not responsible for the credit card debts as they were Monica's separate debt, not made for the "benefit of the community." Monica would argue that at least the $8,000 of debt she acquired during the marriage were community debts. Brian will have difficulty avoiding liability for the land purchase. Either spouse may separately acquire community property, and the land was bought with the intention, at least on Monica's part, of benefiting the community.

Most of Brian's assets will probably not be classified as community property. He acquired his house before the marriage, and Monica's payment of one-half of the mortgage for a short time should not convert it to community property. The same is true of his inheritances, unless the court finds that the $5000 lost its separate character when Brian commingled it in their joint account. Monica could also argue that the increased value of the stock was due to her efforts, and so even if the original stock was separate, the increased value ($1,250) is community property. She might try to make a similar, but weaker, argument regarding the increased value of the ring ($500). Community assets include the land ($2,000) and the couple's earnings ($5,000). Therefore, Commercial Savings could collect $7,000 against the outstanding debt of $18,000.

According to the statute, once community assets are exhausted, the remaining community debt should come "from the separate property of the spouse contracting the debt." As Monica is essentially penniless, the remaining debt will go unpaid.

Finally, all of the community assets will have been exhausted in payment of the community debt. Therefore, there will be nothing left for Monica to claim one-half of as a result of the couple's divorce.

(Note, the worst case scenario for Brian is if the court sees $8,000 of the credit card bills and the land purchase as community debts and all of the following as community assets: the house's value ($20,000), the $5,000 placed in the joint checking account, and the increased value of the stocks ($1,250) and the ring ($500) along with the above mentioned land ($2,000) and earnings ($5,000). This would result in a total of $26,000 in community debts and $33,750 in community assets. Once the debts were paid, there would remain $7,750, of which one-half would be Monica's.)

CASE DISCUSSION QUESTIONS, page 506 for *Woodworth v. Woodworth*

1. In deciding how much to compensate the wife, the *Woodworth* court stated that there were two basic methods. The award could be a percentage share of the present value of the future earnings attributable to the law degree, or the award could be limited to the amount of money the wife actually contributed to the cost of earning the degree. Which formulation would you argue for if you were representing the wife? The husband? The court chose the first method. What problems do you foresee this created in this and future cases?

If you were representing the wife, you would argue for the present value of the future earnings as these are likely to be much greater than the amount of money she actually contributed towards his earning of the degree. The husband would argue that reimbursement of her costs is sufficient. The problem with the first method lies in the difficulty in determining what the present value is.

2. The court noted that some courts have held that

> [a]n educational degree, such as an M.B.A., is simply not encompassed by the broad views of the concept of 'property'. It does not have an exchange value or any objective transferable value on an open market. It is personal to the holder. It terminates on death of the holder and is not inheritable. It cannot be assigned, sold, transferred, conveyed, or pledged. An advanced degree is a cumulative product of many years of previous education, combined with diligence and hard work. It may not be acquired by the mere expenditure of money. It is simply an intellectual achievement that may potentially assist in the future acquisition of property. In our view, it has none of the attributes of property in the usual sense of that term.

> Should the outcome of this and similar cases be determined by whether an educational degree is "property?" On what other factors might the court base its decision?

There are many types of intangible property such as copyright interests. This does not make them any less property. If property is defined as something of value, then the degree is property. It can be liken to any other marital asset, such as a house, that was acquired through the work and sacrifice of the spouses.

Legal Reasoning Exercise, page 507

2. Michael and Bonnie were married. The couple separated, and Michael began living with Donna. Bonnie filed for divorce. On February 10 a hearing was held to end the marriage, but because Bonnie's attorney sent Michael a notice with the wrong date, a new hearing date was set. In the meantime Michael and Donna won a $2.2 million jackpot in the Arizona state lottery. At the rescheduled hearing Bonnie claimed an interest in one-half of the winnings. Should the judge award it to her? Note: Arizona is a community property state. Would your answer be different if it was not?

This is based on the case of *Lynch v. Lynch*, 791 P.2d 653 (Ariz. App. 1990). The Arizona statute states that all property acquired "during the marriage" is community property. Therefore, even though the wife went to the hearing on February 10 thinking she would be divorced that day and have no further interest in her husband's acquisitions, the divorce was not granted. Therefore, the winnings were acquired during the marriage, and one-half belongs to the wife. Also, the facts did not indicate that the husband acquired his interest in the winning ticket in reliance that his marriage would

end on February 10. He and his girlfriend had been sharing weekly tickets for some time even though he was still married. As the court stated: "Fortune favored husband with a jackpot, but, because his marriage had not ended, fortune dealt his wife a share."

CASE DISCUSSION QUESTIONS, pages 509-10 for *Carroll v. Carroll*
1. Do you agree with the *Carroll* court's decision in this case? Why?
This will depend on whether the students agree that child support and child visitation should be treated as separate issues. Parents often do not see this distinction, and for example, withhold visitation if support payments are late.

2. Should the court have considered the needs of the two other children in reaching its decision?
Unfortunately, decisions in family court that effect one family member effect others as well. In this case, eliminating the child support for one child will not decrease the cost to the custodial parent. Having no other source of income, necessarily the lesser amount of money will have to be spread thinner so that all members of the family will receive less.

3. Do you think the court would have reached a different result if it had found that Mrs. Carroll had "orchestrated" her son's decision to terminate visitation? Most courts will not relieve a parent of his or her obligation to supply child support solely on the basis that the custodial parent had denied that parent his or her court-ordered visitation rights. Do you agree with this? Why should the noncustodial parent have to continue to pay child support if he or she is being denied visitation rights?
The child support is for the benefit of the child, not the custodial parent. Even if the custodial parent is violating a court order, if the other parent stops support payments, the one hurt is the innocent child. The proper approach is to go to court and have the court deal with the noncomplying parent.

[Note: On the other side are parents who pay support but who do not seem interested in exercising their visitation rights. Now at least fifteen state are providing a child support credit for non-custodial parents who spend time with their children. Opponents are worried that the wrong message is being sent — that the parent is only seeing the child to save money. Also, there will be less support money to pay for the child's needs. Proponents say that ultimately the child will benefit through increased parental contact.]

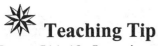 **Teaching Tip**
Pages 511-12: In an interesting variation on the stepparent theme, recently the North Carolina Supreme Court granted custody to a non-biological "father" over the natural mother. In that case, the mother had told the man he was the child's father, and they had raised the child together for three years. Then she left them both for three years. When she tried to reclaim her child, the court looked to the best interests of the child rather than to a bright line test based on biology. *Price v. Howard*, 484 S.E.2d 528 (N.C. 1997).

12. A husband and wife decided to try in vitro fertilization. They signed an agreement that provided in the event of their separation, the wife could use the embryos. The procedure was successful and the wife gave birth to twins. When the couple separated, the wife sought "custody" of the remaining frozen embryos. The father objected. How do you think the court ruled?

In the case of *AZ v. BZ*, the probate and family law judge stated that the wife would not be allowed to the use frozen embryos, despite the agreement. Since the embryos were frozen, the wife had given birth to twins. The court was concerned about the legal responsibilities of the husband who would become a father against his will. Reported in Mass. Lawyers Weekly, October 7, 1996.

13. In settling custody issues the courts are supposed to use a "best interest of the child" standard. To what extent do you think it is appropriate for the courts to take into consideration such things as a parent's gender, age, or religion? In determining custody how much, if any, consideration should be given to the fact that one of the parents smokes and would therefore be exposing the child to secondhand smoke? What if the new partner of one of the parents is of a different race than the child? What if one of the parents openly lives with his or her new homosexual partner?

What is in the best interests of a child is obviously a subjective standard and one that is open to variation based on changing societal values. Some may think that material benefits are more important while others view the only necessity to be that of being able to provide a nurturing home.

14. To what extent should children at various ages be permitted to help determine which parents should have custody?

In recent years courts have been more willing to listen to the wishes of children. However, many psychologists warn that it is tremendously unfair to put any responsibility on the children for choosing with whom they want to live. No matter their choice, they are bound to feel guilt for not having chosen the other parent. They may also make choices based on criteria (such as feeling sorry for one parent) that are not necessarily the best reasons for choosing a custodial parent.

15. What should the courts do if a child refuses to visit the noncustodial parent? In the case of *In re Marriage of Marshall*, 663 N.E.2d 1113 (Ill. App. 1996), nine-year-old Rachel and thirteen-year-old Heidi flatly refused to visit their father. The court "found both Rachel and Heidi to be in direct civil contempt. The court 'grounded' Rachel, and ordered that she not leave her mother's home. Rachel could not watch television or have friends over to the house, but she could read and do crafts. The court ordered [the mother] to enforce these measures. The court placed Heidi in a juvenile detention facility until she agreed to go to North Carolina. The judge indicated that the girls' conduct arose from the efforts of adults to manipulate the system." Id. at 1119. Do you agree that such sanctions are appropriate? What other remedies do you think the court could have pursued?

Many commentators were outraged that the judge would place a thirteen-year-old in a

juvenile detention facility under these circumstances. As the judge recognized in *Carroll v. Carroll*, there is little anyone can do to force a teenager to visit a parent if the teenager refuses to do so.

16. Which of the following two provisions for child visitation do you prefer? Do you think your answer might vary depending upon the couple involved? Why?

●The parties shall determine visitation schedules between them. At a minimum the husband will see the children at least two weekends a month and one day or early evening during the week.

●The husband will have visitation with the three children every other weekend, commencing at 6:00 P.M. on Friday evening, when he will pick up the children at the wife's home. He will return them at 6:00 P.M. on Sunday evening.

The second leaves much less room for interpretation and problems. However, the first might be more appropriate in situations in which the divorce is amicable and the couple can use the flexibility for the benefit of the children.

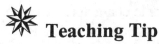 Teaching Tip

A new concern that has arisen over advances in medical technology for treating infertility concerns multiple offspring created by anonymous donors. While many clinics limit the number to ten, reportedly it is not uncommon for one man to father twenty or more children. In one case a man and a woman who planned to marry found out through a blood test that they had been fathered by the same anonymous sperm donor.

DISCUSSION QUESTIONS, page 516

17. Do you agree with a policy that denies welfare assistance to a child because the mother refuses to cooperate with authorities in identifying the child's father?

On the one hand, this policy certainly interferes with the mother's privacy interests. She may have very valid reasons for not wanting the name of the father revealed. However, if she expects the state to support the child, then the government has a stake in locating the father in an effort to recoup its costs.

18. A 15-year-old girl was raped and found herself pregnant. She decided not to have an abortion but to give the child up for adoption. The rapist, however, had other plans. He threatened to assert his paternity rights by signing the state's putative fathers' registry unless the girl dropped the charges against him. What actions do you think a state can take to protect the rights of unwed fathers, while preventing such abuses of the system?

This statute was enacted by the Illinois legislature in reaction to the Baby Richard case. The drafter of the legislation was appalled that this had happened as they obviously had not intended to protect rapists. The added delimna was that if DNA tests were used to prove the rape, it would also establish the paternity claim. However, the rapist never did sign the registry, and the young woman was able to go ahead with her plans for the

adoption of her child. **The students may think of a variety of safeguards including an automatic relinquishment of parental rights in the case of rape.**

19. Do you think the courts should continue to follow the conclusive presumption that a child born of married parents is their child?
Students may see this as a hangover from the days when there was a great deal of stigma attached to being born illegitimate. Those who still feel that way will agree with the presumption. However, many find it hard to understand how the court can support such a legal fiction in the face of irrefutable medical evidence to the contrary. In a recent Arkansas Supreme Court decision, the court stated that a child born during a marriage could not sue the man that DNA test proved was the father to a 99.97% certainty. The court stated that the presumption that children born during marriage are legitimate is irrebuttable. The dissent argued that based on the DNA test results that presumption should have flown "out the window." *Hall v. Freeman*, 936 S.W.2d 761 (Ark. 1997).

DISCUSSION QUESTIONS, page 517
20. Do you agree with the placement criteria included in the California statute discussed above? What is the justification for matching the child's racial and ethnic characteristics with those of the adoptive parents? Should these factors take preference over the economic and lifestyle advantages that an alternative placement might have?
A relative may not necessarily be the best first choice, especially if the child has been in long-term foster care. However, even acknowledging the rights of the foster parents is a progressive step. Many feel that matching racial and ethnic characteristics should be taken into account so that the child can be raised in his or her natural culture and so that cultural and ethnic pride can be preserved.

21. Should children be allowed to "divorce" their parents so that they can be adopted by others?
This obviously could set a dangerous precedent if children were allowed to divorce their parents every time the children felt there was an irretrievable breakdown in the family's relationship. On the other hand, there may be rare instances, especially in the case of older children, where it would be in the child's best interest to sever ties to the natural parents.

CASE DISCUSSION QUESTIONS, pages 519-20 for *In re Doe*
1. The trial court stated: "Fortunately, the time has long past when children in our society were considered the property of their parents. . . . [W]e start with the premise that Richard is not a piece of property with property rights belonging to either his biological or adoptive parents. Richard 'belongs' to no one but himself. . . .A child's best interest is not part of an equation. It is not to be balanced against any other interest." Obviously, the Illinois Supreme Court disagreed. Articulate the standard adopted by the Illinois Supreme Court. Which standard, that of the appellate court or that of the supreme court, produces the more just result? Just to whom?
This quote came from *In re Petition of Joe Doe & Mary Doe*, 627 N.E.2d 648, 651 (Ill.

App. Ct. 1993). The Illinois Supreme Court said that the best interest of the child was not even to be considered, because the father's parental interest was improperly terminated. The standard is whether the natural father was unfit with the burden of proof on the adoptive parents. This was not done and therefore, the court stated that the best interest of the child should not have been considered. Students will disagree about which standard is more just depending on who they see as the victim here: the father who was deceived as to the birth of his child or the child who has lived for the first three years of his life with his adoptive parents.

2. The Illinois Supreme Court's decision in the "Baby Richard" case brought on a great deal of negative media coverage, including Chicago Tribune columns by Bob Greene entitled "Damn them all," "The Sloppiness of Justice Heiple," and "Supreme Injustice for a Little Boy." Following Greene's columns the governor publicly backed legislation designed to change the court's decision. Do you think this is the type of decision that should be left to the courts, or could it be better handled through legislation? Why?
Legislation might give everyone notice of what their rights would be in a similar situation. However, as each situation is bound to differ on the facts, ultimately the courts will still be involved in resolving individual cases.

3. If you were drafting a statute to cover the type of situation that occurred in this case, what balance would you strike between the parents' rights to their natural-born children and the rights of adoptive parents? In drafting your statute consider the proper balance between the natural parents' rights to keep their children and the "best interest of the child."
Possibilities include legislation that would give a conclusive presumption to the natural parent, absent proof of parental unfitness, up until a child had resided for a certain amount of time with adoptive parents. Then at that stage the best interests of the child standard could govern.

4. In January 1997 it was reported that Otakar Kirchner had moved out of his home, leaving custody of Baby Richard to his birth mother. Does this have any impact on your view as to whether the court reached a just decision in this case?
With hindsight this may seem very unfair that the birth mother who originally gave up the child for adoption and lied about its death to the father should be the one to end up with the child.

CASE DISCUSSION QUESTIONS, page 521 for *In re Roger B*
1. Do you agree with the Illinois Supreme Court's ruling? Why? What do you think the proper balance should be between the adopted child's interest in knowing about his or her parents and the natural parents' interest in protecting their privacy?
Students will easily argue for releasing some types of medical information. More than that is problematical. Arguably, many women choose to go the route of adoption instead of abortion only when assured that their name will be kept confidential. Interestingly, until the 1920s most adoption records were not sealed. Recently, Tennessee enacted legislation creating a presumption that adult adoptees could receive identifying

information from their adoption files. Currently, only Alaska and Kansas give adult adoptees full rights to receive their original birth certificate. Other states while not automatically releasing information, have created a presumption in favor of giving information to adult adoptees.

2. What, if any, types of medical conditions justify giving a child or a child's guardians access to sealed adoption records?
Possibilities for releasing records include the need for information regarding any type of genetic abnormalities or situations where a close blood type or other match is necessary, such as a bone marrow transplant.

CASE DISCUSSION QUESTIONS, page 524 for *In the Matter of Baby M*
1. Opponents of surrogacy contracts argue that they should be outlawed because they amount to baby selling. Defenders of surrogacy contracts claim such contracts do not involve the purchase of a baby--they merely provide compensation to the surrogate mother for her time and expenses. With which position do you agree? Did the judges in the Baby M case treat this as a case about the "sale of a child"?
The court definitely saw this as the sale of a child or at least the sale of the mother's right to her child with the court thought the profit motive predominating, especially as there was a middle man who was solely propelled by profit who promoted the "sale."

2. Opponents of surrogacy contracts also argue that they should be outlawed because they exploit women. Defenders counter that they are not exploitive because the women who agree to be surrogate mothers do so voluntarily and wish to help other women have babies of their own. Whose arguments do you find most persuasive and why? What kind of protections, if any, could be built into surrogacy contracts to prevent exploitation?
To many people the idea that women need protection from themselves smacks of the now outdated work laws that prohibited women from working certain hours and from lifting certain weights. On the other hand, if one is truly concerned that women will simply be unable to resist the temptation of "easy money," safeguards could be instituted by, for example, capping the amount of money that could be paid.

3. Why did the court think the surrogate mother's consent to the arrangement was irrelevant?
The court stated that "[t]here are, in a civilized society, some things that money cannot buy. In America, we decided long ago that merely because conduct purchased by money was 'voluntary' did not mean that it was good or beyond regulation and prohibition." [Page 523 in the text.]

4. If you lived in New Jersey and wanted the court to uphold a surrogacy arrangement like the one in this case, what avenues would be open to you to change the law? Under what circumstances would the court enforce a surrogacy arrangement? How should the surrogacy contract be drafted to be enforceable?
If you wanted to change the law, you could lobby the legislature for change. Given the current law, the best way to write an enforceable surrogacy contract would be to ensure

that the natural mother is given the right to change her mind after the baby is born and that she perform the service without compensation. In addition, some method should be devised to assure the court of the parental fitness of the adopting parent.

DISCUSSION QUESTION, page 525
22. Jane and John Doe entered into an arrangement with a surrogate mother. The result of that arrangement was the birth of a girl. Since birth she has lived with Jane and John Doe. However, there was never any legal termination of the parental rights by the surrogate mother and her husband. Jane and John Doe are now divorcing. The girl is thirteen years old. Through blood testing John Doe was determined to be the natural father. The surrogate mother, not Jane Doe, is the natural mother. Both Jane and John Doe are seeking custody or, in the alternative, visitation rights. How do you think the court should rule?
The court was in a quandary but determined that because Jane Doe had never adopted the girl, she had no legal standing to request custody or visitation. Luckily, John Doe agreed to visitation, but the court noted this was simply voluntary on his part and could be withdrawn at any time. (Reported in the Springfield Sunday Republican, page B7, 3/23/97.)

Legal Reasoning Exercise, page 525

3. Mark and Chris Cooley were unable to have children because Chris had undergone a hysterectomy. They decided to enter into a surrogacy arrangement whereby a zygote formed of the gametes of the husband and the wife would be implanted in the uterus of Anna Johnson. Therefore, Mark and Chris were the natural parents of the child, and Anna served as the host surrogate. Anna was a co-worker of Chris's and had volunteered to serve as the surrogate. In return for agreeing to act as surrogate, the Cooleys agreed to reimburse Anna for her medical expenses and any loss of wages for time she had to take off from work, both during and after the pregnancy. In return, Anna agreed to relinquish all parental rights to the child. Shortly before she was to give birth, Anna announced that she would not go through with the agreement unless the Cooleys gave her an additional $20,000. The Cooleys responded with a lawsuit asking that they be declared the parents of the unborn child. Evaluate the arguments both for and against having the court rule in favor of the Cooleys. Base your arguments on *In the Matter of Baby M*, as well as on any additional policy considerations that you think should matter to the court.
This hypothetical has two factors that distinguish it from the *Baby M* case. First, the surrogate mother was "holding up" the parents for additional money. Also, this was a gestational surrogacy as opposed to the more traditional surrogacy arrangement. This situation is based on the case of *Johnson v. Calvert*, 851 P.2d 776 (Cal.), cert. denied, 510 U.S. 874 (1993). In that case the court held that normally the determinates for establishing a mother and child relationship are genetic consanguinity and giving birth. However, "when the two means do not coincide in one woman, she who intended to procreate the child — that is, she who intended to bring about the birth of a child she intended to raise as her own — is the natural mother. . . ." Id. at 782. Therefore, the court determined that the intent to procreate and to raise a child should be the method used to identify the mother, thereby replacing both genetics and birth as the test. They

found that under this standard, the surrogate mother was not the "natural" mother. In a case of a traditional surrogacy, the California Appellate court declined to extend this holding in *In re Marriage of Moschetta*, 30 Cal. Rptr. 2d 893 (Cal. App. 1994). Also, an Ohio court refused to follow the *Johnson* test because of "(1) the difficulty in applying the *Johnson* intent test; (2) public policy; and (3) *Johnson's* failure to recognize and emphasize the genetic providers right to consent to procreation and to surrender potential parental rights." *Belsito v. Clark*, 67 Ohio Misc. 2d 54, 644 N.E.2d 760 (Ohio Court of Common Pleas 1994). The public policy problems the court saw with the test were three: first, that it conflicted with the public policy against surrender of parental rights by agreement; second, that under the traditional adoption laws the state is the only one able to select the "adoptive" parent so as to protect the best interests of the child; and third, the court adoption process provides a clear delineation of when the rights and responsibilities of the biological parents ends and those of the adopting parents begins. Therefore, the court found that the parent is the genetic parent. This then avoids the issue of the surrogate selling her parental rights as she has none. Also, if there are any factual doubts, DNA testing can resolve them. Therefore, while the result in both cases was the same, the surrogate parent lost, the two courts reached that result using very different standards.

DISCUSSION QUESTIONS, pages 527-28
23. To what extent should child abuse protection laws apply to the actions of pregnant women? Should the fact that a pregnant woman smokes or drinks alcoholic beverages be treated as child abuse?
In *Wisconsin v. Kruzicki*, 561 N.W.2d 729 (Wisc. 1997), the Wisconsin Supreme Court narrowly held that the legislature had not intended that a viable fetus be considered a child. Therefore, the county had no authority to detain a 24-year-old pregnant woman for drug treatment. The woman was in her ninth month of pregnancy and had tested positive for drugs four times in four months. Those who want to change the law face some interesting questions: when is a fetus a child — at viability or at any stage? Also, what behaviors would constitute abuse other than ingesting illegal drugs? These are obviously all difficult questions as protection of the fetus bumps up against the privacy rights of the mother to be in control of her own body.

24. When deciding whether to terminate parental rights, some argue that a "clear and convincing" standard gives abused children too little protection. They would advocate a "preponderance of the evidence" standard. On the other hand, parent advocates argue that termination of parental rights is such a final determination that parents should be judged unfit only if the court can find them so "beyond a reasonable doubt." Which standard do you think best balances the needs of the children and the parents?
This will depend on whether the students sympathize with the parents, who are in essence receiving a life time sentence of separation from their children, or the children who, faced with a standard that is almost impossible to prove, move from foster home to foster home throughout their childhood because they are never legally released for adoption.

25. Recently a New York judge ordered a couple from procreating until they could prove they can take care of their children. The mother had four children between 1998 and 2003. As newborns, all four babies tested positive for cocaine and were placed in foster care. The judge ruled the woman could not be a mother again until she could prove that she could care for the children she already had. A representative of the Civil Liberties Union argued that this ruling was inconsistent with fundamental principles of privacy and autonomy. What do you think about the judge's ruling? Can you think of other approaches to the problems presented by pregnant women suffering from drug addiction and poverty?

The judge stated that for all practical purposes the last child had been born into a "no-parent" family. In discussing this case, Lynn Paltrow, who is the executive director of National Advocates for Pregnant Women said that "it would be better to be proactive by preventing situations like this from occurring through increasing "access to drug treatment programs, mental health services, and affordable housing." See *Negligent Upstate Couple is Told Not to Procreate*, The New York Times, May 11, 2004, at 6.

REVIEW QUESTIONS, page 529

1. What are some of the legal benefits of marriage?

Benefits include the right to be supported by the other spouse not only during the marriage but often even after a divorce; property purchased by one spouse may be seen as marital property, in which both have rights; through a legal right known as a *forced share*, each of the married partners is given a statutory right to inherit from the other, even if the other spouse seeks to prevent it. One spouse may also be immune from being sued by the other spouse for torts committed against the first spouse (although spousal immunity at least as to motor vehicle accidents has been abrogated in many states); if a spouse is injured, the other spouse may recover loss of consortium damages; marital spouses may qualify for employer and governmental benefits not available to nonmarried couples; the right to be taxed as a marital unit; and marital partners generally may not be forced to testify against each other.

2. What is the difference between solemnized and common law marriages?

A solemnized marriage is one in which the couple has obtained the proper marriage license from a local government official and has taken marriage vows before either a recognized member of the clergy or a judge and a designated number of witnesses (usually two). A common-law marriage is one in which the parties have mutually agreed to enter into a relationship in which they accept all the duties and responsibilities that correspond to those of a marital relationship and have openly cohabitated together but have never obtained a marriage license or had their marriage solemnized by someone who is legally recognized to do so. Most states no longer recognize the validity of such common-law marriages unless the couple established their common-law marital relationship in one of the few states that still formally recognize common-law marriages and then moved into the state.

3. What requirements does the state usually impose before allowing a couple to marry?

States usually impose the following requirements before allowing a couple to marry: that

163

they be members of the opposite sex, over a minimum age (usually 18), not be too closely related by blood, be "of sound mind" (i.e., mentally capable of giving consent), and undergo blood tests.

4. What is the purpose of a prenuptial agreement? What restrictions are placed on the enforceability of such agreements?

The basic purpose of a prenuptial agreement is to set forth the financial arrangements should one of the parties die or the marriage end in divorce. The restrictions include the need to satisfy the statute of frauds by being in writing and fulfilling the normal contract requirements of offer, acceptance, and consideration. Normally the courts will not enforce provisions relating to third parties, such as those dealing with child custody. Also, normal contract defenses are also available. For example, if the agreement was not based on full disclosure of all financial assets or was the result of undue influence, the courts might see it as against public policy and either modify its provisions or refuse to enforce it.

5. What is the difference between void and voidable marriages?

Marriages are considered completely invalid, or void, in certain situations, as when they involve incest or bigamy. A voidable marriage, on the other hand, is one where the marriage remains valid until a court has determined that it should be voided.

6. How does an annulment differ from a divorce?

An annulment proceeding has the effect of rescinding the marriage and returning the parties to the status they had before the marriage took place. A divorce or disillusionment ends but does not erase the existence of the marital relationship.

7. What are some of the "costs" of divorce?

The "costs" of divorce include the couples relinquishing to the state the power to make major life decisions for them. State courts can oversee a divorced family's financial arrangements in ways not permitted for intact families. Divorce can have severe economic consequences. This is especially true for women. The money that may have been insufficient to maintain one household is now being asked to maintain two homes. The text points out that studies have consistently shown that in the first year after divorce the standard of living for men increases anywhere from 17 to 43 percent, while that for women and children decreases by 29 to 73 percent. Finally, for many divorcing parents the greatest cost is the loss of daily contact with their children.

8. Describe the basic procedural steps involved in obtaining a divorce.

The basic procedural steps for obtaining a divorce are as follows. First, the grounds, even under no-fault, must exist to end the marriage. Then the party wishing a divorce must file a petition or complaint, requesting the divorce and including the reasons why one should be granted. Usually other documents, such as affidavits, must be filed along with the petition. Once the petition is filed with the court, the opposing party must be notified. The other party can indicate he or she does not want to contest the divorce or can countersue. Then both sides may engage in discovery.

After the filing of the petition, the court will hold a hearing to deal with such

matters as temporary child custody, child and spousal support. At any point in this process a settlement agreement can be reached and submitted to the court. Many states incorporate alternative dispute resolution mechanisms into the decisions regarding distribution of property and child custody and support. In those instances in which the parties cannot reach agreement, a trial is held at which witnesses testify to such things as the spouses' fitness as parents, how and when various financial assets were obtained, the fair market value of various assets, and the nature of the children's or spouses' future financial needs. The judge then renders a decision on the basis of this evidence and issues the final divorce decree and related orders. The court retains jurisdiction in matters of child and spousal support.

9. How do courts determine what qualifies as marital property and how it should be divided at divorce?
Under a community property statute everything acquired during the marriage, with the exception of gifts or inheritances, is owned 50/50. In non-community property states courts follow the doctrine of equitable distribution and award a "marital interest" in any property that was acquired during the marriage through the efforts of both spouses. This acknowledges the contributions of both spouses, whether that contribution be financial or through a spouse's work in the home, regardless of whose name is on the legal title.

10. When dividing marital property how have the courts handled professional degrees?
Some courts have not seen professional degrees as property at all. Others have factored professional degrees into a property settlement but have disagreed as to how to value them. Some reimburse the non-degree holding spouse for his or her efforts in helping the other spouse attain the degree. Others award a portion of the net present value of the degree.

11. What is the difference between physical custody and legal custody?
Physical custody determines with whom the child will live and who will supervise the child's day-to-day activities. Legal custody relates to who will have authority to make legal decisions for the child relating to such things as health care and education.

12. Is the right to visitation directly tied to the obligation to provide support payments? Why?
The right to visitation is not tied to the obligation to provide support payments. These are independent obligations and privileges.

13. How are the courts handling the requests of nonparents for visitation and custody?
The courts are gradually enlarging the scope of those individuals who can request visitation and custody. Traditionally, the only persons qualified were the natural parents. Today, however, stepparents, lesbian partners, and grandparents are all making strides in this area.

14. What must happen to the natural parents' rights before a child can be freed for adoption?
The natural parents' rights must be severed either through voluntary consent or through a court order after a showing by clear and convincing evidence that the parent is unfit.

15. Why are adoption records normally sealed? Are there any exceptions?
Adoption records are normally sealed to protect the privacy of all involved. There are routine exceptions for medial reasons. Also, many states are now making it easier for adult adoptees to obtain records. (See the answer to Case Discussion Question 1 for the case of *In re Roger B*.)

16. What is a surrogacy contract? What factors would tend to make such a contract enforceable? Unenforceable?
A surrogacy contract is one in which a woman agrees to conceive a child, usually through artificial insemination; deliver the child to its natural father after birth; and then terminate her parental rights so the father's wife can become its adoptive mother. A court would be more likely to enforce such a contract if it was done without pay and if the surrogate mother was given the right to withhold consent until after the baby was born. Conversely, the courts are likely to frown on those contracts whereby the surrogate is paid for more than her medical expenses and where she is presumed to have relinquished all parental rights before the child is born.

17. When are parents responsible for the negligent acts of their children? When are they liable for the intentional torts of their children?
Parents are normally not liable for their child's negligent acts unless the injury was caused by the parents' own negligent failure to properly supervise the child. Conversely, most states have statutes making parents strictly liable for the intentional torts of their children. However, when only property is damaged, there is often a liability cap, usually set to a relatively low amount of no more than a few thousand dollars.

18. What is the difference between child neglect and child abuse?
In reality it is often hard to know when neglect crosses the line into abuse. However, generally, child neglect can be defined as the negligent failure to provide a child with necessaries, such as food, clothing, shelter, and education. Child abuse involves intentional misconduct.

19. Describe the normal procedure that is followed when child neglect or abuse is suspected.
Normally the state first becomes aware of a potential neglect or abuse situation when someone reports suspicions of child neglect or abuse. The state then investigates such reports. Usually, the first step is to try to get voluntary compliance. If that is not possible, the investigating agency may request court ordered physical examinations of the child, visits to the home, and a general psychological evaluation of the family. During this process the court may appoint a guardian ad litem to represent the child. If the end result of the investigation is a determination that the child is in danger, the court may remove the child from the home and place the child in foster care. The final and most drastic remedy is termination of parental rights.

20. In what ways does the law favor the rights of minors? In what ways are minors legally disadvantaged?

The law favors the rights of minors in allowing them to treat the contracts they enter as "voidable." The minor may either enforce the terms of the contract or "disaffirm" it within a reasonable time period. Also, if a minor commits a crime, the case is ordinarily handled by a special juvenile court system, which is designed to be less punitive and more focused on rehabilitation. Disadvantages include having to rely on their parents or other guardians to act on their behalf in enforcing those rights. For example, minors cannot file lawsuits on their own. Also, minors have more limited rights than do adults in regard to making major life decisions, such as whether to obtain an abortion. A minor who wants an abortion may be required to get the consent of a parent or the authorization of a trial court judge.

21. Who is an emancipated minor?

An emancipated minor is someone who is still under the legal age of adulthood but who has nevertheless been released from parental authority and given the legal rights of an adult. Such emancipated status is usually given when a minor has entered into a valid marriage or is on active duty in the armed services. It can also be given at the discretion of the courts in situations where the minor is living independently, physically and financially, from his or her parents.

Chapter 15

Criminal Law and Procedure

Because criminal law is so state specific, make sure the students understand that they must research the statutes in their own state in order to know whether any specific behavior is "against the law." Like family law, this is another area where you may find you have a class full of "experts." Hopefully, that expertise comes more from watching TV than from real life, but nonetheless, you will probably find that your students have much more definitive ideas about criminal law than they exhibited when you were discussing contract or commercial law.

DISCUSSION QUESTIONS, page 535

1. Think back to the last movie or television program you watched about the criminal justice system. Was the system portrayed in a realistic light? How would you describe the portrayal of the attorneys' behavior, both prosecutors and defense attorneys? If the system did not work in that instance, who was portrayed as being at fault? Do you agree?
Generally, students are anxious to discuss what they have seen and heard about the legal system, especially the criminal justice system. Rather than always treating students' questions as digressions, time should be spent to help students connect what they learn in the classroom with what they see and hear on television, in the movies, and in classic and current literature. Devoting a part of one class to this issue now helps the students to control their questions (that do not relate to the subject at hand but rather to the plight of their friends or relatives) during the substantive lectures. This discussion will also help prepare them for the "real world" of the law as opposed to what they see on TV and to gain some insight in how to cope with criminal law related questions from their families and friends.

2. What would you say to a friend who replies to your desire to work for a defense firm by stating, "But why would you want to do that? Defense attorneys are just hired guns."
This question may be an entre into a discussion of legal ethics in the criminal arena. The criminal client's rights to confidentiality and attorney client privilege, as well as his or her right to zealous representation, should be discussed here. In addition, this question may spark a discussion of the constitutional questions that arise in this area of practice. You may also remind the students that *all* attorneys are hired to work for their clients and criminal practice is not for everyone.

3. A "Victim's Rights Amendment" has been introduced in Congress that would give victims the right to be present at court and parole proceedings, to be heard at sentencing, and to be notified about the release or escape of a defendant or prisoner. Would you support such an amendment? Some 450 law professors submitted a letter saying the amendment would hamper prosecutions by placing new burdens on law enforcement agencies. What do you think would be the basis for reaching such a conclusion?

During this discussion, students will consider the impact that crime has on the victim, and the family of the victim and discuss the goals and priorities of the criminal justice system. Arguments for such an amendment include the following: this amendment would allow victims a proactive role in the proceedings and an opportunity to remind the jury that the victim, as well as the criminal, has a right to be heard. While criminals currently are protected by the Constitution, victims are not. By making this a Constitutional amendment, it would ensure that victim's rights are enforced in all states. Allowing the victim to testify will also remind the court that an actual human being has suffered. Having an opportunity to be part of the process, may also make it easier for victim's to accept the court's decision. If victims are notified of the defendant's release, they may be able to take precautions that will prevent further crimes from occurring. Arguments against such an amendment include the following: currently the states are making great progress in protecting victims' rights through legislation. They should be allowed to continue with this process without interference from the federal government. Also, the process of approving a Constitutional amendment is both lengthy and burdensome. Such a process might stall the progress the states are making through legislation. Until legislation is proven to be inadequate for the task, it should be allowed to develop unhindered. Also, there are some definitional problems, for example, it may not always be easy to determine who the "victim" is. Finally, some of the procedures would place a tremendous burden on the system by requiring the criminal justice system to track released or escaped prisoners and the families of victims. How long should this tracking go on? What happens to record keeping and tracking when victims and perpetrators move from one jurisdiction to another? Would there be liability when the tracking system failed?

Students may want to share their experiences with the criminal justice system, as their experiences, whether as victims, family members of victims, or as defendants will affect their opinions as they discuss this issue.

Legal Reasoning Exercise, page 540

1.   Review the Robbery and Armed Robbery statutes from the Illinois Criminal Code. What crimes were committed under the following circumstances?

   a) Martin waited until the bartender turned her head. Then he slipped $10 from the cash register into his pocket.

   The crime of robbery or armed robbery may not have been committed here. Robbery requires that the property be taken from "the person or presence of another." Presence may require the victim to know that the property is being taken. Also, even if the robbery was in the presence of the bartender, there did not appear to be a "use of force" or the threatening of the "imminent use

169

of force." If there is no robbery, there can be no armed robbery, as robbery is the lesser included offense. Even if there was a robbery, there is no indication of a "dangerous weapon."

b) Kamil broke the lock on the kick stand and stole a bike while the owner was in the grocery store.

There may not be a crime of either robbery or armed robbery in this example. This theft may have been committed outside the "person or presence" of another. Again, there does not seem to be a weapon involved to raise this crime to armed robbery.

c) David drove his car slightly behind a woman walking on the side of the road. When she stopped for the light, David reached out of the car window and grabbed her purse. The set of knives that David just won while playing Bingo were on the front passenger seat of the car.

These actions could be construed as robbery because all of the elements are met. This robbery may be considered armed robbery if the knives are considered "dangerous weapons" and if keeping them on the seat of the car is considered carried "on or about" his person. An argument could be made that because the knives were within his reach, they were about his person.

d) After everyone left the party, Rosie took a fur coat that had been left behind, hid it in a shopping bag, left the apartment, and pushed the doorman as she left the building.

If the "presence of another" requirement is satisfied by the doorman and her push was sufficient to be considered "force," then these actions could be considered robbery pursuant to the statute.

CASE DISCUSSION QUESTIONS, page 543 for *Smallwood v. State*

1. In general, what must the state prove to show attempted murder?
The crime of attempted murder requires a specific intent to murder and some overt act in furtherance of that intent beyond mere preparation.

2. Why did the majority believe the defendant's conviction for attempted second degree murder should be sustained?
The specific intent to murder could be inferred from the defendant's knowledge that he was infected with HIV, his knowledge it was a fatal disease, and his knowledge that it could be transmitted through sexual conduct. The attempted first degree rape constituted the overt act.

Do you agree, or do you think the dissent was correct in saying that he did not have the specific intent required for a murder conviction?
The dissent thought the current facts could also raise the inference of an intent to rape with a reckless disregard for the risk of infecting the victim. This is not the specific intent

170

required for an attempted murder conviction. Here the dissent thought that if the defendant had the specific intent to murder he would have used the gun in his possession rather than the less sure method of rape.

Legal Reasoning Exercises, pages 547-49

2. Apply the Model Penal Code, Article 210, Criminal Homicide, to each of the following situations. What crimes, if any, have been committed?

a. Sam, a hired assassin, pulls out a gun and points it at Mary's head. He pulls the trigger, the bullet strikes Mary in the temple, and she is killed instantly.
§210.2 (1) (a) Murder, committed purposely or knowingly. Without any additional information, it appears from the facts given that Sam committed this act after obtaining a loaded weapon, deliberately pointing it at a specific human, and pulling the trigger. This information seems to be sufficient to prove the "purposely or knowingly" elements of this section.

b. Janet, to protest what she views as the increasing decadence of modern society, leaves a bomb in an empty adult movie theater. Later that night the bomb goes off and kills the janitor who was there cleaning the theater.
§210.2 (1) (b) Murder, committed recklessly under circumstances manifesting extreme indifference to the value of human life; or §210.3 (1) (a) Manslaughter, committed recklessly.

§210.2 (1) (b) specifically determines that the recklessness and indifference required to prove this crime are presumed "if the actor is engaged or is an accomplice in the commission of, or an attempt to commit, or flight after committing or attempting to commit . . . arson." If the bombing meets the elements of arson, then recklessness and extreme indifference are presumed. Even without this presumption, there is little doubt a jury could determine leaving a bomb where anyone might come on it where many people could be injured or killed is reckless under circumstances "manifesting extreme indifference to the value of human life."

In the alternative, a jury could consider this behavior merely reckless, and therefore find the defendant guilty of the lesser charge of § 210.3 (1) (1), manslaughter, committed recklessly. The jury would have to look carefully at whether the defendant had a reasonable explanation or excuse for a level of extreme mental or emotional disturbance which would have influenced her actions and reduce the murder to manslaughter.

c. Rita accompanies John while he robs a store owner at gunpoint. The gun goes off, and the owner is killed by the gunshot.
§210.2 (1) (b) Murder, committed recklessly under circumstances manifesting extreme indifference to the value of human life. This recklessness is presumed by statute when the actor is engaged or is an accomplice in the commission of a burglary. Like the sample above, this may also be reduced to § 210.3 (1)(a).

171

d. Five boys are playing a game of "chicken" in which they pass a partially loaded gun (one of six chambers contains a live bullet) around the circle. Each player takes a turn spinning the cylinder, pointing the gun at his head, and pulling the trigger. When Dan takes his turn, the gun goes off, and he dies instantly. **With this exercise you can help the students to explore the true meaning of "actus reus." What actions did the boys actually take to be charged with any crime under this statute? Perhaps none if the students look to the exact action that caused the death — the actions of Dan alone. Because the actor, Dan, is dead, he cannot be charged with any crime. The other boys may be charged with §210.5 (2) Causing or Aiding Suicide if it is determined that they purposely aided or solicited Dan to commit suicide. Without this determination, the boys may not be charged with any specific crime listed in this exercise. The boys could, however, be charged with some other crime, especially weapons charges.**

The boys might also be charged with §210.2 (1) (b) Murder, if their behavior is considered reckless under circumstances manifesting extreme indifference to the value of human life.

This is a good opportunity to review the requirements for lesser included offenses. You can also discuss plea bargaining as an effective method for helping the prosecution get quick convictions and helping the defense team limit the exposure of their clients to more serious penalties attached to more serious crimes.

3. Your firm represents Jimmy Jones. He and his best friend, Bobby Smith, are both twenty-year-old, high school dropouts. They have held several part-time jobs in the past but are currently unemployed.

Last Saturday night Jimmy and Bobby, along with their friend Doris, were restless with nothing to do. Bobby then had a brainstorm, and what started out as a frolic has since ended in a nightmare for Jimmy.

For "fun" and money the three decided to hold up the local 7-11 store. Doris volunteered the information that the only person on duty at that time of night would be an elderly gentleman who would give them no trouble. Shortly before leaving for the store Doris had a change of heart and told the other two that she would not be coming along.

Neither Jimmy nor Bobby owns a gun. Unbeknown to Jimmy, Bobby decided to take along his kid brother's very realistic looking water pistol. When they got to the store, no customers were present. Jimmy and Bobby went up to the counter and demanded that the clerk hand over the money in the cash register. When the clerk simply stared at them, Bobby pulled out the water pistol, which had been concealed under his jacket. He said, "Hand over the money, old man, or I'll spray you with acid." Actually, the gun only had water in it. The clerk, who was an elderly, overweight man, began to perspire and shake. He placed the money on the counter. Then he suddenly clutched his chest and fell to the floor. Bobby grabbed the money and ran from the store.

Although very frightened by the turn of events Jimmy decided to stay and try to help the clerk. He called the police, telling them to send an ambulance right away. When the police arrived, Jimmy turned himself in. Unfortunately on his way to the hospital the store clerk died.

a. With what crimes do you think Bobby could be charged?
Robbery — took property from the "presence of another" by threat of the imminent use of force. It will be armed robbery if the gun is seen as a "dangerous weapon." While it was only a water gun, he said it had acid in it. May be charged with Murder, Section 210.2(1)(b) if his actions caused the death and if he was committing robbery as recklessness is presumed if the defendant was engaged in a robbery.

b. What would be the major weaknesses in the prosecution's case?
For armed robbery, the major weakness would be in having to prove that the gun was a "dangerous weapon." For Murder, the major weakness would be in having to prove that the man died because of the robbery.

c. Do you think Doris could be convicted of any crimes? If so, which ones?
The question is whether she could escape being charged as an accomplice. Even though she backed out before the commission of the offense, it is doubtful that she either deprived it of its effectiveness or acted in any way to prevent the crime.

d. What about Jimmy?
If Jimmy is an accomplice, then he will be convicted of the same crimes as Bobby unless as to the armed robbery, he can convince the court that he did not know of the "gun" and so could not have the requisite intent. Also, even though he did call the police, he terminated his participation in the crime after and not before its commission.

4. Apply the Model Penal Code, Article 210, Criminal Homicide, to the following situations. Have any homicide crimes been committed?

Last summer, Willie Albano stabbed and killed Roberto Basso during an argument outside of a convenience store. Willie was apprehended by police only ten minutes and one block away from the scene. A knife, the alleged murder weapon, was recovered at the scene and only the defendant's fingerprints were on it.

Two months later, the victim's parents, Peter and Maria Basso, and their only other child, Michael, attended a pretrial hearing. At the hearing the Bassos discovered that the police department had lost the knife, and the judge agreed to dismiss all charges against Willie Albano. The defendant turned toward the family and smiled. He slowly walked toward the Bassos, leaned over them and said, "Too bad. Better luck next time — after I kill you other son." To Michael he said, "Watch out, buddy. You're next."
Students should be directed to consider and interpret the actus reus and the mens rea for each scenario. Students should especially consider the level of passion that might reduce murder to manslaughter and the existence of a "cooling off" period that would restore purpose and knowledge to what otherwise might be considered manslaughter. It is

especially important to help students realize that these are adversarial situations and that there should be an argument for the prosecution and one for the defense, and the two sides would most likely not agree as to the outcome. Rather than ask students what they think the crime should be, ask them what the prosecution and in the alternative, the defense, might argue. That may keep students from simply voicing their personal opinions.

a. Mr. Basso jumped from his courtroom seat, grabbed the defendant's neck with a force so great that they both fell to the floor. A few seconds later, Willie Albano was dead from a broken neck and other injuries inflicted by Mr. Basso.
§210.2 (1) (a) or §210.3(1) (b) **Students should consider the immediacy of the action and the purpose and the level of the "influence of extreme mental or emotional disturbance for which there is reasonable explanation or excuse." However, the prosecution could argue that there was sufficient time during the hearing for the defendant Basso to form the necessary purpose and knowledge to amount to murder.**

b. After Willie's comments Mr. Basso walked next to Willie out of the courtroom. Once outside the building Mr. Basso grabbed Willie by the neck and strangled him.
§210.2 (1) (a) or §210.3(1)(b) **Again, timing may be the key. Students should consider manslaughter but should begin to see the possible existence of a "cooling off period" that might reduce the level of mental or emotional disturbance allowing for manslaughter and lead the jury to a murder conviction.**

b. Mr. Basso stayed in his seat as Willie walked past. When Willie exited the courtroom, Mr. Basso was waiting with a loaded pistol he had stolen from an unsuspecting guard. He aimed the gun at Willie but shot and killed the prosecutor who was standing near Willie.
§210.2 (1) (a) or §210.3(1) (b) **Students should discuss recklessness and what it means to manifest "extreme indifference to the value of human life" Again, the "cooling off period" seems to be extended and students will consider how long is too long to sustain the level of extreme mental or emotional disturbance needed for manslaughter consideration.**

c. Mr. Basso waited in his seat until Willie left the courthouse, and then he brought his family home. The next day he purchased a rifle from the local sporting goods store. Later that day he waited outside of Willie's apartment, and when Willie returned, Mr. Basso called out, "You'll never touch anyone in my family again." He pulled the trigger and killed Willie.
§210.2 (1) (a) or §210.3(1) (b) **The length of time between the hearing and the alleged crime, the deliberate actions of Mr. Basso, especially the purchase of a rifle, will lead students to reconsider, and possibly abandon, the manslaughter charge in favor of murder. Yet, the argument could be made that the grief**

over the murder of the first son and the fear of threat of murder to the surviving son would not disappear and in fact, may increase as time went on.

d. Three days after the hearing, Mr. Basso waited with his shotgun outside Willie's apartment for several hours. While he was waiting, Mr. Basso drank six cans of beer and two small bottles of whiskey. Finally giving up on his plan, Mr. Basso sped away from the apartment. He failed to notice a stop sign and killed a pedestrian with his car. The pedestrian was Willie Albano.

§210.4 (1) Negligence should be reexamined here and students should again consider the mens rea necessary to perpetrate a crime. Students may argue that the only evidence of wrongdoing here consists of motor vehicle offenses. Most likely, students will not believe the factual scenario and should be reminded that sometimes a criminal defendant's story seems not to be consistent with common sense. Even so, that may not make the story untrue — just harder for the defense to work with.

e. Mr. Basso arrived at Willie's apartment and forced his way inside. While he held a gun to Willie's head, Willie slit his own wrists with a kitchen knife. Willie died from those wounds six hours later.

§210.5 (1) requires a show of force, duress, or deception that causes another person to commit suicide. Holding a gun to the head of another is usually considered adequate evidence of force or duress. There may still be an argument here for manslaughter, or even murder, depending on the students' interpretation of the scenario.

This is another good exercise for helping students hone their adversarial skills and could be used as a group exercise or oral exercise. This could also be used as a mock hearing or mock oral advocacy assignment.

CASE DISCUSSION QUESTIONS, page 554 for *People v. Wolf*

1. Why did the court refuse to accept the testimony of the experts regarding the defendant's sanity?

The court stated that "[t]o hold otherwise would be in effect to substitute a trial by 'experts' for a trial by jury, for it would require that the jurors accept the psychiatric testimony as conclusive on an issue — the legal sanity of the defendant — which under our present law is exclusively within the province of the trier of fact to determine."

Do you agree that there should be a difference between the legal and the medical definitions of insanity? Why?

This discussion should raise some troublesome issues as to why the legal definition should not be the same as the medical definition, especially as the science of medicine advances and we have more insights into why the "insane" behave as they do.

175

2. Do you think the result would have been different in this case if the court had been following the standard for insanity set out in the Model Penal Code?
The evidence in this case demonstrated that the defendant did know what he did was wrong (the M'Naughton test as used by the court), but not necessarily that he could control his conduct. Therefore, it could be argued under the Model Penal Code test that he could have been found insane.

DISCUSSION QUESTIONS, page 554
4. If children engage in criminal behavior, how old do you think they should be before being treated the same as adult criminals? Do you think that answer should change based on the crime committed?
This question may afford students another opportunity to discuss their personal encounters with the criminal justice system and their feelings about juvenile offenders in general. Students should consider the impact of juvenile crime on society, the impact of criminal involvement on the juvenile perpetrators, and the age at which students believe juveniles could really form the mens rea necessary to be found guilty instead of delinquent. Students may consider the type of crime committed when they consider this question and may find that when juveniles commit particularly violent crimes, their legal status should be reconsidered.

5. Why do you think we have not been able to settle on one definition of legal insanity?
Students should explore the connection between medicine/psychiatry and the criminal justice system and the changing expectations that society has about both systems.

6. Do you think anyone should ever be found guilty on the basis of insanity? If so, under what circumstances?
"Only a crazy person would do that!" If most crime is incomprehensible to the average citizen, aren't most criminals insane to do what they do? Then again, is the insanity defense simply a way for criminals to avoid responsibility for their actions? This question will help students see beyond the common misconceptions about who qualifies for the insanity defense and how attorneys interpret the insanity defense for the jury and for society.

Legal Reasoning Exercise, page 555
5. Working as a member of the defense team, apply each of the three tests for insanity to determine whether this defendant might succeed with an insanity defense.
Emanuel Jones had been on medication for several years to stop the voices he heard in his head. He recently stopped taking his medication because it made him feel sleepy. Five days ago, during a visit with his best friend, Sam, Emanuel became angry and confused. He attacked Sam with a golf club, and Sam died as the result of the wounds he sustained.
The defense may be able to allege, because Emanuel was on medication, that he had been diagnosed with a mental disease or defect. Naturally, the prosecution

176

may want Emanuel to be examined. Once the disease or defect is established, Emanuel may be eligible for the insanity defense, depending on the test used in his jurisdiction and depending on whether the court would find that he lacked the ability to know what he did was wrong or to control his behavior. Working for the defense as the question suggests helps students look critically at available facts and draw valuable inferences from available facts. Then, by switching sides and reexamining the facts pursuant to the prosecution's point of view, the students can gain an appreciation for the necessity of preparing for litigation. Students should be instructed to prepare arguments for both sides. Then, in a classroom exercise, students could be asked to argue Emanuel's case from the perspective of each test.

a. Emanuel walked out of the house and stopped at a nearby restaurant for a hamburger. When the waiter asked him how Sam was, Emanuel replied he thought Sam was at home sleeping.
Perhaps Emanuel could succeed here with any level of insanity test unless the jury believed he was simply lying to cover up his knowledge of his crime.

b. Before leaving the house Emanuel put the golf club and his bloody clothes in the bath tub and filled the tub with water. He changed his clothes and ran home.
Perhaps the attempt to cover up his crime and his flight are indications that Emanuel was aware of his actions and the criminal complications that his actions would bring. These facts could, however, simply be interpreted as more bizarre actions without explanation or reason.

c. When the police questioned Emanuel the next day and asked him about Sam, he replied, "I killed him. He'll be back tomorrow."
Without knowledge of the nature or quality of his actions, Emanuel could be eligible for the insanity defense, unless these statements are perceived as lies.

d. When the police questioned Emanuel the next day and asked him about Sam, he replied, "I killed him. I tried to stop, but he just kept laughing at me."
These fact could lead to an argument for the insanity defense based on the irresistible impulse test. He may not have been able to control his conduct, or under the substantial capacity test, to conform his conduct to the requirements of law.

e. Several weeks after the incident and his return to his medication Emanuel expressed great grief and guilt over the death of Sam.
The return to sanity and appropriate emotional response after returning to his medication may indicate in the negative that, without it, his reactions were not controllable. Unfortunately, these facts illustrate a perplexing dilemma for litigators. If convicted, the medicated Emanuel will suffer the consequences, yet it was a seemingly different, unmedicated man who perpetrated the crime.

Consider the same facts as a member of the prosecution team. Do you come to the same conclusions?

While the conclusions may differ, the thought process is the same. Some students will be amazed they can create effective arguments for each side.

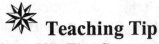 **Teaching Tip**

Page 557: The *Goetz* case gives you an opportunity to show the students how the states have responded to the development of the Model Penal Code and that they have not all chosen to adopt it verbatim. It also provides another opportunity to discuss the differences between a subjective and an objective standard.

CASE DISCUSSION QUESTIONS, page 559 for *People v. Goetz*

1. The *Goetz* case gives an excellent example of how critical the choice can be as to which standard, objective or subjective, to apply. First, define each standard, and then discuss which standard you think should be applied to similar situations in the future.

The objective standard looks at what a reasonable person in the defendant's position would have done. The subjective standard looks at what the defendant actually believed, whether or not that belief was reasonable. The students should discuss the dangers of the subjective standard but also the unfairness in individual cases of applying a reasonable standard.

2. How does the New York penal law differ from the Model Penal Code on the use of deadly force in self-defense? Which do you think is the better approach?

Under the Model Penal Code the defendant charged with murder or attempted murder need only show that he *believed* that the use of deadly force was necessary to protect himself. New York did not choose to follow the MPC in its equation of a mistake as to the need to use deadly force with a mistake negating an element of the crime. Instead, New York choose to use a single section which would provide either a complete defense or no defense at all by inserting the word "reasonably" before "believes."

3. After nearly eight weeks of trial, Goetz was acquitted of attempted murder but convicted of illegal gun possession. If you could read the jurors' minds, what do you think was a determining factor in their verdict?

This may be an example of jury nullification — that is, even though all of the elements for attempted murder might have been present, the jury did not want to convict Goetz of that crime so they substituted a conviction for illegal gun possession.

DISCUSSION QUESTIONS, pages 569-70

7. Which of the following areas do you think should be considered "private" and therefore require a warrant to be searched?

      a. your bedroom in your parent's home
      b. your garage
      c. your office at work

d.   your school locker
e.   your garbage that you have placed at your roadside curb

Students should discuss the varying degrees of the expectation of privacy and should recognize that the more private the setting, the higher the expectation of privacy. The issue of third party consent, especially for a., should also be discussed. This question is also a great opportunity to create a mock adversarial situation in the classroom. Rather than ask the question to the entire group, create a defense and prosecutorial team. Help students realize that the argument they make is shaped by the party they represent — and that there may be a valid argument for each side.

8. How "plain" does plain view have to be? For example, in which of the following situations do you think the marihuana was in plain view?

a.   Using a helicopter, the police fly over your fenced back yard and see it growing in pots on your back patio.
b.   Standing across the street the police use binoculars and see it growing inside your sunroom.
c.   Walking down the street the police dog that has been especially trained to smell marihuana and other illegal drugs, "points" to your briefcase.
d.   Aiming a thermal-imaging device at your house, the police find suspicious "hot spots," indicating the probable presence of marijuana growing within your home.

These factual scenarios should serve to facilitate general discussion on search and seizure, plain view, and a more general discussion of the limits on police power. This area of the law changes rapidly. The boundaries are being tested by inventive perpetrators as technologically trained law enforcement officers continue to expand the limits of "plain view." While almost any area capable of being seen from outside your house is generally considered plain view, the outcomes of the factual examples will very depending on the jurisdiction. Generally, the police dog may give the law enforcement officials reasonable suspicion/probable cause and may be enough to allow a stop and frisk search. Also depending on the jurisdiction, without permission, officers can not usually open a closed briefcase, but they could get a warrant based on this information.

A recent case covering the plain view doctrine involved the use of thermo imaging equipment to spot a "hot spot" in the garage of someone who law enforcement authorities thought to be involved in growing marijuana. In *Kyllo v. United States*, 533 U.S. 27 (2001) the U.S. Supreme Court held that the plain view exception did not apply and government agents needed to get a warrant before they could use a thermal-imaging device aimed at a private home from a public street for the purpose of detecting evidence of a crime.

Students could use these factual scenarios as jumping off points for research in their own jurisdiction.

CASE DISCUSSION QUESTIONS, page 577 on *Rhode Island v. Innis*
1. How did the *Innis* court define *interrogation*?
Interrogation is express questioning or its functional equivalent when the person is in custody, that is, police words or actions that the police should know are reasonably likely

to elicit an incriminating response from the suspect. This depends largely on the perceptions of the suspect, rather than the intent of the police.

2. Applying that definition of interrogation, why did the Court believe the officers' remarks were not a form of interrogation? Do you agree with the Court's decision?

The court concluded that the defendant had not been interrogated because the conversation between the two patrolmen included no express questioning of the defendant. Rather it was just a dialogue between the two officers. The dissent, of course, disagreed. They saw it as a calculated appeal to the defendant's conscience to get him to reveal the location of the weapon.

Legal Reasoning Exercise, page 578

6. Using the standard discussed in this chapter did custodial interrogation take place during the following incidents?

    a. A suspect ran up to the police officer and cried, "Help! I killed him. I killed him. I didn't mean to do it!"

       This appears to be a spontaneous outburst, without either custody or interrogation.

    b. An officer walked up to a group of boys hanging around a street corner and said, "Hey, guys. What are you doing here?"

       This could be construed as a type of routine police procedure, not including custodial interrogation. However, considering the circumstances is important here. The time of day, the presence of other witnesses, the location, the level of police power, the officer's attitude, and the age and experience of the boys may convince a judge that the boys did not feel free to leave (custody) and were asked questions which could result in inculpatory information (interrogation).

    c. While at the police station the suspect explained how he stole the car from the parking lot down the street.

       The suspect's presence at a police station may indicate custody and the statement could have been at the direction of or pursuant to questioning from police officers. On the other hand, the suspect could be simply volunteering information without questioning.

    d. As an officer asked questions, the suspect wrote answers on a piece of paper.

       These facts have the appearance of a police directed statement, usually considered custodial interrogation, especially when given at a police station.

    e. In the case scenario being used in this chapter the police questioned Grant on the ride to the police station.

       Custodial interrogation seems likely here. Even if the police did not ask him any direct question, any conversation intended to convince the suspect to respond may be considered custodial interrogation.

9. How do you reconcile the purpose behind a motion for a view with the traditional belief that jurors are supposed to base their decision solely on what they hear and see in the courtroom?

Traditionally, jurors are only allowed to gather evidence and make inferences from what they hear presented to them through witnesses. While encouraged to use their common sense to interpret evidence, they are not allowed to investigate the case themselves or to gather additional evidence outside of the courtroom. Yet, in many criminal cases, jurors are taken from the courtroom to the crime scene. Usually, however, the jurors are brought to the scene through a witness, who guides the jurors with testimony. The courts consider a view to be like exhibits in the courtroom, used to enhance the juror's understanding.

CASE DISCUSSION QUESTIONS, page 588 for *Mapp v. Ohio*
1. According to the Supreme Court, what is the main justification for the exclusionary rule?
If items illegally seized could be used against a citizen, then the protection of the Fourth Amendment to be secure against such searches and seizures would be of no value. Use of illegally seized evidence involves a denial of the accused's constitutional rights.

2. What negative consequences arise out of application of the exclusionary rule?
If someone is guilty but the only evidence the police have is excluded, than the guilty will go free.

3. What problems would be created by having one set of rules for the federal courts and a separate set of rules for the state courts?
It would look as though the states by admitting evidence unlawfully seized were disobeying the federal constitution.

4. The dissenting justices in *Leon* saw that decision as a step toward the destruction of the Fourth Amendment. They wrote that "[t]he right to be free from the initial invasion of privacy and the right of exclusion are coordinate components of the central embracing right to be free from unreasonable searches and seizures." Do you agree?
The conflict is between sometimes letting the guilty go free versus allowing the government to fail to observe its own laws.

Legal Reasoning Exercise, page 588

7. Suppose someone fired a bullet through the floor of an apartment into the apartment below. The police entered the shooter's apartment looking for the shooter, other weapons, and possibly for victims. While they were in the apartment, the police discovered weapons and a stocking cap. The police also noticed stereo equipment and, suspecting that it was stolen, recorded the serial numbers. In order to read all of the numbers, the police moved some of the equipment. When the police headquarters notified the police that the equipment was stolen, the police officers seized it.

a. If you worked as a paralegal for the defense team, what arguments would you make to convince the court to suppress the evidence?

Because the serial numbers were not in plain view, the officer should have obtained a warrant before moving objects in the apartment. Naturally, any plain view objects in the apartment could be accessible to the officer if the court considers the officer's entrance into the apartment to be because of exigent circumstances. If no exigent circumstance exist, then all information gathered after the officer entered the apartment should be suppressed pursuant to the exclusionary rule and the fruit of the poisonous tree doctrine.

b. If you worked for the prosecution, what arguments would you make to convince the court that the search was legal?

Exigent circumstances required entry into the apartment and everything thereafter was covered by plain view.

c. Which side has the most persuasive arguments?

The defense probably has a better argument but the results of the motions to suppress may depend on human factors, like the credibility of the witnesses and the current status of search and seizure law in any particular jurisdiction.

This may be an opportunity for students to participate in a mock motion hearing.

DISCUSSION QUESTION, page 591

10. Criminals are guaranteed a jury of their peers. If you were on trial for a criminal offense, what factors would you consider when trying to select a jury of your peers? Is there such a thing?

Students should explore the factors that contribute to the art of jury selection. Consider the effects of age, race, nationality, economic and education level, language barriers, and gender. Discuss jury psychology and the impact the lawyer's ethnic and racial background and sex may have on the jury.

DISCUSSION QUESTIONS, page 594

11. How might you respond to your neighbor who says the judicial system is "falling apart" because of plea bargaining?

Learning to give an intelligent response to comments about the criminal justice system will help students gain confidence in themselves and in their profession. Students should discuss the prosecution's duty to see that justice is accomplished, and the interrelationship between the police, the prosecution, and the defense. Explain that after research and considering the totality of the circumstances, the charges may need to be adjusted. Judicial economy and the expenses of litigation are legitimate concerns. Plea bargaining, when accomplished correctly, is beneficial to both prosecution and defense and in many cases, it accomplishes justice. Abuse of this legal technique, like the abuse of any system, is problematic and reduces confidence in the system.

12. "It is better that ten guilty men go free than one innocent man be convicted" is an often quoted legal expression. Do you agree or disagree? Why?

Students will agree or disagree with this statement depending on the political and social climate. Most students seem comfortable with the concept that many guilty perpetrators go free as the result of dealings in the criminal justice system. Students are not so comfortable imagining that innocent suspects may be convicted. Students should be reminded that for the criminal system to work perfectly, all the law enforcement and court room participants must perfectly perform their jobs. While much of the country has adopted a "tough on crime" attitude, it's not a bad idea to remind students that any system driven by humans is subject to human error and confusion.

13. Discuss the manner in which the death penalty serves each of the major theories of punishment. Do you support or oppose the use of capital punishment? Why?

Specific deterrence — Because the goal of this theory is to keep the perpetrator from committing other crimes, the death penalty is the ultimate guarantee that this perpetrator will not err again.

General deterrence — Experts tend to disagree about whether the death penalty discourages others from perpetrating crimes. Because many murders occur as the result of some type of passion, perpetrators may not actually analyze the likelihood of getting caught, convicted, and sentenced to death prior to committing the crime. Proponents of the death penalty believe many more crimes would be committed but are deterred by the threat of the death penalty.

Incapacitation — No one can argue that capital punishment incapacitates the perpetrator! Capital punishment exceeds the goal of incarceration, since most perpetrators are incarcerated for a period of years, and then released.

Rehabilitation — Capital punishment does not serve this theory of punishment unless one could argue that death is the ultimate rehabilitation in preparation for the next life. Usually, however, opportunities for rehabilitation cease when capital punishment is applied.

Retribution — If society, the victim, or the victim's family seek retribution, capital punishment may meet the goal of this theory of punishment. Especially in murder cases, capital punishment appears to exact revenge and bring the 'eye for an eye' philosophy to fruition.

Whether someone supports the death penalty is a personal decision, driven by all the factors that shape us as human beings. Be prepared for a wide range of comments and some passion on this issue. Even though this topic has long been debated, it can still raise heat in the classroom. An important byproduct of this type of question is to facilitate discussion in the classroom without allowing personal attack or anger to intrude on meaningful discussion and sharing. One approach might be to ask the students to consider why their state law does or does not allow for this penalty and how that policy differs from the policies of surrounding states.

14. How much discretion should the judge have in sentencing? Why?

This question returns to a debate over the appropriateness of federal sentencing guidelines and mandatory sentencing in general. One could argue that the only person who should

exercise discretion is the one who listened to all the facts, evaluated the credibility of all the witnesses, who was a first-hand witness to the victim impact statements, and who, over the course of a trial, had an opportunity to evaluate the defendant on and off the stand. That theory works when the judge exercises that discretion without the "baggage" human beings sometimes bring to decision making. Sentencing guidelines take the bulk of the discretion away from judges and could reduce the number of defendants who are not treated equally.

15. On November 4, Leandro Andrade stole five videotapes worth $84.70 from a Kmart store. Fourteen days later, Andrade entered a different Kmart store and placed four videotapes worth $68.84 in the rear waistband of his pants. (The tapes included "Batman Forever" and "Cinderella.") The police arrested Andrade for these crimes. At trial, Andrade was found guilty of two counts of petty theft. The jury also made a special finding that he had previously been convicted of three counts of first-degree residential burglary. (One case involved his attempt to steal a bicycle.) Each of his petty theft convictions for stealing the videotapes triggered a separate application of the three strikes law. Therefore, the judge sentenced him to two consecutive terms of 25 years to life, with no chance for parole. Does it seem as though his punishment was proportionate to his crime? How would you argue that his case is similar to or different from the *Ewing* case discussed above?

These were the facts in Lockyer v. Andrade, 538 U.S. 63 (2003). The court upheld his sentence, stating "[t]he gross disproportionality principle reserves a constitutional violation for only the extraordinary case.. . . . [I]t was not an unreasonable application of our clearly established law for the California Court of Appeal to affirm Andrade's sentence of two consecutive terms of 25 years to life in prison." Souter, joined by Stevens, Ginsburg, and Breyer in dissent noted that Andrade's "criminal history is less grave than Ewing's, and yet he received a prison term twice as long for a less serious triggering offense. . . .If Andrade's sentence is not grossly disproportionate, the principle has no meaning. [Note: In California, petty theft is a defense that can be punishable either as a misdemeanor or as a felony at the discretion of the prosecutor. The trial court also has discretion to reduce the charge to a misdemeanor at the time of sentencing. In this case, the prosecutor choose to charge Andrade with felonies which the judge did not reduce at the time of sentencing. The three-strike law had been enacted largely in response to the murder of a young girl by a paroled repeat criminal. It is doubtful that the legislature had cases such as Ewing's and Andrade's in mind when they enacted the legislation. Andrade's case is similar to Ewing's in that both were convicted of shoplifting, not of any crime involving serious bodily injury. Indeed, two consecutive twenty-five year sentences would seem to be more appropriate for murder than for shoplifting.]

REVIEW QUESTIONS, pages 595-97

1. Why is "[n]o behavior a crime unless the law makes it a crime?
No act, no matter how troublesome or destructive to society, is considered a criminal act unless the governing body makes it a crime by enacting a statute explicitly prohibiting

that behavior. For example, some behaviors that were considered tolerable in years past, like spousal abuse, became politically and socially incorrect. As the result of a change in public climate which led to the enacting of statutes, this behavior is now criminal in most states.

2. Who has the burden of proving a criminal case?
The prosecution (the government) has the burden of proving a criminal case.

Why is the standard of proof not the same in criminal and civil cases?
The standard of proof in a criminal case (beyond a reasonable doubt) is higher and more difficult to prove than the standard of proof in a civil case (preponderance of the evidence). In addition to financial penalties available in civil cases, conviction of a criminal offense could result in the loss of the defendant's liberty and in some jurisdictions, could result in the loss of the defendant's life. This loss of life and/or liberty is seen as a more serious penalty than the loss of money and so criminal guilt should be determined by a higher standard.

3. What alternatives are there to incarceration?
In addition to incarceration in either a jail (local or county) or a prison (state or federal) the defendant could be sentenced to a suspended sentence, probation, day reporting, restitution, property forfeiture, and could, after serving a portion of the sentence, be paroled.

4. What is the Model Penal Code?
The Model Penal Code is a set of criminal statutes drafted by the American Law Institute in 1956.

What was the intent of its drafters?
The drafters intended to create (and intended that the states adopt) a uniform set of criminal statutes hoping that this would lead to uniform criminal laws and prosecution throughout the country.

Has that intent been accomplished?
The intent of the drafters has only partially been realized. While many individual provisions have been adopted by individual jurisdictions, the Model Penal Code has not been universally adopted. Criminal laws still vary from state to state.

5. What are the differences between felonies and misdemeanors?
Felonies are generally considered more serious crimes, accompanied by more serious penalties — including capital punishment in some jurisdictions. Misdemeanors, generally are considered less serious. Felonies and misdemeanors can usually be distinguished by the duration and location of incarceration, the location of incarceration, and the title of the court hearing the matter.

Misdemeanors occupy a large portion of the court calendar. Occasionally the legislature considers de-criminalizing various misdemeanor crimes to free the court's time for "more serious" and more complicated cases. With the advent of the "three strikes" rule, crime classification and the availability of plea bargaining from a felony to a lesser included misdemeanor takes on even greater significance than it had in the past.

6. What is the *actus reus* of a crime?
The *actus reus* is the action that the defendant must commit to be charged with a crime. That act must be voluntary. The action itself need not do any harm.

What is the *mens rea* of a crime?
The mens rea is the nature of a person's intent. Evidence of a "guilty mind" must be present for the act in question to be considered a crime.

7. How do you determine whether one crime is a lesser included offense of another crime?
Look to both crimes. If all of the elements of crime one are contained in crime two, but the second crime has extra elements, crime one may be a lesser included offense of crime two. Look carefully at those extra elements and whether they really exist in your case. If not, maybe you can plea bargain from crime two to crime one.

8. What is an inchoate crime?
When the defendant attempts a crime, but is prevented from successfully completing the crime, the behavior may be classified as an inchoate crime. The prosecution must prove that the defendant intended to commit the crime and that the defendant did some overt act in furtherance of that intent.

9. What is the difference between general and specific intent?
Under the common law, intent was divided between general and specific intent. If the defendant intended to act only, without regard to causing the results of the act, then the defendant had general intent. If the statute required the defendant to do the act and to intend to cause the harm that resulted from the act, then the defendant possessed specific intent.

10. Define and describe the categories of intent used by the Model Penal Code.
The Model Penal Code abandoned the use of the categories of general and specific intent found in the common law. The Model Penal Code divides intent into four categories that incorporate the common law standards.

     Purposeful — desiring to cause the harm that resulted
     Knowing — knowing or having reason to know the resulting harm would occur
     Reckless — disregarding a substantial likelihood that the resulting harm would occur and that the law will be violated
     Negligent — failing to be aware of the substantial risk of harm

Purposeful intent is considered the most serious form of intent and is usually punished the most severely.

11. Who is the principal of a crime?
The principal of a crime in the first degree is the person who actually commits the crime.

What is the difference between the principal and the accessory to a crime?
Unlike a principal, an accessory need not be present at the scene of the crime. The accessory, also known as the accomplice, could simply have been involved in the planning or the coverup of the crime. According to the Model Penal Code, an accessory could be held accountable for the commission of a crime by another under several circumstances unless that person terminates involvement or informs authorities or otherwise acts to prevent the commission of the crime.

12. What defenses might be available to the following individuals?
   a. The Elliots complained to the police that the son of their next-door neighbor broke their garage windows with rocks. They wanted him arrested. The police went next door to arrest the boy, and they discovered that he is seven years old. They arrested him and brought him to the police station. He was charged with destroying the Elliot's property.
   Infancy —The age that determines infancy currently varies from state to state.

   b. Marcus was arrested for the murder of his cousin Michael. At the time that Michael was killed Marcus claimed that he was on a business trip 300 miles away.
   Alibi — The defendant could allege that because of his location at the time of the crime, it would have been impossible for him to commit the crime.

   c. Every day on the way to school, Rosa pushed Carmen to the ground and stole her lunch. On Tuesday, Carmen hid behind a car on the way to school, and when she saw Rosa walking toward her, she jumped out and hit her. Rosa pushed Carmen to the ground and walked away without taking her lunch.
   Rosa has the defense of self-defense only after Carmen hid behind the car and attacked her. Carmen does not have a defense for striking Rosa. She is not allowed to use physical force to protect her property under these circumstances.

   d. As Paula walked toward her car after work, she was confronted by Terry, who pointed a realistic toy gun at Paula and demanded that Paula hand over her wallet. Paula took a gun out of her purse and shot and killed Terry.
   Self-defense — Paula may have this defense if all the circumstances point to her fear for her own safety. The prosecution may argue that she may have had an opportunity to escape and should have tried to escape before resorting to deadly force.

   e. After his car was forced off the road, Patrick tried to stop the bleeding on his wife's face. When she passed out, Patrick ran to a nearby home, jumped over the fence, and banged on the front door. When the occupants would not let him in, Patrick broke a window of the house, climbed through, and ran toward the

187

telephone. The homeowner grabbed a rifle and shot Patrick in the back.
Patrick may have the necessity defense if he can prove that the chain of events forced him to break and enter to avoid further injury to his wife. The homeowner may have the right to self-defense, or defense of his family and property, unless there was no threat of harm from Patrick or the force seems excessive considering Patrick's behavior. The court will carefully consider the facts, especially that Patrick broke into a home, usually considered the most private place deserving the most respect and protection. The court will also look carefully into why Patrick was shot in the back and whether the family could have escaped harm without resorting to excessive force.

f. During a grocery store robbery a thief held a gun to a customer's head and demanded he put all the money from the store safe into a bag, which he did. When the police arrived, they arrested the customer for robbery.
Duress — The customer could claim that the thief used unlawful force against his person and coerced him to act.

g. During the last five years of their marriage, David beat his wife, Mary, so severely that she was hospitalized four times. About six months after the last beating Mary stabbed David to death while he was sleeping. She was arrested for murder.
Battered Woman Syndrome, also called Battered Spouse Syndrome, is available in some jurisdictions to give battered individuals the right to self-defense even though there may not be immediate danger at the exact moment of retaliation.

h. Officer Kaplan responded to an emergency call for a store robbery in progress. When the masked thief shot at the officer, Officer Kaplan shot and killed the thief. The man's family wanted Officer Kaplan charged with murder.
Justifiable homicide if it is determined that the officer killed the victim as part of his official duties as a police officer.

13. What is the difference between a complete and a partial defense?
Complete — if perfect, will result in not guilty verdict.
Partial — if perfect, will result in reducing a crime to a lesser included offense.

14. Describe the various tests that have been developed to determine whether a defendant was insane at the time he or she committed the crime.
The insanity defense is based on the belief that the defendant was incapable of formulating the required element of mens rea to be found guilty of the defense charged. The major tests for insanity, the M'Naughton Test, the Irresistible Impulse Test, and the Model Penal Code Substantial Capacity test each present a different standard for analyzing the defendant's lack of mens rea. The tests center around the defendant's ability to understand right or wrong because of a mental disease or defect (M'Naughton);

the inability, because of mental disease or defect, to control actions (irresistible impulse); and, because of mental disease or defect, lacking the appreciation of the wrongfulness of actions (substantial capacity).

15. What are the possible results of successfully proving an insanity defense?
The results vary from state to state. The defendant could be found "not guilty" due to insanity and could be set free. Some states have adopted a "guilty but insane" verdict to allow the defendant to escape the penal system of punishment and to be hospitalized instead. If the defendant is then cured, the defendant could be sent to a penal institution to complete the sentence.

16. What is the difference between the duress and necessity defense?
Duress occurs when one person uses unlawful force against another and forces the other to commit a crime. According to the Model Penal Code, the force used should amount to coercion and should be of a level that a reasonable person would be incapable of resisting. The necessity defense is similar, except that the force is exerted by nature, like a tornado, that forces a person to commit a crime. The necessity defense is also used when one crime is committed to avoid a more serious crime.

17. What does a defendant have to show to prove entrapment?
The elements of this crime may differ depending on the jurisdiction, but usually the defendant would have to show that he or she was tricked or led to commit a crime by a law enforcement agent when he or she would not have otherwise committed the crime. If the law enforcement official simply paved the way for the criminal to commit the crime, entrapment would not exist.

18. When can a potential victim use deadly force to protect himself or herself?
Deadly force can only be used when the actor believes that there is an immediate threat of serious bodily harm or death. Only the Battered Woman's or Spouse's Syndrome would allow the use of deadly force without imminent harm.

19. What is the retreat exception to the self-defense doctrine?
In many jurisdictions a person in danger should try to flee, or should give up possessions, before resorting to the use of deadly force. Life, even the life of an alleged criminal, should not be taken or even endangered unless other avenues of safety are explored.

20. What problems arise with using battered woman's syndrome as the basis for a self-defense argument?
Until the introduction of this defense, self-defense was not allowed without the fear of immediate harm. The battered woman's syndrome defense could be seen as a "slippery slope" towards allowing self-defense in other circumstances not involving immediate harm. Some may see this broadening of self-defense as increasing the risk for private retribution for past wrongs.

21. What protections are afforded by the double jeopardy clause?

Once jeopardy attaches, usually when the jury is sworn in, the defendant can not be tried again for the same offense. This does not prohibit civil trials in addition to criminal trials. It also does not prohibit a new trial post appeal, or a second trial based on different charges.

22. When might a statute be challenged for vagueness?

A statute may be challenged for vagueness when the law is too vague to discern the limits or parameters. An example of a statute that might be challenged based on vagueness is one prohibiting vagrancy.

For overbreadth?

A statute may be considered overbroad when there is a great potential for abuse and such abuse would lead to interference with lawful activities.

23. What is a stop-and-frisk search?

Law enforcement officers are permitted to briefly stop, briefly question, and pat down the outside of an individual's clothing when that individual is suspected of illegal activity. There is no Fourth Amendment violation because the intrusion into the individual's privacy is so slight.

24. What is the difference between reasonable suspicion and probable cause?

According to *Terry v. Ohio*, reasonable suspicion required for a stop and frisk search must be based on "specific and articuable facts which, taken together with rational inferences from those facts, reasonably warrant that intrusion." An officer must be able to articulate to the court the facts that led to the suspicion that the individual has committed, is in the process of committing, or is about to commit a crime.

Probable cause is a higher standard than reasonable suspicion. To find probable cause, law enforcement officers must rely on knowledge of the suspect and information provided by witnesses and victims.

Why does it matter?

The differences between the standards matter because the intrusions into the lives of citizens may not exceed that allowed under the Fourth Amendment. The lower reasonable suspicion standard is applied during the minimally intrusive stop and frisk search. The higher probable cause standard is applied when the intrusion is higher at arrest or during a complete search of a suspect's body or home.

25. Why does the court consider the suspect's expectation of privacy when evaluating a search?

The Fourth Amendment protects only against unreasonable searches. The higher the level of expectation of privacy, the more closely the court looks at the behavior of law enforcement officials to make sure that the search was not unreasonable.

26. What is a warrant?

A warrant is the court's permission, after a showing of probable cause, to search, seize, or arrest.

27. List some specific facts that must be included when police officers apply for a warrant to search a suspect's home.

Facts that must be included are name, address (including apartment number or floor), description of specific items searched for in as much detail as possible (including brand name, size, age, model numbers, weight), and any other available details.

28. What is a no-knock warrant?

A no-knock warrant allows law enforcement officials to execute a warrant at night with no announcement. Police must convince the judge that without this special privilege, evidence would be destroyed or police officers would be in danger.

In *Richards v. Wisconsin*, 117 S. Ct. 1416 (1997), the Supreme Court held that the Fourth Amendment does not allow a blanket exception to the knock-and-announce requirement for felony drug investigations. Rather, as with any case, the police must have a reasonable suspicion under the particular circumstances that knocking and announcing would be dangerous or futile or that it would allow for the destruction of the evidence. In *Richards* the Court found that the police officer's no-knock entry into the defendant's hotel room was justified. On the facts of the case, it was reasonable for the police officers to believe that the defendant knew they were police, and they were searching for drugs which by their nature are easily disposable.

29. What exigent circumstances may allow police to search without a warrant?

Exigent circumstances include plain view, consent, third-party consent, emergency (plain view only), preservation of evidence, hot pursuit, and incident to lawful arrest.

30. What are *Miranda* warnings, when are the police required to give them, and under what circumstances might a defendant waive them?

Pursuant to the Fifth and Sixth Amendments and from such landmark cases as *Escobedo v. Illinois*, 378 U.S. 478 (1964) and *Miranda v. Arizona*, 384 U.S. 436 (1966), a suspect under custodial interrogation is entitled to be informed of the right to remain silent, that statements made may be used against the suspect in a court of law, that the suspect has the right to consult with an attorney, and if he or she can not pay for an attorney, one will be appointed. Because these rights belong to the suspect, he or she can waive them so long as the waiver is done knowingly, intelligently, and voluntarily. The state has the burden of proving that the suspect properly waived his or her *Miranda* rights.

31. What extra protection do juveniles usually get when they are given their *Miranda* rights?

The court recognizes that children, even children in trouble, may depend on the help of adults when making decisions, especially important decisions concerning their legal futures. In addition to the *Miranda* rights, juvenile suspects are given added protection by the court. Any juvenile suspect is given an opportunity to speak with an interested

adult, like a parent or guardian, prior to signing a *Miranda* card and determining whether to waive *Miranda* rights.

32. What might a defendant expect to occur during booking?
The booking process usually includes taking the suspect's personal information, an inventory of the suspect's personal belongings on his person at the time of the booking, an opportunity to read and sign a *Miranda* card, and an opportunity to use a telephone. The police may photograph or fingerprint the suspect and may conduct relevant examinations, like a breathalyzer exam or sobriety tests. The suspect may expect this process to be videotaped. Depending on the circumstances, the suspect may be released, with instructions to go to court at a later date, or be held at the police station or other lock up until the court date.

33. What is the exclusionary rule?
Under the exclusionary rule, if evidence against the defendant has been obtained in violation of the suspect's constitutional rights, it cannot be used against the defendant during legal proceedings. Additionally, the "fruit of the poisonous tree" doctrine prohibits the use of any evidence discovered as the result of the excluded evidence.

34. How do motions to suppress affect the prosecution's case against defendants?
If allowed by the court, a motion to suppress limits the prosecution's use of evidence against a defendant. Once evidence is suppressed, the prosecution must proceed without it and may not make any reference to it. If the motion to suppress is not allowed by the court, the questioned evidence remains available for use by the prosecution during trial.

35. What are the differences between a guilty plea and a plea of nolo condendre?
Nolo contendere, or no contest, means that the defendant neither admits nor denies the charges. By this plea, the defendant only admits that if the case should go to trial, the prosecution would have sufficient evidence to obtain a guilty verdict. Because the defendant never admits guilt, the case cannot be used against the defendant during any subsequent civil proceedings. With a guilty plea, the defendant must admit the facts presented by the prosecution are true. The defendant must also admit that he or she committed the acts as described.
This may leave the defendant open for civil liability.

36. If you worked for the prosecution, would you consider the following items to be potentially inculpatory or exculpatory? Could this evidence be potentially inculpatory *and* exculpatory?

    a.   The finger of a second person on the murder weapon
        This evidence could be exculpatory if it omits the defendant as the shooter, inculpatory if it is determined that the two acted in concert.

b. A statement that the defendant gave to the police shortly after the arrest disclosing the location of the missing body
This evidence would probably be considered inculpatory, since the jury could infer possession of this knowledge signifies guilt.

c. Samples of hair and skin found at the scene of the crime
Depending on the ownership of the samples, these items would likely be considered inculpatory. Scientific tests could aid in the identification of these materials. Mere location of samples, however, does not necessarily provide inculpatory evidence at trial, especially if they are found at a location often frequented by the defendant.

37. If the following facts were true, what pretrial motions might you file on behalf of the defendants?

a. All of the local papers have reported that the judge on the case used to be married to the victim.
Motion to Recuse (to remove the judge who may be biased); Motion for a Change of Venue (to move the case to where the pre-trial publicity may not have been seen); Motion to Sequester Witnesses/Jury (if the jury has not yet seen the local papers)

b. Each of the two defendants claims that the other defendant was the sole assassin.
Motion to Sever

c. The defendant, who was represented by a public defender, needs to conduct an independent drug evaluation, especially since the defendant alleged the green, leafy substance was oregano bought to add spice to spaghetti sauce.
Motion for Funds; Motion to Suppress

d. There were seven witnesses prepared to testify at trial. Four of the witnesses were related by blood or marriage.
Motion to Sequester Witnesses

38. Describe the basic steps that occur in a criminal trial.
If it is a jury trial, the trial begins with jury selection. Opening statements, while not evidence, introduce the jury to the facts in question. The prosecution opens first, and presents its case because it has the burden to prove each element beyond a reasonable doubt. After each witness is examined by the prosecution, the defense has the opportunity to cross-examine. When the prosecution closes, the defense has an opportunity to make a motion for a required finding of not guilty, indicating to the court that the prosecution failed to meet its burden. If allowed, the trial is over and the case is dismissed. If not allowed, the trial goes forward and the defense has the opportunity to

call witnesses, including the defendant, who can then be cross-examined by the prosecution. The defense is not required to call any witnesses and the defendant is not required to testify. After the defense closes its case, each side has an opportunity to address the jury one last time in a closing argument. The closing is not evidence. After the judge charges the jury, it retires to deliberate and, hopefully, comes to a verdict. If the verdict is not guilty, the case is dismissed and the defendant is released. If the verdict is guilty, the defendant may be scheduled for sentencing or may be sentenced immediately.

39. Why is there no requirement that the defendant take the stand?
The Constitution provides that the defendant has a right to remain. The defendant need not testify, unless, after strategic planning by the defense team, or the introduction of a defense, the defendant's testimony is necessary and advised. The prosecution is prohibited from referring to the defendant's failure to testify.

40. What is the purpose of charging the jury?
In charging the jury, the judge explains the law, usually including instructions on reasonable doubt, an explanation of the charges and the elements of each charge, and some instructions on the duties and responsibilities of the jury. After the charge, the jury is sworn and usually leaves the courtroom, to be held in some convenient place, guarded by a court officer, until the verdict is reached.

41. What are the theories of punishment?
Theories of punishment include specific deterrence, general deterrence, incapacitation, rehabilitation, and retribution.

Which theory or theories do you think would be the most effective in eliminating crime in society?
Students should discuss the various theories. Inevitably, some students will favor rehabilitation while others will voice a strong desire for personal rather than social retribution. A discussion of capital punishment as an alternative to incapacitation will spark some debate, if not argument. The instructor should encourage students to focus on whether they seek reform of the criminal individual or reform to society as the goal of punishment.

42. What are the U.S. Sentencing Guidelines, and why are they controversial?
Federal sentencing guidelines attempt to regulate sentencing to reduce the uneven results that may occur when judges use their discretion in sentencing. By these guidelines, the government hopes to eliminate a judge's prejudice and bias during sentencing. Guidelines are controversial because they attempt to treat all criminals alike, regardless of certain mitigating factors. As noted in the text, recently the Guidelines were called into doubt by the United State Supreme Court in *Blakely v. Washington*, 124 S.Ct. 2531 (2004).

43. Why is it not double jeopardy for the prosecutor to appeal an intermediate appellate level decision?

Because once the defendant has in effect "waived" his or her rights by appealing a conviction, the appeal must run its course. Also, if the defendant appeals a conviction and wins the appeal, the appellate court may remand the case for a new trial.

Appendix A

Excerpts from the United States Constitution

While a bit unconventional, we opted to include only excerpts from the United States Constitution. My experience has been that when I assign the entire Constitution students skim it at best. Because it seems overwhelming and because they do not know how to decipher which parts are the most important, they often elect to simply not read it. By giving them only excerpts, you can expect them to give this assigned reading their full attention.

Appendix B

Fundamentals of Good Writing

While many lament that student writing skills are at an all time low, I have not really noticed a major decline. As always, students have a great deal of trouble recognizing sentence fragments and run-ons in their writing. A fairly recent development, however, has been the increasing use of the word "of" instead of "have." I suspect this is because students are reading less, and in conversation the word have often sounds like of.

It is important to emphasize to students that their word simply will not be taken seriously if it is full of spelling and grammar errors. Good legal writing is judged not only on its content but also on its style.

REVIEW QUESTIONS, pages 628-29

Correct the following sentences.

1. On any given day, a paralegal can be asked to perform any of the following tasks, to interview clients, research in the library, drafting of documents, filed pleadings, or writing client letters.
An attorney can ask a paralegal to perform any of the following tasks: to interview clients, research in the library, draft documents, file pleadings, or write client letters. [Excessive verbiage, passive voice, and lack of parallel construction.]

2. The complaint, which contains theories based on both tort and contract law, alleging that the product was defective, was filed with the wrong court.
Containing theories based on both tort and contract law, alleging that he product was defective, the attorney filed the complaint with the wrong court. [Passive voice; intrusive phrase.]

3. Even though the attorney made a long-winded and impassioned plea to the jury at the end of the trial.
Even though the attorney made a long-winded and impassioned plea to the jury at the end of the trial, his client lost. [Sentence fragment]

4. The attorney made a long-winded and impassioned plea to the jury at the end of the trial the jury found the defendant guilty.
The attorney made a long-winded and impassioned plea to the jury. At the end of the trial the jury found the defendant guilty. [or (;) — run-on]

5. In <u>Jones</u>, a child is injured by his father's negligence. The court decides that children were able to sue for parental negligence.
In <u>Jones</u>, a child was injured by his father's negligence. The court decided that children are able to sue for parental negligence. [Verb tense]

6. Even though a criminal defendant may engage in plea bargaining, they still may receive a different sentence from the judge.
Even though criminal defendants may engage in plea bargaining, they still may receive a different sentence from the judge. [Noun/pronoun agreement]

7. The judge, denied the plaintiff's request, ordered a new trial and set the new trial date.
The judge denied the plaintiff's request, ordered a new trial, and set the new trial date. [No comma between subject and verb; use a serial comma.]

8. All paralegals, who are members of the local paralegal association, have access to the job bank information.
All paralegals who are members of the local paralegal association have access to the job bank information. [There should be no commas because the phrase contains essential information.]

9. He went over to Bob Browns house where he saw the Browns collection of stamps.
He went over to Bob Brown's house where he saw the Browns' collection of stamps. [Possessive]

10. The witness stated that "he ran away from the accident", and he testified that he was "scared".
The witness stated that "he ran away from the accident," and he testified that he was "scared." [Commas and periods to be included within quote marks.]

11. In <u>Black</u> the court held that only involuntary intoxication could be a defense to the formation of a contract. (First sentence in a paragraph.)
This sentence needs a lead in, for example: There are several defenses to the formation of a contract. For example, in <u>Black</u> the court held that only involuntary intoxication could be a defense to the formation of a contract.

12. It is interesting to note that notwithstanding the fact that the defendant was found guilty, at that point in time clearly the defendant still felt his attorney had done a good job of defending him.
Although the defendant was found guilty, at that point in time clearly the defendant still felt his attorney had done a good job of defending him. [Excessive verbiage.]

13. The decision by the jury to convict the defendant surprised no one.
The jury's decision to convict the defendant surprised no one. [Passive voice.]

14. In <u>Jones v. Warner</u> the court felt that only those who were involuntarily intoxicated could be excused from their contractual obligations.
In <u>Jones v. Warner</u> the court stated (or thought, etc.) that only those who were involuntarily intoxicated could be excused from their contractual obligations. [Do not use words that suggest emotion regarding a court's statements.]

15. Said court also stated that two beers wouldn't be sufficient to prove intoxication.
The court also stated that two beers would not be sufficient to prove intoxication. [Do not use legalese; do not use contractions.]

16. Will the court in our case say that four beers are sufficient to prove intoxication? Would six be enough? What of two whiskeys?
The issue is how many beers the court will require to find intoxication. [Do not ask your reader questions.]

17. There are 5 cases that deal with intoxication.
There are five cases that deal with intoxication. [Write out numbers under one hundred.]

18. Defendant driving car after drinking five beers was found to be intoxicated.
The police determined that the defendant who was driving his car after drinking five beers was intoxicated. [Do not use the "headnote" method of writing. Include all necessary articles.]

19. The plaintiff can bring suit for negligence against the city for injuries he sustained in the accident. Even though his contributory negligence may bar him from recovery.
The plaintiff can bring suit for negligence against the city for injuries he sustained in the accident, even though his contributory negligence may bar him from recovery. [Sentence fragment.]

20. The woman was frightened by a man she described as seedy, it was only after she struck him with a rock that she discovered he was an undercover police officer.
The woman was frightened by a man she described as seedy. It was only after she struck him with a rock that she discovered he was an undercover police officer. [Run-on.]

21. During an autopsy, looking for the cause of death, the deceased is examined by the pathologist.
During an autopsy, looking for the cause of death, the pathologist examined the deceased. [Misplaced modifier; passive voice.]

22. The new computer system offers four advantages for our firm:
    1) it includes 15 software packages
    2) the warranty extends to 160 days
    3) provides a full-scale training program
    4) state-of-the art features are included.

The new computer system offers four advantages for our firm:
    1) 15 software packages;
    2) a 160 day warranty;
    3) a full-scale training program; and
    4) state-of-the art features.

[Lack of parallel construction.]

23. The enclosed forms should be completed by you no later than August 15.
You should complete the enclosed forms no later than August 15. [Passive voice.]

24. The depositions proved to be very revealing, however, our client has decided to settle.
The depositions proved to be very revealing. However, our client has decided to settle. [Run-on.]

25. <u>Dillon</u> holds that under certain circumstances a bystander may recover for emotional distress.
The court in <u>Dillon</u> held that under certain circumstances a bystander may recover for emotional distress. [Make the court and not the opinion the subject; use past tense for actions that occurred in the past.]

200

Appendix C

The Basics of Citation Form

The rules on citation form are bound to change rapidly as soon as electronic research becomes as common as book-based research. While many have argued that such an event will never happen, it is rapidly becoming a reality. Also, be sure to alert your students if your state courts alter any of the Bluebook rules.

REVIEW QUESTIONS, pages 658-59

Give the correct citation for each of the following.

1. A 1988 Massachusetts Supreme Court decision. The appellant was James Bennett; the appellee was William Buckley. The opinion begins on page 55 of volume 108 of North Eastern Reporter Second, and on page 119 of volume 329 of the Massachusetts Reports.
Bennet v. Buckley, 329 Mass. 119, 108 N.E.2d 55 (1988).

2. A 1993 Illinois Supreme Court decision. The appellants were Sally Field and James Connor; the appellee was the Fine Gun Shooting Gallery, Company, Inc. The opinion begins on page 999 of volume 109 of North Eastern Reporter Second, and on page 40 of volume 232 of Illinois Reports. You want to direct the reader to a specific page within the opinion, that is page 1001 in North Eastern Reporter Second and page 43 in the Illinois Reports.
Field v. Fine Gun Shooting Gallery, Co., 232 Ill. 40, 43, 109 N.E.2d 999, 1001 (1993).

3. A 1989 Massachusetts Appeals Court decision. The appellant was Matthew Brown; the appellee was Christine White. The opinion begins on page 225 of volume 555 of the Massachusetts Appeals Court Reports and page 1019 of volume 446 of North Eastern Reporter Second.
Brown v. White, 555 Mass. App. Ct. 225, 446 N.E.2d 1019 (1989).

4. A 1980 Massachusetts federal District Court decision. The appellant was Janet Smith; the appellee was Judy Green. The opinion begins on page 448 of volume 509 of the Federal Supplement.
Smith v. Green, 509 F. Supp. 448 (D. Mass. 1980).

5. A 1979 First Circuit decision. The appellant was Frank Pierce; the appellee was Grant Coleman. The opinion begins on page 1058 of volume 559 of the Federal Reporter Second. **Price v. Coleman, 559 F.2d 1058 (1st Cir. 1979).**

6. A 1960 United States Supreme Court decision. The petitioner was Shirley Temple; the respondent was Sylvia Porter. The opinion begins on page 45 of volume 354 of the United States Reports, on page 558 of volume 997 of the Supreme Court Reporter, and on page 68 of volume 199 of the United States Supreme Court Reports. **Temple v. Porter, 354 U.S. 45 (1960).**

7. A 1988 Minnesota Supreme Court decision. The appellant was Robert Recht; the appellee was Louise Wrong. The opinion begins on page 787 of volume 556 of the Northwestern Reporter Second. Minnesota stopped publishing its official reports in 1977. **Recht v. Wrong, 556 N.W.2d 787 (Minn. 1988).**

Please give the correct citation for each of the following. Use the information contained in this Appendix and especially the examples for Massachusetts state statutory and regulatory citations as found on page 762.

8. The 1973 Massachusetts statute on comparative negligence. You have located it in the Lexis Law Publishing's Massachusetts Annotated Laws hardbound volume. The copyright date on the inside page of that hardbound volume is 2001. The statute is chapter 231, section 85 of the Massachusetts General Laws. **Mass. Ann. Laws ch. 231, § 85 (Lexis Law Pub. 2001).**

9. The 1963 Massachusetts statute on spousal immunity. It is chapter 209, section 6 of the Massachusetts General Laws. You have located it in the 2005 pocket part of volume 34 of the West Massachusetts General Laws Annotated, beginning on page 174. **Mass. Gen. Laws Ann. ch. 209, § 6 (West Supp. 2005).**

10. A 1964 federal statute. It is section 108 found in title 29. You have located it in volume 42 of the United States Code Annotated. The copyright date on the inside page of that hardbound volume is 2004. **29 U.S.C.A. § 108 (West 2004).**

11. A federal regulation that you found in the 2005 edition of the Code of Federal Regulations. It is title 47, section 73.609. **47 C.F.R. § 73.609 (2005).**

12. A Massachusetts regulation. It is title 603, section 7.00. In Massachusetts the regulations are published in a looseleaf binder. As changes are made to the regulations new pages replace older ones. At the bottom of the pages you can see the effective date of the new provision: 12/31/00. **Mass. Regs. Code tit. 603, § 7.00 (2000).**

13. The federal constitution, article two, section two.
U.S. Const. art. II, § 2.

14. Assume you have cited to <u>Smith v. Brown</u>, 99 Mass. 432, 301 N.E.2d 404 (1983). You have cited no other authority. You want to cite to the opinion as a whole again. What would be the easiest way to do that?
<u>Id.</u>

15. Assume you next cite to an Illinois court decision. You now want to cite to the Massachusetts court decision in question number 14 again, but now referring specifically to material located on page 435 in the Massachusetts Reports and page 406 in North Eastern Reporter Second. What would be the easiest way to do that?
<u>Smith</u>, 99 Mass. at 435, 301 N.E.2d at 406.

Appendix D

Finding the Law

The best approach to legal research is to talk as little as possible and to have the students do as much actual researching as possible. Therefore, I suggest you have the students read this appendix before going to the library. Tell them there is no need to memorize the information. The purpose is simply to give them an overview now and a reference for later. In class, you may want to spend just a short amount of time going over the example pages. Although these examples are all based on Massachusetts law, the approach described can be applied to any state as well as to federal research. To broaden the range of examples, however, you might also want to use the *Sample Pages* published by West.

Legal Reasoning Exercise, page 673

1. Read the first full paragraph of Exhibit D-8 carefully. Given what the court said about negligence actions in *Lewis*, do you agree with the analysis, which states that "spouses are not permitted to maintain actions for personal torts against each other such as assault." Do you think that if the court no longer thinks spousal immunity is a bar in negligence cases, it would keep it as a bar when one spouse intentionally hurts the other?

The purpose of this exercise is to reinforce for students that secondary authority is only some other person's idea of what the law is. It is not the law. Here is a graphic example of where the writer may be technically correct — that is, the Massachusetts Supreme Judicial court may not have held that spouses can sue based on intentional torts. But that is more likely because it has not yet been faced with that case, rather than because it would not hold that there was such a right if asked to do so.

 Teaching Tip

Even if you do not have access to Lexis or Westlaw, you can give your students a solid grounding in the basics of Boolean logic and proximity searching using various Internet sources, such as FindLaw. I have found that having students develop terms and connectors searches is one of the best ways to teach them how to focus on the precise legal issue that is raised by a specific fact pattern.

Legal Reasoning Exercise, page 714

2. Assume you work for a law firm in Pennsylvania. One of your firm's clients, Melba Street, had a pet poodle, Suzie, whom she dearly loved. She left the poodle one weekend at the local kennel. On Saturday, a new kennel worker accidentally let Suzie loose in the fenced in yard with Butch, a vicious German Shepard. Unfortunately, that was the end of Suzie. Melba would like to sue the kennel for the emotional distress she suffered in having her pet killed.

a. What terms and connectors search would you construct to try and find cases that would answer whether she can recover for her emotional distress?
Students are tempted to use very specific factual terms, such as "kennel" and "poodle." If they do, they will retrieve no cases. They should be encouraged to think about the underlying legal issue - Melba suffered emotional distress because her pet died. Based on that legal issue, they might construct a search similar to the following.

> **mental or emotional w/3 anguish or distress or suffering w/10 dog or cat or pet w/10 destr! or kill or harm or hurt**

b. What natural language search would you construct?
Can a woman sue a kennel for "emotional distress" she suffered in having her pet killed?

REVIEW QUESTIONS, pages 716-18

1. What is your main goal when conducting legal research?
The main goal is to find primary authority.

2. In what type of books can you read general background information on a particular legal topic?
You read general background information in secondary authority, for example, encyclopedias.

3. What is the difference between primary and secondary authority?
Primary authority is the law — constitutions, statutes, court opinions, and regulations. Secondary authority is source information about the law.

4. What are TAPP and TARP, and how do they aid a legal researcher?
TAPP and TARP are acronyms developed to help the researcher think of words that might be located in an index. TAPP stands for *Thing, Acts, Person,* or *Place.* TARP stands for *Thing, Cause of Action, Relief, Parties.*

5. What are the two major legal encyclopedias? In what ways are they the same and how do they differ?
The two major legal encyclopedias are Am. Jur. 2d and C.J.S. They both give a general description of the law with footnote references to primary authority, principally cases.

Am. Jur. 2d tends to include more text and fewer footnote references. C.J.S. claims to be more inclusive in its coverage.

6. Why should you never end your research with an encyclopedia?
You should never end your research with an encyclopedia because they are too general, they are not updated frequently enough, they just represent their editor's opinions, and they are not the law itself.

7. What is a law review and what type of articles does it contain?
A law review is published by law school students. The articles are either scholarly pieces by well-known authorities or shorter student notes.

8. How do you locate relevant law review articles?
By using the Index to Legal Periodicals. (Also Westlaw and Lexis.)

9. How dos A.L.R. differ from an encyclopedia?
A.L.R. contains more detail on a few selected topics.

10. Why do you think the general rule is that it is O.K. to cite to a law review article, but not to an encyclopedia?
Law review articles not only describe but also analyze the law. An encyclopedia only describes the law.

11. When researching primary authority, should you generally begin your research with statutes or court opinions? Why?
You should generally begin your research with statutes, because if there is one, the courts have to follow it.

12. What makes an annotated statutory code "annotated"?
Annotated refers to editorial features.

13. How are digest summaries and headnotes similar? What is the function of each?
Textually digest summaries and headnotes are identical. Functionally, headnotes help to summarize a case and point the reader to where specific information is located in the case. They will also tell the researcher where to go in the digest to read more cases on the same topic. Digest summaries organize all cases on a single point by topic.

14. Assume you are researching the topic of whether minors can get out of their contractual obligations and that you have found a New Hampshire case directly on point. That case's third headnote lists the topic as Contracts 211. How would you go about locating a Kansas case dealing with that same issue?
Go directly to the Kansas Digest and look up the topic Contracts, key number 211. Because West uses the same topic and key number system in all fifty states, once you have found one case, you can find cases digested under the same topic in other states by looking in that state's digest.

15. What is the difference between saying a case has been reversed versus overruled?
Reversed means the same litigants have a retrial. Overruled means a later case changes the law.

16. When using the digest topic method, what steps do you need to take to make sure your research is up to date?
[See Figure D-5, page 671.]

17. What are the three main reasons for using Shepard's?
The three main reasons for using Shepard's are as a source of parallel citations, to find subsequent history, and to find treatment.

18. In Shepard's, what is subsequent history and what is the treatment of a case?
Subsequent history is what happened later to the same litigants. Treatment is how later cases treated the issues of law raised in your cited case.

19. In Shepard's, to what do the terms *citing case* and *cited case* refer?
Cited case is the case you are Shepardizing. Citing case is a case listed in Shepard's that cites your case.

20. Your boss has asked you to Shepardize 89 N.E. 542.
    a. What is your first step? What do you do next?
    b. In Shepardizing you found the following information. What does it mean? Is there any history of the case? How do you know?

-542-
(203Mas364)
f90NE^{2}864
94NE^{1}691
129NE718

First find the appropriate Shepard's including all updates. Then locate the correct volume and page number. The first reference in parenthesis is to the parallel cite. There is no history, because history always starts with a letter and is always first. The first cite starts with an "f" for followed, a treatment abbreviation. The first case has cited your case for the proposition found in headnote 2. The second case has cited your case for the proposition found in headnote 1. The third case's treatment of your case was too general for Shepard's to assign a specific headnote number to it.

21. Your boss has asked you to Shepardize a case giving you only the official citation. Describe the steps you would take to Shepardize the case.
First find the appropriate Shepard's including all updates. Be sure you are in the part of Shepard's that contains the official citations. Then locate the correct volume and page number.

22. Your boss knows of a California case, *Tarasoff v. The Regents of the University of California*, 551 P.2d 334 (Calif. 1976), that stands for the proposition that if a psychiatrist knows a patient is a threat to another person, the psychiatrist must warn that person. If you want to find out if any New York cases have followed the *Tarasoff* decision, which Shepard's would you use and why? (Note: California is in the Pacific region, and New York is in the Northeast region.)
You would use the Pacific Shepard's because you always start with the Shepard's that is from the region of your case, not of the case you want to find. You use a regional Shepard's because it contains cites to your case from around the country (not just from that region).

23. Last month the police saw your client Bill Black exchange money for a packet of white powder. Without a warrant the police placed an electronic tracking device on your client's car. The police then followed him to an alley where he handed the packet to a woman who gave him money in return. They arrested your client for selling illegal drugs. Your boss would like to make a motion to have the evidence excluded by arguing that it was unlawful for the police to put the electronic tracking device on your client's car without a warrant.
Assume that in the course of your research you have found *Commonwealth v. Boven*, 413 Mass. 755, 306 N.E.2d 222 (1986). The headnotes in the NorthEastern Reporter, Second Series, appear as follows:

1. Searches and Seizures [Key] 7(26)
Defendant did not have standing to challenge X-ray search of suitcase, where the suitcase belonged to his co-defendant.

2. Searches and Seizures [Key] 7(10)
Utilization of electronic tracking device, without prior court approval, may be justified by probable cause and exigent circumstances.

3. Criminal Law [Key] 1144.13
On appeal from jury conviction, Court must view evidence, both direct and circumstantial, and all reasonable inferences to be drawn therefrom.

4. Criminal Law [Key] 696(1)
Trial court did not err in failing to grant defense motion to strike testimony of agent, although all of agent's investigatory notes had been destroyed.

Using the information *from the headnotes*, describe how you would go about finding out if there are any other court opinions in Massachusetts dealing with the subject of when agents can place electronic surveillance devices on cars without first obtaining a warrant. Describe the steps you would take in as much detail as possible. Include a description of how you would bring your research up to date, using both the digest and the Shepard's approaches.
First you could use the topic method and rely on the topic criminal law, searches & seizures 7(10). You would start with the digest, including the pocket part. Then you would check the closing table in the digest pocket part to see the number of the last

208

volume of the regional report included within the digest. Finally, you would check all of the reporters and advance sheets that have been published since the digest pocket part. Second, you would Shepardize the case, paying particular attention to cases that dealt with headnote number 2.

24. In updating your research what is the advantage of using the digest method over Shepardizing? In using Shepard's over the digests?

By using the digests, you can find cases that are on the same topic but that do not cite your case. By using Shepard's you can find cases in which the court cited your case but that West has not digested under the topic you have been researching. Therefore, while you will usually find the same cases using both methods, there will be times when one method will give you a case that the other method will not.

25. Your boss asks you to Shepardize *Brown v. Smith*, 322 Mass. 89, 78 N.E.2d 640 (1946). You determine that headnotes 4 and 8 are most relevant to your client's problem. In Shepard's you find the following information.

-640-

99 N.E.2d^3 888

99 N.E.2d 904

q101 N.E.2d 44

102 N.E.2d^8 99

102 N.E.2d^1 301

Explain which citations you would look up, in what order, and why.

You would first look up 101 N.E.2d 44 because it has a "q" for questioned in front of it. This means the case may no longer be good law. Then you would look up 102 N.E.2d^8 99 as it related to one of your headnotes. Finally, you would look up 99 N.E.2d 904 because there is no headnote reference so you cannot tell if it might be relevant or not.

26. How does the use of on-line research differ from traditional book research?

On-line research is based on doing full-text searches of the actual court opinion or statutes, as opposed to using an index or digest system. It can be faster, it is more current, and it gives you access to a wider range of information. It can also be more costly. Finally, it allows you to do searches, for example by deciding judge, that you could not do otherwise.

27. What are the two main methods for conducting full-text research in an on-line database, and how do those two methods differ from each other?

The two methods are 1) terms and connectors and 2) natural language. In terms and connectors you must think of specific terms that would describe the legal issue. It is important to include synonyms and proximity connectors. Every term or its synonym must be included within the documents that are retrieved. In natural language searching you simply type your request in normal English. This may result in a large number of "hits" as it is not mandatory that any of the terms be included in the documents found. However, the most relevant documents will be at the top of the list.

28. You need to find cases dealing with free speech, and using the terms and connectors method, you type in the following search: free speech. How do you think Westlaw and Lexis would differ in the ways they would interpret that search request?

Lexis would look for the phrase "free speech." Westlaw would look for documents that contain either the word "free" or the word "speech."

29. Your boss represents a client who was injured when his Handy Hardy riding tractor tipped over. You searched through the on-line sources that contained primary authority but did not find any appellate decisions involving the Handy Hardy riding tractor. In what other types of on-line databases might you want to search and why?

You would want to check news sources to see if the Handy Hardy company had been sued in the past and perhaps settled the claims. You might also want to search for experts and look for jury verdicts in similar cases. Remind your students that very few cases reach the appellate level. That does not mean that similar cases have not been filed in the past.

Appendix D

NetNotes

Your students will find NetNotes throughout the text. To act as an easy reference, they are also included here in Appendix D. You may want to warn your students that they should not be surprised if they do not all work. The web is a dynamic place and while we double-checked all of these links at the time of publication, some of them could easily have changed by the time the students try to access themselves.

Sample Syllabi
and Assignments

As mentioned at the beginning of this manual, if you want your students to have the time to really develop their critical thinking skills, this course is best taught over two semesters. In this section, I first include sample syllabi based on a two semester model with classes meeting twice a week. This is followed by a sample syllabus based on a one semester model with classes meeting once a week for 15 weeks. Finally, I have included the assignments that I use in my two semester course.

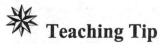 **Teaching Tip**

The following are the syllabi for a two semester course, meeting twice a week.

SYLLABUS — Semester I

Required Text: *The Study of Law: A Critical Thinking Approach*
Recommended: Any law dictionary

- All readings, review, and discussion questions are to be done PRIOR to the class indicated.
- Hand in all assignments on the day indicated.

TUESDAY	THURSDAY
	#1 Introduction to the Course
#4 Introduction to Legal Reasoning **Ch. 1, Intro. to the Study of Law** Prepare for class discussion Legal Reasoning Exercise.	#3 Constitutional, Statutory, and Common Law **Ch. 2, Functions and Sources of Law; Appendix A, Excerpts from the U.S. Constitution**

TUESDAY	THURSDAY
#5 How Lawyers Classify Law Ch. 3, **Classification of the Law** Assign. #1 - Report on News Article (P/F)	**#6 Understanding the Courts** Ch. 4, **Structure of the Court System**
#7 Civil Litigation - Pre-Trial Ch. 5, **Litigation and Its Alternatives** Read App. B - Fundamentals of Good Writing and then do Assign. #2, REVIEW QUESTIONS, 1-25 (P/F)	**#8 Civil Litigation - The Trial** Ch. 5, **Litigation and Its Alternatives**
#9 Statutory Interpretation Ch. 6, **Finding and Interpreting Statutory Law** Prepare for class discussion Legal Reasoning Exercises 1-5.	**#10 Statutory Interpretation** Assign. #3 - IRAC Analysis A, Legal Reasoning Exercise 8 (P/F)
#11 Case Analysis Ch. 7, **Finding and Interpreting Court Opinions** **Assign. #4 - IRAC Analysis B (Graded)**	**#12 Power of Judicial Review** Ch. 7, **Finding and Interpreting Court Opinions** Assign. #5 - Brief of *Johnson* (P/F)
#13 Citation Form App. C - **Citation Form** Assign. #6 - App. C REVIEW QUESTIONS 1-15 (P/F)	**#14 MIDTERM EXAM**
#15 Applying Established Law Ch. 7, **Finding and Interpreting Court Opinions** Prepare for class discussion Legal Reasoning Exercise 1. **Assign. #7 - Brief of *Keller* (P/F)**	**#16 Creating New Law** Ch. 7, **Finding and Interpreting Court Opinions,** **Prepare for class discussion Legal Reasoning Exercise 2.** Assign. #8 - Brief of *Callow* (P/F)

TUESDAY	THURSDAY
#17 Case Analysis 　Ch. 7, Finding and Interpreting Court 　Opinions Legal Research 　App. D, Finding the Law **MEET IN LIBRARY** Assign. #9, Report on Courtroom Visits Due (P/F)	#18 Legal Research **MEET IN LIBRARY** Assign. #10 - Brief of *Lewis* (Graded)
#19 Legal Research **MEET IN LIBRARY** Assign. #11, Research A (P/F)	#20 Legal Analysis 　Ch. 8, Applying the Law
#21 Holiday - No Class	#22 Updating Your Research **MEET IN LIBRARY** 　App. D, Finding the Law, updating Assign. #12, Legal Research B (Graded)
#23 Discuss Courtroom Visits Review Shepardizing Assign. #13 , Legal Analysis A (P/F)	#24 Legal Research **MEET IN LIBRARY** Assign. #14, Legal Research C (Graded)
#25 Review of Researching Strategy Assign. #15, Research D (Graded)	#26 Holiday - No Class
#27 View "This Honorable Court" Assign. #16, Brief From Research D Due (Graded)	#28 Review Legal Analysis
#29 Individual meetings	#30 Review for Final Exam Assign. #17, Legal Analysis B (Graded)
#31 FINAL EXAM	

Your grade in this course will be based on your work throughout the semester. Some assignments will be graded on a pass/fail basis. In order to pass the course, you must pass each of those assignments. The other assignments will be graded numerically.

Assignment #1 -	Legal News Report	P/F
Assignment #2 -	Grammar Review Questions	P/F
Assignment #3 -	IRAC Analysis A	P/F
Assignment #4 -	IRAC Analysis B	5 pts
Assignment #5 -	Brief of Johnson	P/F
MIDTERM		20 pts
Assignment #6 -	Citation Review Questions	P/F
Assignment #7 -	Brief of Keller	P/F
Assignment #8 -	Brief of Callow	P/F
Assignment #9 -	Report on Courtroom Visit	P/F
Assignment #10 -	Brief of Lewis	5 pts
Assignment #11 -	Library Exercise A	P/F
Assignment #12 -	Library Exercise B	5 pts
Assignment #13 -	Legal Analysis A	P/F
Assignment #14 -	Library Exercise C	5 pts
Assignment #15 -	Library Exercise D	10 pts
Assignment #16 -	Brief	5 pts
Assignment #17 -	Legal Analysis B	15 pts
FINAL EXAM		30 pts

TOTAL POSSIBLE POINTS   100 pts

REWRITE POLICY:

1) If you do not pass a pass/fail assignment, I will ask you to rewrite all or part of the assignment. When you have completed your rewrite, please turn it in along with your original graded pass/fail assignment.

2) At your option, you may rewrite any graded assignment other than the researching assignments, the midterm, and the final. Turn in the rewrite with the original graded assignment. I will award you the difference between your original grade and the rewrite. I do not grade on a curve. Therefore, please, do not feel compelled to do rewrites. View this policy as a safety net for those few occasions when you find that you have somehow really missed the mark and you want a second chance.

REQUIREMENTS FOR WRITTEN ASSIGNMENTS:
1)   All papers must be either typed or word processed.
2)   Single space case briefs. Double space all other written work.
3)   Leave margins at the top, bottom, and both sides of your paper that are between one and one and a half inches wide.
4)   Number all pages of your paper after page one.

5) Staple the pages of your paper in the top left corner. Do not use paper clips, folders, or binders.

6) Follow basic English grammar rules. Doing any of the following will give your writing an unprofessional appearance. It will also cause you to lose points.
   a) Using sentence fragments and run-ons.
   b) Using contractions.
   c) Using first person.
   d) Using slang. Be particularly careful to distinguish between how things sound versus how they are written. It may sound like "would of," "could of," etc., but it is would <u>have</u>, could <u>have</u>, etc.
   e) Misusing its and it's.
   f) Asking questions of your reader.

7) If a particular court or statutory rule is in question, quote it. Otherwise, use quotations sparingly. Generally, it is better to paraphrase. If you do quote, use quotation marks around quoted material. The failure to do so is plagiarism.

8) Proofread your paper before you turn it in. If you find errors and do not have time to retype or reprint a corrected copy, make the corrections neatly in ink.

NOTE ON STUDY TECHNIQUES:

Learning about the law is a lot like learning a foreign language. Initially you may feel overwhelmed by the terminology and amount of material that you are expected to cover. Unfortunately, much of legal writing, such as court opinions, is written for attorneys and not for students. Therefore, the writers presuppose a knowledge of the law that you, of course, do not have. With persistence, however, you will find that studying will become progressively easier as the semester proceeds. In the meantime, I suggest the following:

1) Plan on reading everything at LEAST twice. The first time through do not be too concerned with understanding every detail. Rather, try to gain an overview of the material. The second time through be more meticulous. Take notes, circle or highlight especially important points, and bring your questions with you to class.

2) Do not plan on doing all of an assignment at one sitting. Also, do not put off beginning an assignment to the night before it is due.

3) If there are too many distractions at home, do your studying elsewhere.

4) Buy and use a legal dictionary.

SYLLABUS -- SEMESTER II

Required Text: *The Study of Law: A Critical Thinking Approach*
  - All readings, review, and discussion questions are to be done PRIOR to the class indicated.
  - Hand in all assignments at the beginning of the class indicated.

Tuesday	Thursday
	#1 Introduction to the Course and to Ethical Issues
#2 Ethical Dilemmas The Adversarial System; Confidentiality Read ch. 9, pages 241-62.	**#3** Legal Ethics Confidentiality; Client Perjury; Inadvertent Disclosure Hand in Assign. #1, Discussion Questions 6 and 7, (P/F). Read ch. 9, pages 263-74.
#4 Legal Ethics Conflict of Interest Read ch. 9, pages 275-81.	**#5** Legal Ethics Access to Justice Read ch. 9, pages 282-92.
#6 Intentional Torts Assault and Battery False Imprisonment Read ch. 10, pages 295-307.	**#7** Intentional Torts Defamation Invasion of Privacy Infliction of Emotional Distress Harm to a Person's Property Hand in Assign. #2, Legal Reasoning (Graded). Read ch. 10, pages 307-15.

Tuesday	Thursday

#8   Negligence
    Duty
    Breach
 	
Hand in Assign. #3, Brief of *Woods* (Graded)
 	
Read ch. 10, pages 316-24.
	#9 Negligence
	    Cause
	    Duty of Care to Third Parties
	    Harm
	
	Read ch. 10, pages 325-34.

#10   Negligence
    Defenses
    Immunities
 	
Hand in Assign. #4, Brief of *Greaves* (Graded).
 	
Read ch. 10, pages 334-40.
	#11 Strict Liability
	    Ultrahazardous Activities
	    Products Liability
	New Torts
	    Wrongful Life or Birth
	    Battered Woman's Syndrome
	    Drug Dealer Liability Act
	
	Hand in Assign. #5, Legal Reasoning (Graded).
	
	Read ch. 10, pages 340-55.

#12   Contract Law
    The Uniform Commercial Code
    Types of Contracts
    Offer
    Acceptance
    Quasi-Contract
 	
Read ch. 11, pages 357-72.
	#13 Contract Law
	    Consideration
	    Promissory Estoppel
	    Defenses/Lack of Contractual
	Capacity
	    Minors
	    Intoxication
	    Mental Incompetence
	
	Read ch. 11, pages 372-88.

Tuesday	Thursday

#14 Contract Law
Defenses
    Illegal Contracts
    Contracts that Violate Public Policy
    Lack of Genuiness of Assent
    Breach of Warranty
Termination
Third Party Rights
Damages
Drafting and Reviewing Contracts
 	
Hand in Assign. #6, Legal Research/Contract Law (P/F).
 	
Read ch. 13, pages 388-401
	#15 *MIDTERM EXAM*

#16 Property Law
    Ownership of Real Property
    Rental of Real Property
    Transfer of Real Property
 	
Hand in Assign. # 7, Legal Reasoning (P/F).
 	
Read ch. 12, pages 407-21.
	#17 Estate Law
	    Wills
	    Living Wills
	    Trusts
	    Probate Process
	    Intestate Succession
	
	Read ch. 12, pages 421-31.

#18 Laws Affecting Business
    Four Business Forms
      Sole Proprietorship
      Partnership
      Corporation
      Limited Liability Company
    Commercial Paper
    Secured Transactions
    Agency Law
    Respondeat Superior
 	
Read ch. 13, pages 431-54
	#19 Laws Affecting Business
	    Title VII
	    Overt Discrimination and BFOQ
	    Intentional Discrimination
	
	Read ch. 13, pages 454-65.

Tuesday	Thursday
#20 Laws Affecting Business Disparate Impact Sexual Harassment ADEA ADA At-Will Employment **Hand in Assign. #8, Legal Reasoning (Graded).** Read ch. 13, pages 465-80.	**#21 Family Law** Marriage Premarital Agreements Annulment Divorce Procedures Read ch. 14, pages 480-501.
#22 Family Law Property Settlements Alimony Custody, Visitation, and Child Support Read ch. 14, pages 502-14.	**#23 Family Law** Paternity Actions Adoption Surrogacy Child Neglect and Abuse Read ch. 14, pages 514-29
#24 Criminal Law The Criminal Justice System Classifications of Crime Elements of Crimes Specific versus General Intent Parties to the Crime **Hand in Assign. #9, Legal Research/Employment and Criminal Law (Graded).** Read ch. 15, pages 531-49	**#25 Criminal Law** Defenses including Insanity and Self-defense Read ch. 15, pages 549-62.
#26 Criminal Procedure Stop and Frisk Arrest Searches and Seizures Questioning Suspects **Hand in Assign. #10, Legal Reasoning (Graded).** Read ch. 15, pages 562-78	**#27 Criminal Procedure** The Court System The Exclusionary Rule Motion Practice Read ch. 15, pages 578-94.

Tuesday	Thursday
#28 FINAL EXAM	

GRADING POLICY: There are 10 assignments for this class. You must pass the pass/fail assignments to pass the course. If for some reason, you cannot pass a pass/fail assignment, 2 points will be deducted from your final course grade. You may redo any assignment, other than the researching assignments, once. For graded assignments, your grade will be the average of the original grade and the grade on the redone assignment.

Assignments:

#1	Legal Ethics Discussion Questions	P/F
#2	Legal Ethics Reasoning Assignment	5%
#3	Brief of *Woods*	5%
#4	Brief of *Greaves*	5%
#5	Legal Reasoning Exercise	10%
	MIDTERM	20%
#6	Researching Exercise in Contracts	P/F
#7	Legal Drafting Exercise (Contracts)	P/F
#8	Legal Reasoning Exercise	5%
#9	Research in Employment/Criminal Law	5%
#10	Legal Reasoning Exercise (IRAC)	10%
	FINAL	35%
	Total	100%

✻ Teaching Tip

The following is a sample syllabus based on a one semester model with classes meeting once a week for 15 weeks. Note that it would be very difficult to cover all fifteen chapters in one semester. You may want to skip one or more of the substantive law chapters, while devoting more than one week to the analytical chapters, as suggested below.

Syllabus for the Study of Law

Week 1   Introduction to Legal Reasoning and Critical Thinking
        Ch. 1, Intro. to the Study of Law

Week 2   Constitutional, Statutory, and Common Law
        Ch. 2, Functions and Sources of Law
        Appendix A, Excerpts from the U.S. Constitution

Week 3   How Lawyers Classify Law
        Ch. 3, Classification of the Law
    Understanding the Courts
        Ch. 4, Structure of the Court System

Week 4   Civil Litigation
        Ch. 5, The Litigation Process and Its Alternatives

Week 5   Statutory Interpretation
        Ch. 6, Finding and Interpreting Statutory Law
    Fundamentals of Good Writing
        Appendix B

Week 6   Case Analysis
        Ch. 7, Finding and Interpreting Court Opinions
    Citation Form
        Appendix C

Week 7   Case Analysis
        Ch. 7, Finding and Interpreting Court Opinions

Week 8   Legal Analysis
        Ch. 8, Applying the Law
    Midterm

Week 9   Ethical Dilemmas
        Ch. 9, Ethical Dilemmas Facing Attorneys

Week 10 Tort Law
> **Ch. 10, Torts**

Week 11 Contract Law
> **Ch. 11, Contract Law**

Week 12 Business Forms and Employment Law
> **Ch. 13, Laws Affection Business**

Week 13 Family Law: Same Sex Marriages, Divorce, Custody
> **Ch. 14, Family Law**

Week 14 Criminal Law
> **Ch. 15, Criminal Law and Procedure**

Week 15 Final Exam

 Teaching Tip

The following are the assignments that I use in the first semester based on the two semester course model. I have included grading sheets that I use for most of the graded assignments (as opposed to the pass/fail assignments). As you can see from the grading sheets, I believe very strongly that all grading should be made as objective as possible. I also think all assignments that result in something being handed in should be in writing. This eliminates any possibility that the students don't hear you correctly, a common occurrence if you give verbal instructions only.

ASSIGNMENT #1
LEGAL NEWS REPORT

Go to the library and locate current issues for each of the following: Legal Assistant Today, the ABA Journal, Lawyers Weekly USA, and the National Law Journal. Please scan through recent issues of each of these publications. Find an article that interests you and that describes one of the following:
1) a change in the practice of law as it effects paralegals (such as increased computerization of the courtrooms);
2) a developing trend in the law (such as the controversy over living wills);
3) a recent trial court opinion; or
4) a recent appellate court decision.

Then write a report. At the beginning of your report indicate the title, source, and date of the article. Next summarize the article. Finally, give your thoughts as to why the change or development is important. If you quote directly from the article, be sure to enclose the quoted material in quotation marks. Please attach a copy of the article to your report.

Bring your report to class and be prepared to discuss it with your classmates.

ASSIGNMENT #2
GRAMMAR REVIEW QUESTIONS

Appendix B, **Fundamentals of Good Writing**, contains a series of review questions. They are located on pages 628-29. Please correct each of the sentences **and** tell me what was wrong with the sentence as originally written. Please note: a sentence may have more than one grammatical or stylistic error. For example, the first sentence has the following problems: excess verbiage, passive voice, and lack of parallel construction.
[Instructor's note: See this Teacher's Manual, Appendix B, for answers to these questions.]

****
ASSIGNMENT #3
IRAC Analysis A

Prior to our next class meeting, please do the following:
1) Reread the factual scenario presented in Legal Reasoning Exercise 6 on page 145.
2) Using IRAC, write a one paragraph analysis for the issue you were assigned in class. Be sure to include both sides of the argument in your analysis and be sure to include your reasoning as to why one argument is better than the other. Conclude by letting me know which of the two arguments is the most compelling. Bring this one paragraph written analysis with you to class. NOTE: If you can, bring it to class on disk in WordPerfect or Word format.

In class, our task will be to review what each of you has written, to improve on it, and then to write a complete analysis, including a road map paragraph, an IRAC paragraph on each issue, and a concluding paragraph.

Sample Answer Based on Class Group Effort*

Carl has been charged with burglary which requires the satisfaction of five separate elements. Burglary requires a "breaking and entering of a dwelling at nighttime with the intent to commit a felony." This case presents four issues, the first being whether Carl was guilty of breaking into a motel room when the door was already open. The element of entering is not an issue. The second issue, whether a motel room qualifies as a dwelling, and the third, whether 5:00 P.M. is nighttime also have to be determined. The final issue involving the "intent to commit a felony" is unresolved, as the price of the T.V. was $600 new, whereas its resale value is $400 used. If the T.V. is determined to be used, the felony requirement of "over the value of $500" would not be satisfied.

The first issue is whether or not Carl was breaking into the motel room. The door had been left ajar by the occupant as she was temporarily leaving the room. Carl pushed open the door further as he entered the room but had not been given permission to do this. Carl did not use force to enter the room but he did violate the lady's privacy. Under a strict construction approach, as there was no damage, the court should not find that this constitutes a breaking. However, as the policy of the statute is to protect people, not

just their property, the entry need only be unlawful to constitute a breaking. This interpretation of breaking makes Carl guilty of "breaking" into the room.

The second issue is whether a motel room constitutes a dwelling. A motel room is not a permanent home in the usual sense. There is not the same expectation of privacy as maids and others are normally allowed entry into the room. However, paying for the temporary use of the facilities allows the occupant the privilege of residing within. Hence, in effect a motel room is a home away from home. Therefore in conclusion, a motel can constitute a home (albeit, a temporary one), so this element is also satisfied.

The third issue is if the attempted burglary was at night. The statute reads "nighttime." The attempted burglary took place at 5:00 P.M. This could be considered nighttime because people are arriving home from work at this time. However, during most of the year it is not yet dark by 5:00 P.M. and that is not the normal time for sleeping. Therefore, as it is less likely that people would be at home, made defenseless by dark or sleep, any justification for adding the extra penalty of burglary occurring at nighttime would not be met. Therefore, the element of the statute has not been met.

Finally, in order for Carl to be convicted of burglary, it must be shown that he intended to commit a felony. A separate statue requires that for a theft to be viewed as a felony, Carl had to commit "theft of personal property over the value of $500.00. . . ." While it is true that the T.V.'s were purchased for $600.00 and their purchase was recent, the facts are they are now considered used T.V.'s and have a resale value of only $400.00. The resale value should be used as that is their actual value. Because the statute states that "theft of personal property of a value less than $500.00 is a misdemeanor," Carl did not satisfy the necessary element of committing a felony. The resale value of the T.V. at $400.00 makes this offense a misdemeanor. As burglary requires the intent to commit a felony, that element of the statute is not met.

In conclusion, although the first two elements are satisfied — breaking into a dwelling, because the requirement that the burglary occur at night was not met and the value of the T.V. was not over $500, Carl cannot be found guilty of burglary.

*Note this is an actual answer that was developed by one of my classes while working together using an overhead projecting computer.

****
ASSIGNMENT #4
IRAC Analysis B

Your firm represents Irma Brown. She has been charged with burglary in the first degree. Briefly, the facts are as follows:

Irma used to work as a cleaning woman for the Smiths. The Smiths regularly provided Irma with a key for a door leading into their attached garage so that she could enter their house to clean it when they were not at home. Once when she had the key, she secretly took it to a local hardware store and had a duplicate key made. Last June she returned to school and quit her cleaning job.

Shortly after Irma quit her job, she decided it was time to give her lawn the first mowing of the season. Unfortunately, she could not get her old mower to start. She then remembered that the Smiths owned a beautiful new John Deere mower. She also remembered that they normally took a cruise in the Bahamas at that time of year. Thinking that they would be away and that they would not mind if she borrowed their mower, she got into her pick-up truck and drove over to their house, arriving around 7:00 p.m., shortly before sunset. She parked her truck in the driveway and used her duplicate key to let herself into the garage. She located the mower and loaded it into her truck. She went back into the garage to look for a gas can.

The Smiths were indeed away on vacation, but their eldest son, John, was home and had been in the house studying for his final exam in Business Law. On hearing Irma in the garage, John ran into the garage, yelled "Get out of here," and started towards Irma. Frightened, Irma grabbed the closest thing she could reach, a lightweight wooden garden rake. She waved it in front of her while she backed towards the garage door. John tripped over a coiled up garden hose, and Irma was able to get out of the garage and make it to her truck. She dropped the rake, jumped into the car, and drove away. Based on the description John gave the police, Irma was arrested the next day.

The following statutes govern this situation.

Ch. 100, sec. 1
Burglary is defined as the breaking and entering of a dwelling at nighttime with the intent to commit larceny therein.

Ch. 100, sec. 2
Burglary is a felony of the first degree if, in the course of committing burglary, the actor is armed with explosives or a deadly weapon. Otherwise, burglary is a felony of the second degree.

Ch. 120, sec. 8
Larceny is the taking and carrying away, with the intent to steal, the property of another.

Please write an analysis of whether or not you think Irma can be convicted of burglary in the first degree. Read these instructions before beginning to write your analysis.

1. Do not do any additional research. Rely only on the information I have given you. In real life, you would want to research other statutes as well as court opinions. For the purposes of this problem, however, confine your analysis to these three statutes.

2. Read the statutes very carefully. Based upon their language, do you see any ambiguous words or phrases? If so, think about how you could argue that the language of the statutes supports Irma. How might the prosecutor use that same language against Irma?

3. Think about the policy behind the statutes, i.e., why do you think the legislature enacted such statutes, and would that policy be served by convicting Irma of first degree burglary?

4. Write an outline. The outline can be very brief, and it does not have to conform to any formal outline style. Its purpose is simply to help you plan the order and substance of your answer and to remind you of what you want to say as you begin the process of writing your answer. Your outline can take the form of a series of single words or phrases or even of a flow chart, just so long as it does four things:

1) lists all of the issues;
2) lists facts that raise arguments on both sides of each issue;
3) lists arguments as to why you think particular facts are important; and
4) lists your points in a logical order.

5. Write your analysis of Irma's situation based on the language of those statutes, the policy behind the statutes, and the facts. In writing your analysis, follow this format:
  1) begin with a road map paragraph;
  2) follow that with an IRAC analysis of each issue; and
  3) end with a conclusion that wraps up your analysis of all of the issues.

Do NOT repeat the facts in a separate paragraph. In your roadmap paragraph you should include just enough of the facts to set the stage. Save the detailed facts for the analysis section of each of your IRAC paragraphs.

In the road map paragraph state the issues you will be discussing. In stating the issues remember that an issue consists of the rule and the specific facts that make the outcome problematical. In other words, be sure to tell me enough about the law and facts so that I will know why the issues are issues. For example, a mere listing of the statutes to be discussed would not tell me what issues are raised by those statutes and our particular facts.

When writing the paragraphs between your first and last paragraphs (the IRAC paragraphs), discuss each issue in a separate paragraph. In each paragraph you should do the following:

a)   deal with only <u>one major issue</u>;
b)   begin with a <u>topic sentence</u>;
c)   <u>quote</u> the relevant language of the rule;
d)   discuss the problem's <u>facts</u> relevant to that part of the rule;
e)   <u>analyze</u> whether or not you think the rule will apply to Irma's situation given the specific language of the rule and Irma's specific facts;
f)   <u>conclude</u> on that issue; and
g)   possibly include a <u>transition</u> to the next paragraph.

In your analysis of each issue be sure to raise any arguments that either your side or the state's prosecutor would make. Evaluate the strengths and weaknesses of each argument and conclude as to which is the better argument <u>on each issue.</u> If you think the answer on any issue is uncertain, say so, but be sure to explain why. Use the facts to show how those particular facts, when coupled with a rule of law, lead to a certain result. Be sure to include transitions to lead me easily from one issue to the next.

Discuss all of the possible issues. Do not write half an answer. Even if you think your conclusion as to your first issue definitively resolves Irma's case, do not stop there.

Assume you may be wrong and go on to discuss the other issues.

In your last paragraph give me your conclusion and brief reasoning as to why Irma most likely would or would not be convicted of first degree burglary. Therefore, as part of your conclusion include a summary of the logic that led to your conclusion.

6. Read and EDIT your answer for spelling and grammatical errors. Ask yourself--Do I know what I am trying to say; will the reader known what I am trying to say? If the answer is no or even maybe, figure out how to say it more clearly.

7. Please hand in your outline and your finished answer.

Answer Sheet
  Roadmap
   Issues   3
   Specific enough 2

Breaking		3
duplicate key=no breaking		2
but was unlawful		2
Dwelling		3
garage	2	
attached to house		2
Nighttime		3
hour prior to sunset		2
7:00	2	
Intent to commit larceny		3
intent was to borrow, not		
steal mower		2
did take it		2
Transition - If burglary, to be	3	
lst degree need		
Deadly weapon		3
Lightweight rake		2
Could poke him/waved at him		2

Conclusion	5	
Issue statements	4	4=always 3=usually
Gave conclusions as went along	4	2=rarely 0=never
Used transitions	4	
No major grammar errors	5	
Handed in Outline	10	

Total 75 + 25 for handing it in = 100

ASSIGNMENT #5
BRIEF OF <u>JOHNSON</u>

Please brief <u>Texas v. Johnson</u>. Follow the briefing format that we discussed in class: citation, facts, rule, issue, holding, reasoning, and criticism. Recall that the facts should include any fact that you think affected the court's decision as well as the main procedural facts. The rule should be the rule as it existed prior to this decision.

The issue statement should contain two main components: the rule (label plus definition) and specific facts. After reading the issue, the reader should know exactly why each side thought it had a chance of convincing the court that it should win.

The holding should be very specific so that your reader will know the limits that the court placed on its decision.

The reasoning section should be as complete as possible so that your reader can fully understand why the court decided as it did.

Finally, the criticism section should include a short accounting of what the dissent had to say. Your criticism section should also point out any logical failings or limitations that you found in the majority opinion's thinking. Make sure anyone reading your criticism section can tell when you are giving your own criticism versus when you are simply reporting on what the dissent had to say.

[Instructor's Note: See the earlier discussion regarding Chapter 7 in this manual for a sample copy of the *Johnson* brief.]

****
ASSIGNMENT #6
CITATION REVIEW QUESTIONS

Appendix C, **The Basics of Citation Form**, contains a series of review questions. They are located on pages 658-59. Please give the correct citations. Because spacing, punctuation, and capitalization are crucial, you must word process or type this assignment. **[Instructor's note: See this Teacher's Manual, Appendix C, for answers to these questions.]**

****
ASSIGNMENT #7
BRIEF OF <u>KELLER</u>

Please brief <u>Keller v. DeLong</u>. Follow the briefing format that we discussed in class: citation, facts, rule, issue, holding, reasoning, and criticism. Recall that the facts should include any fact that you think affected the court's decision as well as the main procedural facts. Be sure to include facts, not conclusions. For example, to say someone was driving 80 mph is to state a fact. To say someone was speeding is to give a conclusion. The rule should be the rule as it existed **prior** to this decision.

The issue statement should contain two main components: the rule (label plus definition) and specific facts. After reading the issue, the reader should know exactly why each side thought it had a chance of convincing the court that it should win. The holding should be very specific so that your reader will know the limits that the court placed on its decision. The reasoning section should be as complete as possible so that your reader can fully understand why the court decided as it did. Finally, your criticism section should point out any logical failings or limitations in the court's thinking.

[Instructor's Note: See the earlier discussion regarding Chapter 7 in this manual for a sample copy of the *Keller* brief.]

****

ASSIGNMENT #8
BRIEF OF <u>CALLOW</u>

Please brief <u>Callow v. Thomas</u>. Follow the briefing format that we discussed in class: citation, facts, rule, issue, holding, reasoning, and criticism. Recall that the facts should include any fact that you think affected the court's decision as well as the main procedural facts. However, remember that sometimes it is more important to make a chronology of events clear than it is to give every detail. The rule should be the rule as it existed prior to this decision.

The issue statement should contain two main components: the rule (label plus definition) and specific facts. After reading the issue, the reader should know exactly why each side thought it had a chance of convincing the court that it should win. The holding should be very specific so that your reader will know the limits that the court placed on its decision. The reasoning section should be as complete as possible so that your reader can fully understand why the court decided as it did. Finally, your criticism section should point out any logical failings or limitations in the court's thinking.

[Instructor's Note: See the earlier discussion regarding Chapter 7 in this manual for a sample copy of the *Callow* brief.]

****

ASSIGNMENT #9
COURTROOM VISIT

Please visit a courtroom while a trial is in session. Before going to court, or shortly after arriving, you should talk with either the civil or criminal clerk of court as to what trials are scheduled for that day. Also, do not be afraid to get up from one courtroom and visit another if nothing is happening where you are sitting.

There are no rules as to the visit other than that you should: 1) visit a minimum of two hours (need not all be on the same day) so that you can see at least part of one trial; 2) hand in a report on your visit; and 3) be prepared to report orally about your courtroom visit to the class.

In writing your report, please answer the following questions:

1. Which court did you visit?
2. Did you sit in on a criminal or civil matter?
3. Were you able to view a trial? If not, what did you sit in on?
4. What was the case about?
5. Describe the actors present, i.e., the judge, jury, attorneys, clients, court reporter, interpreter, social worker, etc.
6. What happened while you were there? Specifically, answer the following questions and add anything else that you think is relevant.
   a) Were witnesses called? If so, about what did they testify? Did you see both direct and cross-examinations? If so, how did they differ?
   b) Was demonstrative evidence introduced? If so, what evidence?
   c) Were any objections raised either to questions asked or to evidence introduced? If so, what were the objections?
   d) Did the attorneys ever confer privately with the judge either in her chambers or beside the judge's bench? If so, could you tell what the conference was about?
7. In your estimation, how well did each of the attorneys do in presenting his or her case?
8. Was visiting a trial what you had expected it to be? Why or why not?
9. Feel free to add any other comments that you would like to make regarding your courtroom visit.

****
ASSIGNMENT #10
BRIEF OF <u>LEWIS</u>

Please brief <u>Lewis v. Lewis</u>. Follow the briefing format that we discussed in class: citation, facts, rule, issue, holding, reasoning, and criticism. Recall that the facts should include any fact that you think affected the court's decision as well as the main procedural facts. The rule should be the rule as it existed prior to this decision.

The issue statement should contain two main components: the rule (label plus definition) and specific facts. After reading the issue, the reader should know exactly why each side thought it had a chance of convincing the court that it should win. The holding should be very specific so that your reader will know the limits that the court placed on its decision. The reasoning section should be as complete as possible so that your reader can fully understand why the court decided as it did. Finally, your criticism section should point out any logical failings or limitations in the court's thinking.

The numbers represent how I grade this assignment.

	1 (Names correct) 1 (Mass. cite)
5	<u>Lewis v. Lewis</u>, 370 Mass. 619, 351 N.E.2d 526 (1976)
	1 (Underlining) 1 (N.E.2d cite) 1 (date)

15 FACTS: The plaintiff wife was injured while a passenger in the <u>car negligently driven</u> (2) by <u>her husband</u>, (5) the defendant. The plaintiff sued her husband for injuries received in the accident. (3) The husband's motion for summary judgment was allowed. (2) The plaintiff was granted direct appellate review. (1) Judgment vacated. (2)

10 RULE: Under the common law, spouses may not sue each other for torts committed during coverture. Mass. Gen. Laws ch. 209, § 6 provides that a married woman may sue but does not authorize suits between husband and wife. (5 only if only give statute.)

10 ISSUE: Whether interspousal immunity, which generally prohibits spouses from suing each other, (2) bars a wife (3) from suing her husband in tort for personal injuries received in an uninsured car accident. (5)

10 HOLDING: No. Interspousal immunity does not bar claims between spouses, (5) but the holding is limited to accidents arising out of motor vehicle accidents.(5) [Note: no credit for procedural statement, i.e., judgment vacated. Also, 1/2 credit if students see issue as whether the court should reconsider the common law rule of spousal immunity. That is "the issue" as stated by the court, but not the issue as we have defined it.]

20 REASONING: The realities and principles of today's society have antiquated the interspousal immunity doctrine. Any public policy arguments relating to the doctrine's prevention of collusion and marital discord are insufficient grounds to continue the doctrine. (5) The court interpreted the state statute as neither abolishing nor mandating the continuance of the doctrine. Therefore, the court retained the power to abrogate the doctrine. (5) Because the courts stated that tortious injuries should have a remedy, (5) it abrogated the doctrine in this case, an automobile accident situation, but said that further abolition of the doctrine must await future cases. "Conduct, tortious between two strangers, may not be tortious between spouses. . . ." (page 532) (5)

5 CRITICISM: The court seemingly stretches the language of the statute to fit its desired result. The future is very unclear as to the viability of other types of tort claims. (3 if no real criticism)

75 + 25 (just for handing it in) = 100

233

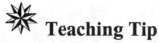 **Teaching Tip**

The researching assignments are all based on Massachusetts law. Obviously, you will have to adapt them to your own jurisdiction. I included them, however, as examples of the types of questions and level of analysis that you might expect from your beginning students. The answers were accurate as of fall 2004.

ANSWER SHEET: Redlined books are ones I have students collect and bring to the table before class so that we have them to consult.

****

ASSIGNMENT #11
RESEARCH EXERCISE A

Instructions: You may do the following problems in any order. If you find yourself becoming frustrated with one problem, switch to another. HINT: Don't forget pocket parts!

Please be considerate of your classmates:

        Do not hoard books.
        Do not write in library books.
        Do reshelve all books as you finish with them.

PLEASE MAKE A COPY OF YOUR ANSWERS and bring it with you to class, as I will ask you to hand in one copy at the beginning of class and to keep the second copy for yourself.

LOCATING COURT OPINIONS - STARTING WITH A CITATION

I. Your boss would like you to locate a court decision about a person who fell, allegedly due to the negligent application of wax on a landing at the bottom of a hotel's stairs.

    1.   Locate <u>Peacock v. Ambassade Realty Corp.</u>, 336 Mass. 115, <u>142 N.E.2d 775</u> (1957).

    2.   What are the names of the justices who took part in this decision?
        Wilkins, Ronan, Spalding, Counihan, & Cutter

    3.   How many headnotes are there?
        2

    4.   What is the topic and key number assigned to headnote #1?
        Negl Key 10

    5.   Assume that you wanted to find more court decisions that dealt with the issue covered in headnote #1. In the Massachusetts Digest 2d locate the topic assigned to headnote #1 in <u>Peacock</u>.   Negligence

A. Looking at the analysis section located at the beginning of that topic, find the key number from headnote #1. How is it listed?
10 Unintended Consequences

B. Using that topic and specific key number, find the citations for the most recent court decisions listed in Massachusetts Digest 2d and give the full and correct citation for each of the following:
-the most recent Supreme Judicial Court decision
Flood v. Southland Corp., 416 Mass. 62, 616 N.E.2d 1068 (1993)

-the most recent 1st Circuit opinion
Jorgensen v. Mass. Port Authority, 905 F.2d 515 (1st Cir. 1990)

LOCATING A STATUTE - USING THE INDEX

II. Assume you are working as a paralegal. Your boss has a client who is seeking a divorce. First, the client wants to know whether or not her contributions as a homemaker will be factored into how the court determines alimony. Second, she wants to know whether an inheritance that her husband recently received will be subject to division at the divorce.

1. Find the statute that governs whether or not a homemaker's contributions will be factored into how alimony is determined. Is it a factor?
   Yes

2. Give the correct citation for the statute that gave you that answer.
   Mass. Gen. Laws Ann. ch. 208, § 34 (West 1998)
   Mass. Ann. Laws ch. 208, § 34 (Lexis Law Pub. 1994)

3. Using only the Lawyers Co-operative Annotated Laws of Massachusetts (the black set), read the court summaries following this section of the statute. What is the correct citation for the most recent case dealing with whether an inheritance is subject to division at divorce? (Hint: To narrow your search, first look for your topic in the listing of Case Notes located right before the one paragraph summaries begin.)
   Zeh v. Zeh, 35 Mass. App. Ct. 268, **618 N.E.2d 1376** (1993).

4. Find that court decision. How many headnotes are there?
   7

5. What is the topic and key number of headnote #1?
   Divorce 252.3(3)

6. If you wanted to read more summaries of court decisions on this topic, where would you next look?
   Mass. Digest 2d under topic of Divorce

235

7.   In Mass. Digest 2d, look at the analysis section at the beginning of the topic Divorce. What is the topic and key number that you listed as your answer in number 5 about?

Separate Property and Property Acquired Before Marriage

8.   Use the topic and key number for headnote #1 to locate the citation for the most recent Massachusetts <u>state</u> supreme court decision summarized in the Massachusetts Digest 2d under that topic and key number. (The case does not have to deal with inheritances. It must simply be digested under this topic and key number.) What is the correct citation for that decision?

<u>Baccanti v. Morton</u>, 434 Mass. 787, 752 N.E.2d 718 (2001)
Note: Shows topic broader than the specific case with which we started.

LOCATING A COURT OPINION - STARTING WITH ITS NAME

III. Locate the complete citation for <u>Neagle v. Morgan</u>, a court decision from the 1970's dealing with liability for harm caused by a pet bird.   Table of Cases

1.   What is the full citation for that decision?

<u>Neagle v. Morgan</u>, 360 Mass. 864, 277 N.E.2d 482 (1971).

2.   Under what West topic is that court decision summarized?

Animals

THE VALUE OF WEST EDITORIAL FEATURES

IV. What advantage is there to reading a court decision in N.E.2d rather than in the Massachusetts Reports?

You get the headnotes to help locate information in the case and to summarize the case. Also, through topic and key numbers you can locate other cases in the digest (even from around the country)
Note: show them a volume from the General Digest.

V. What is the relationship between headnotes and digest summaries?

The text is identical but their functions differ. Headnotes are to summarize a specific case and to lead you to information in that case. Digest summaries are to organize all cases by subject matter.

LOCATING A STATUTE - KNOWING ITS CITATION

VI. Locate Mass. Gen. Laws Ann. ch. 152, § 53A, a statute dealing with worker's compensation trust funds.

    1.   When was it last amended?

        2000

    2.   How would you write the correct citation for this statute?

        Mass. Gen Laws Ann. ch. 152, § 53A (West Supp. 2004)

        Mass. Ann. Laws ch. 152, § 53A (Lexis Law Publ. 2000 & Supp. 2004)

USING SECONDARY AUTHORITY

VII. Because of the chain saw accident, Janice Miller has sued George Booth for negligence. In addition, she would like to see him criminally prosecuted for assault and battery. Locate the section in Mass. Practice Series, vol. 32, dealing with the general topic of assault and battery.

    1.   What is the section number?

        322

    2.   Read that section. If George was merely negligent in causing Janice's eye injury, can he be found guilty of criminal battery? **No**   Why or why not?

        Must be an intentional act

    3.   What is the correct citation for the court decision mentioned in footnote 2 of that section?

        Commonwealth v. Welch, 16 Mass. App. Ct. 271, 450 N.E.2d 1120, rev. denied, 390 Mass. 1102, 453 N.E.2d 1231 (1983).

VIII. Locate the section in Am. Jur. 2d that defines common law burglary.

        Burglary

    1. What does Am. Jur. 2d say are the elements of common law burglary?

        Breaking and entering; dwelling; at nighttime; with intent to commit a felony

    2.   Under what topic and section number did you find this information?

        Burglary, § 1 Definition

IX. Using Mass. Jurisprudence. Go to the index for the Personal Injury and Torts volumes and locate where you can find information on spousal immunity.

    1.   What sections deal with spousal immunity?

        2:8 & 2:9

    2.   You will see a footnoted reference to a case called Stamboulis. Give the citation for this case as it appears in the footnote.

        Stamboulis v. Stamboulis (1988) 401 Mass 762, 519 N.E.2d 1299

3. What is wrong with the format of this citation?
   Date in the wrong place

NOTE FOR PROBLEMS X & XI: The most recent issues of journals and newspapers are kept on the main floor. Older issues are stored in alphabetical order on the third floor.

X. Find the article in the November 1988 Boston University Law Review, located in volume 68, No. 5, entitled "Pregnancy and Employment: Three Approaches to Equal Opportunity."
   1. Read the first few paragraphs. What are the three basic approaches?
      Fed. anti-discrimination amend.
      State statutes
      Proposed comprehensive federal legislation

   2. To see how a typical article is written, scan the rest of the article. Who authored the article?
      Marjorie Jacobson

****

ASSIGNMENT #12
RESEARCH EXERCISE B

You may do the following problems in any order. If you find yourself becoming frustrated with one problem, switch to another. As a general rule of thumb, if you find that you have spent a half hour on one problem and you are unable to resolve it, move on. If for any reason you feel that you are "hopelessly stuck," give me a call. Give this assignment your best shot, but do not worry if you cannot answer all of the questions. Simply note the steps that you took in trying to answer those questions.

You will be graded on this assignment. Therefore, please do not share your answers with your classmates. I know that not being able to work with each other will make this project frustrating at times. However, I do feel that now is the time for you to begin to struggle through this on your own. As hard as that is, it is better than finding yourself on the job as a paralegal and unable to solve an assigned researching problem.

PLEASE MAKE A COPY OF YOUR ANSWERS and bring it with you to class, as I will ask you to hand in one copy at the beginning of class and to keep the second copy for yourself.

From your readings and our class discussions, you know that there are several ways to begin researching a legal problem.

APPROACH #1
If you only have a fact situation with which to begin, you will usually want to start your research with the Massachusetts statutes, using their general indexes.

APPROACH #2

If no statute governs your problem, you will begin with the Massachusetts Digest 2d, using its descriptive word index.

APPROACH #3

Third, if you have a partial citation for a court opinion, you might want to first obtain the complete citation by using the Massachusetts Digest or Massachusetts Digest 2d Table of Cases. Then you could begin your research by reading that opinion.

APPROACH #4

A final method would be to begin your research in a secondary source such as American Jurisprudence Second or the Massachusetts Practice Series.

This research assignment is designed to give you practice with all four approaches. It will also introduce you to Shepard's for finding parallel citations.

APPROACH #1 - BEGIN WITH THE STATUTES

A. One night, about a year ago, your client, Dr. Samuel Long, was driving home on I-90 when he saw a car ahead of him spin out of control and drive into the ditch. Dr. Long carefully pulled over to the side of the road, turned on his four-way flashers, and ran to the other car to see if he could be of assistance. He found the driver lying unconscious across the front seat with a large gash in his right leg. Blood was spurting from the gash and for the next ten minutes, until an ambulance and police car arrived, Dr. Long applied a tourniquet to the leg to slow the bleeding. As a result of the accident, the driver lost partial use of his leg. He wants to sue Dr. Long for allegedly contributing to the lose of use of his leg. Dr. Long is a licensed physician and is amazed to think he can be sued for only trying to be a "good Samaritan." For this problem confine your research to Massachusetts statutory law. (15 pts)

1. In Massachusetts can a licensed physician be held liable for the assistance he renders during an emergency situation?

>   **No**

2. Give the <u>correct</u> citation for the statute that gave you that answer. (Give the correct citation for both the West and Lawyer's Co-operative sets.)

>   **Mass. Gen. Laws Ann. ch. 112, § 12B (West 2003)**
>   **Mass. Ann. Laws ch. 112, § 12B (Lexis Law Pub. 2004)**

3. When was this section of the statute last amended?

>   **1993 (added physician assistant)**

4. Using the West Massachusetts General Law Annotated (the green set), give the <u>correct</u> citation for the most recent Supreme Judicial court decision summarized under this statute.

>   **<u>Hooper v. Callahan</u>, 408 Mass. 621, 562 N.E.2d 822 (1990)**

5. Using the Lawyer's Co-Operative Annotated Laws of Massachusetts (the black set), give the <u>correct</u> citation for the most recent Supreme Judicial court decision summarized under this statute.

>   **Same**

B. A client, Ms. Brown, has come into your office because she would like some advice on the Massachusetts adoption laws. She and her husband are planning to adopt a child in the near future. They are strong believers in "bonding" and would like to take the baby home as soon as possible after it is born. They realize, however, that they cannot get a baby until the natural mother has signed a consent form indicating her willingness to give the baby up for adoption. Therefore, they would like to know how soon after the birth the natural mother can sign the consent to adoption.

Second, the Browns realize that although they will have the baby at home with them, there is a waiting period between the time the mother signs the consent and the time the adoption is finalized in court. They are very concerned about what would happen if the mother should change her mind after she signs the consent form but before the adoption is finalized in court. They are worried, for example, that an unwed mother might sign the form but later want to keep the child if the baby's father later agreed to marry her. (15 pts)

1. Find the statute that governs adoptions in Massachusetts. Locate that statute and then find the section that deals specifically with consenting to adoption. Read that section.
   a)   How soon after birth can the mother sign the adoption consent?
        No sooner than 4 calendar days after day of birth = day 5

   b)   Give the <u>correct</u> citation for the section that gave you that answer.
        Mass. Gen. Laws Ann. ch. 210, § 2 (West Supp. 2004)
        Mass. Ann. Laws ch. 210, § 2 (Lexis Law Pub.2003)

2. Look at the summaries of the court opinions that have interpreted the statute.
   a)   Give the complete and <u>correct</u> citation for the court decision where the Supreme Judicial Court stated that a minor parent may consent to the adoption of his or her child.
        Adoption of Thomas, 408 Mass. 446, 559 N.E.2d 1230 (1990).

C. Your client, James Bennett, was recently fired. His boss had asked all employees to take a polygraph test. When Mr. Bennett refused, his boss fired him. Mr. Bennett has now been out of work for six weeks. For this problem confine your research to Massachusetts statutory law. (15 pts)

1. In Massachusetts is it legal for an employer to require that an employee take a polygraph test as a condition of his or her continued employment?
        No

2. Give the <u>correct</u> citation for the statute that gave you that answer. (Give the correct citation for both the West and Lawyer's Co-operative sets.)
        Mass. Gen. Laws Ann. ch. 149, § 19B (West 2004)
        Mass. Ann. Laws ch. 149, § 19B (Lexis Law Pub.1999)

3. When was this statute last amended?
        1985

4. If Mr. Bennet were to sue his employer and win, what might Mr. Bennett expect to recover?
        Treble damages for lost wages or other benefits
        Costs & reasonable attorney fees

<u>APPROACH #2 - BEGIN WITH THE DIGEST</u>
HINT: Although it is always important to plan your strategy BEFORE entering the library, that is especially true if you must start with the digests. Be sure that you have a number of fairly <u>specific</u> words that you plan to use when searching through the index. For example, the words liability or negligence would be too broad. Also trust yourself. Even if the topic you locate seems as though it could not be right, check it out.

A. Last Saturday, your client Wilma Street, drove her son to Bradley International Airport and saw him get on his 9:30 A.M. flight bound for San Francisco. Lather that night, while watching the 11:00 P.M. news, she heard that his plane had crashed while over Colorado and that all passengers had died. There was evidence that the crash may have been due to the airlines negligence in maintaining the airplane. Naturally, Mrs. Street is very upset over her son's death. (15 pts)

1. Assume that the airline was negligent and that their negligence caused the crash.
   a) Can Mrs. Street recover from the airline for the emotional distress she suffered as a result of hearing of the airplane crash?
   No

   b) Using <u>correct</u> citation form, give the citation for a court opinion that gave you that answer. (Base your choice on the court that wrote the appellate decision, the age of the case, and the degree to which the facts are analogous to our client's facts.)
   <u>Cohen v. McDonnel Douglas Corp.</u>, 389 Mass. 327, 450 N.E.2d 581 (1993) = our exact facts. Give partial credit for other emotional distress cases such as <u>Stockdale</u> (kid hurt at work) and <u>Nancy P</u> (mom learns of sexual abuse of daughter)

2. Under what topic and key number in the digest did you find that citation?
   Damages 51

APPROACH #3 - BEGINNING WITH A COURT CITATION OR PARTIAL CITATION
A. Last week your client was dining at a well known local eatery. While eating fish chowder, a bone became lodged in her throat. Luckily someone close by knew the Heimlich maneuver and prevented her from suffering any permanent injury. Nonetheless, she would like to sue the restaurant. Your boss remembers reading a strikingly similar Massachusetts court opinion in law school by the name of <u>Webster v.</u> somebody. Please locate that decision. (15 pts)

1. Using <u>correct</u> citation form, what is the citation?
<u>Webster v. Blue Ship Tea Room, Inc.</u>, 347 Mass. 421, 198 N.E.2d 309 (1964)

2. Was the plaintiff in that case able to recover?
 No

3. Why or why not?
Chef was not forced to reduce fish in chowder to minuscule size.

APPROACH #4 - BEGINNING WITH A SECONDARY SOURCE
A.   In <u>Callow v. Thomas</u>, we learned that there is a difference between voidable and void marriages. (10 pts)

1. Use the Massachusetts Practice family law volumes. What would cause a marriage to be void?
Incest; bigamy; polygamy

2.	What section number(s) in Massachusetts Practice that gave you that answer?
	19.1 - Actions when Validity of Marriage is in Doubt
	19.2 - Void Marriage

B. Your boss wants to know if paralegal time can be included in her request for attorney's fees. Please use American Jurisprudence Second. (10 pts)

1.	What does American Jurisprudence Second say about this issue?
	May be reimbursable, depending on the law.

2.	What was the topic and section number in American Jurisprudence Second that gave you that answer?
	Trial § 1933

USE SHEPARDS TO LOCATE PARALLEL CITATIONS
Use Shepards to find the parallel citations for the following cases. (10 pts)

1. Beginning with a N.E.2d cite,
	a)	What is the parallel citation for 162 N.E.2d 284?
		338 Mass 709

	b)	Now give the full and correct citation for that case.
		Milford v. Casmassa, 388 Mass. 709, 162 N.E.2d 284 (1959)

2. Beginning with a Mass. cite,
	a)	What is the parallel citation for 415 Mass. 309?
		613 ND 881

	b)	Now give the full and correct citation for that case.
		Fontaine v. Ebtu Corp., 415 Mass. 309, 613 N.E.2d 881 (1993).

NOTE: There are a possible 105 points on this assignment. However, the most that you can earn is 100 points.

****
ASSIGNMENT #13
LEGAL ANALYSIS A

Your firm represents Amanda and Sam Baker, grandparents of two-year-old Brian Baker. Brian was recently injured in a home accident. The two-year-old stuck a hairpin into an electrical outlet and was severely burned. Brian's parents had not installed safety plugs in the outlets because they felt the plugs gave a false sense of security. The plugs are easily removed and were not present in many of their friends' homes. The grandparents want to bring a negligence suit on the child's behalf against the parents.

The attorney in charge of the case filed a complaint on behalf of Brian, alleging that the parents' negligence caused Brian's injuries. In response, the attorney for the parents filed a motion to dismiss on the grounds that children cannot sue their parents unless the underlying situation involves a motor vehicle accident. The trial court granted the motion. The case is now on appeal before the Massachusetts Supreme Court. Based upon your understanding of <u>Lewis</u>, as well as of <u>Sorenson</u> and <u>Brown</u> (copies attached), analyze whether you think the Massachusetts Supreme Judicial Court will or will not allow Brian to continue with his suit against his parents.

In writing your analysis, please follow the IRAC (Issue, Rule, Analysis, Conclusion) method discussed in class. Start with a general statement of the issue you will be discussing. Follow that with a statement of the existing rule regarding parental immunity. Follow that with a brief explanation of how that rule, as well as the rule regarding spousal immunity, has been applied in the past, i.e., briefly discuss the facts and holdings of the prior cases as they relate to the facts of our case. Based upon whether you see the facts in the prior cases as being analogous to or distinguishable from our case and also based upon the court's language and general policy views give arguments both for and against reversing the lower court decision. Be sure to give equal weight to both sides of the case. Finally, end with a conclusion as to the most likely outcome in Brian's case.

Remember, you are not to discuss whether you think Brian's parents were negligent. That will be an issue for the trial court, but only if you think that the Supreme Judicial Court would reverse the trial court and allow Brian to sue his parents. Therefore, you are only to discuss the legal issue of whether children should be allowed to sue their parents in situations not involving motor vehicles.

After you have finished your legal analysis, please write a separate paragraph in which you state your PERSONAL views on whether or not you think Brian ought to be allowed to sue his parents. As this paragraph represents your personal opinion as opposed to what you think will happen, the result you reach may or may not coincide with the result you reached as a result of your legal analysis. Because your boss is interested in your legal opinion only, normally your boss would not ask you to give your personal opinion. However, to make sure that you can distinguish between the two, I want you to write this separate personal analysis as well as your legal analysis.

Finally, before writing your analysis, please review the appendix on legal writing style. Pay particular attention to the admonition to avoid starting paragraphs with "In the case of . . . ." Be sure that you double space this assignment, that you do not use contractions nor first person, and that all of your sentences are grammatically correct.

[Instructor's Note: See the suggested analysis for Legal Reasoning Exercise 2 in Chapter 8.]

ASSIGNMENT #14
RESEARCH EXERCISE C

You may do the following problems in any order. If you find yourself becoming frustrated with one problem, switch to another. If for any reason you feel that you are "hopelessly stuck," give me a call.

You will be graded on this assignment. Therefore, please <u>do not share your answers with your classmates</u>.

PLEASE MAKE A COPY OF YOUR ANSWERS and bring it with you to class, as I will ask you to hand in one copy at the beginning of class and to keep the second copy for yourself.

From your readings and our class discussions, you know that there are several ways to make sure that your research is as current as possible:

      1)   Shepardizing;
      2)   checking the mini-digests in the N.E.2d advance sheets;
      3)   reading Massachusetts Lawyer's Weekly; and
      4)   using either WESTLAW or Lexis.

This assignment will give you practice in the first two methods. It will also give you an opportunity to use the Code of Massachusetts Regulations.

NOTE: When Shepardizing, be sure to double check the volume. Is it N.E. or N.E.2d that you are looking for? Also, when faced with a long list of cites, use these shortcuts to narrow your search:

      1)   Are any of the cases preceded by a letter, especially r, o, or q?
      2)   Can you use the headnote numbers to focus your search?
      3)   Remember that the higher volume numbers are the new cases.
      4)   When possible, look for Massachusetts Supreme Judicial Court cases first and Massachusetts Appeals Court cases second.

SHEPARDIZING   BRING ALL SHEPARDS

1. Your boss represents a client who would like to sue his doctor for medical malpractice. The client recently discovered that he has a sponge in his small intestine. It appears that the sponge was left behind when he had surgery in 1985. However, it has only been in the last six months that he has been experiencing pain. In fact, it was the pain that caused him to have the problem investigated. That led to the discovery of the sponge. Prior to the onset of pain six months ago, the client had no idea that there had been a problem with his surgery. Because the surgery occurred so long ago, your boss is concerned that there may be a statute of limitations problem. (21 pts)

      Your boss would like to know whether or not the statute of limitations began to run when the sponge was left behind or when your client first felt the pain. He remembers a case called <u>Pasquale</u> v. somebody, a 1966 Massachusetts Supreme Judicial Court decision, that dealt with this precise issue.

a)   What is the <u>correct</u> citation for that case?
     <u>Pasquale v. Chandler</u>, 350 Mass. 450, 215 N.E.2d 319 (1966)
     2 for correct citation form; 2 for correct case

b)   Read the decision. Based on <u>Pasquale</u> does the statute of
     limitations begin to run when the operation occurs or when the
     patient discovers the problem?
     When the operation occurs. (found clamp more than 2 years after surgery.)

c)   Use Shepard's to determine if that answer is still correct. Is it?
          No

d)   What in Shepard's gave you that answer?
          o 381 Mas 612 or q 381 Mas 621 OR
          o 411 ND 459 or q 411 ND 465

e)   Give the full and <u>correct citation</u> for the decision that you found in Shepard's.
     <u>Franklin v. Albert</u>, 381 Mass. 611, 411 N.E.2d 458 (1980)

f)   What does the court say in that decision about when the statute of limitations
     begins to run?
     Not until learns or reasonably should have learned

g)   What does the court say about the proper role of the court versus the legislature
     in making changes to the rule regarding when the statute of limitations begins to
     run for medical malpractice claims?
     **Legislature's silence may not mean approval but rather a desire to leave
     matter to the courts.**

2. Your boss is writing an appellate brief and would like to rely on <u>Commonwealth v. Wotan</u>, 37
Mass. App. Ct. 727, 643 N.E.2d 62 (1994).   (10 pts)
     a)   Use Shepard's to determine whether or not your boss can safely
          rely on that decision. Can he?
               No.

     b)   What in Shepard's gave you that answer?
               r 665 ND 976 OR
               r 422 Mas 740

     c)   Give the full and <u>correct</u> citation for the court decision you found cited in
          Shepard's.
          <u>Commonwealth v. Wotan</u>, 422 Mass. 740, 665 N.E.2d 976 (1996)

3. Last year your client was in an automobile accident. The accident was the other driver's fault. In his answer, the other driver raised the issue of contributory negligence as your client was not wearing a seat belt at the time of the accident. Your boss has not done any research in this area of the law for several years. He does remember, however, a 1973 case where a car manufacturer was sued by a passenger who was injured when the seat back snapped during a sudden stop. The court stated that the passenger had not assumed the risk of injury by failing to wear her seat belt. (24 pts)

a)   The name of that Massachusetts case is <u>Breault v.</u> somebody. Please locate that decision. Using correct citation form, what is the citation?
Correct citation 2; found case 3
<u>Breault v. Ford Motor Co.</u>, 364 Mass. 352, 305 N.E.2d 824 (1973).

b)   Look at the headnotes to that case. Which headnote <u>topics and key numbers</u> are most relevant to the issue of whether or not the failure to wear a seat belt can be raised as a defense?
Autos 6, 16

c)   Which <u>headnote numbers</u> would you use to help you Shepardize the case on the issue of whether or not the failure to wear a seat belt can be raised as a defense?
2,5,8

d)   Shepardize <u>Breault</u>. What is the correct citation for the two most recent Massachusetts <u>state</u> court decisions to talk about <u>whether or not the failure to wear a seat belt can be raised as a defense</u>? (HINT: Remember to check any case with your headnote numbers or with no headnote numbers.)

<u>Most Recent Case:</u>
Correct citation 2; found case 3
<u>Shahzade v. C.J. Mabardy, Inc.</u>, 411 Mass. 788, 586 N.E.2d 3 (1992). (Evidence not wearing seatbelt insufficient to warrant submission to jury on issue of contributory negligence absent showing was causally related to her injuries.)

<u>Next Most Recent Case:</u>
Correct citation 2; found case 3
<u>MacCuish v. Volkswagenwerk</u>, 22 Mass. App. Ct. 380, 494 N.E.2d 390 (1986)

(Headnote #5 leads here)

e) Locate those decisions. Read the headnotes. Which headnote <u>topic and key number(s)</u> in those decisions are most relevant to our issue?

<u>Most Recent Case:</u>
Automobiles 245(81)

<u>Next Most Recent Case:</u>
Sales 430

THE CODE OF MASSACHUSETTS REGULATIONS

6. Ms. Brown and her husband are thinking about pursuing an "open adoption." An open adoption is one where the birth parents and adoptive parents meet each other. In the last assignment you found a statute governing adoption. In addition to that statute, the Department of Social Services has developed regulations to govern adoption. (10 pts)

  a) Locate those regulations. What are the department's requirements for recommending an open adoption?
   1) Severance harmful to child
   2) All parents consent
   3) Child over 12 consents
   4) Best interest of the child

  b) Give the correct citation for the regulation that gave you that answer.
   Mass. Regs. Code tit. 110, § 7.215 (2) (1993)

7. At one time I was on an ad hoc committee that was trying to establish a day care facility here at Elms College. There is a statute and state regulations that govern how one is supposed to set up and run a day care facility. Unfortunately, one problem here on campus is and was a lack of money. We were afraid we would not be able to comply with all of the regulations. (15 pts)

  a) Locate the <u>regulations</u> that govern group day care <u>centers</u>. Be careful here. You want to find the regulations that govern day care centers and not some other type of arrangement such as group homes. These regulations are written by the Office for Children. What is the <u>correct</u> citation for the regulations that govern day care centers?
   Mass. Regs. Code tit. 102, § 7.00 (1993).

  b) Find the definition of a <u>day care center</u>. We were planning to have a center that would take care of children of students while those students were in class or studying in the library. We did not expect any child to be in the center for more than a few hours a week.

   What language in the definition of a day care center could we use to argue that we do not fit within the definition? Please quote the language and tell me your argument for why you think we do not fit the definition of running a day care center. Give as many reasonable arguments as you can.

separate from parents
occasional care
operated on regular basis
not including any part of a private organized educational system

c)   Give the <u>correct</u> citation for the regulation that gave you that information.
Mass. Regs. Code tit. 102, § 7.02 (1993)

ASSIGNMENT #15
RESEARCH EXERCISE D

Please prepare the following (not necessarily in this order):

1) the citation and a brief summary of any statutes that are relevant to Mr. Baker's problem;

Mass. Gen. Laws, ch. 231, § 85Q   [5 pts]

This section imposes liability on a landowner for   [10 pts]
> **trespassing children**
> **if he maintains an artificial condition**

and the following five conditions are met:

1) the landowner knows or has reason to know children are likely to trespass;

2) the condition involves an unreasonable risk of death or serious bodily harm to children and the owner knows or has reason to know this;

3) because of their youth the children do not discover the condition or realize the risk;

4) the utility of maintaining the condition and the burden of eliminating the danger are slight as compared to the risk; and

5) the owner fails to exercise reasonable care to eliminate the danger or otherwise to protect the children.

2) the citation and a brief one paragraph summary of the four opinions that you think are most relevant to Mr. Baker's problem. Also include a brief explanation as to why you included the opinion (for example, because it is the most recent case, the case with facts the most similar to ours, etc. For this part, be sure to review Chapter 10's description of how to evaluate the precedential value of a case.);

I have listed all of the cases I think they will have found based on their research in the statutes, digest, and secondary authority. I would expect them to list the two I have marked with a ✓. I would then give them credit for any other two that make sense to you based on what the students give as an explanation. I have marked the ones I would consider using with a ~.

[40 points total; 10 for each case - 2 for the cite; 6 for the summary; 2 for explanation of why included.]

✓ Phachansiri v. City of Lowell, 35 Mass. App. Ct. 576, 1124 N.E.2d 623 (1994). An uncovered, drained public swimming pool was closed for the season. It was enclosed by a 10 foot chain link fence, topped by 2 feet of barbed wire. John (7) and Joseph (5) crawled through a hole they had dug underneath the fence. The boys slid into the uncovered pool and John drowned in the five feet of accumulated ground water. The jury found that it was foreseeable that children would trespass

250

(satisfying one element of the statute) but not that the condition involved an unreasonable risk. This court agreed, reasoning that the jury could have concluded either that the danger of a pool should have been apparent to the children or that because of the city's precautions (the double fence) that the pool did not pose an unreasonable risk.
[Included because fairly recent and only case that dealt specifically with swimming pools.]

✓ Soule v. Massachusetts Elec. Co., 378 Mass. 177, 390 N.E.2d 716 (1979)
8 year old Philip and a friend were playing on town land, as they did several times each week. Seeing a switching station, that was enclosed in a wooden structure, the boys decided it would "be a good lookout tower." The station was not enclosed in a fence, and there were no warning signs. Philip climbed the pole, stuck his head through the opening, came into contact with a high voltage wire that was only 6-12" above the opening, and was knocked to the ground, receiving serious injuries. Although Mass. Gen. Laws ch. 231, § 85Q had been enacted by the time of this lawsuit, it was not in effect at the time of the accident. However, the court stated that it was still open to them to change the common law to hold that a landowner owes a duty to prevent harm to foreseeable child trespassers. The court reasoned that where the child is "unable to appreciate danger as intelligently as an adult, . . . the child's presence is foreseeable," and "where the burden of undertaking precautions is not great compared to the magnitude of the risk involved," then the landowner owes a duty of reasonable care to the child. In this case, the jury was entitled to find a breach of reasonable care in the "defendant's failure to fence in the station, post a warning sign, or elevate the high-voltage wires hired above the floor of the station." The court reinstated the jury verdict for the plaintiff.
[Included because it is the landmark case from the SJC establishing liability of landowners.]

[Note: I have arranged the remaining cases by court and year.]

Mathis v. Massachusetts Elec. Co., 409 Mass. 256, 565 N.E.2d 1180 (1991).
16 year old boy climbed utility pole. Jury found he was 75% at fault and therefore could not recover. Court rejected plaintiff's argument that landowners should be held strictly liable. Therefore, if the jury determines the landowner breached a duty, it should then determine any possible contributory negligence of the child. These are not inconsistent standards as a jury could "find that the landowner unreasonably created a dangerous condition, the risks of which would not ordinarily be discovered by children, while at the same time finding that even though the plaintiff failed to realize the risk, he or she acted without the degree of care expected from a child of similar age, intelligence, and experience."
[Include - recent case and decided by SJC. Good discussion on difference between landowner's liability and child's contributory negligence. Exclude - students were to focus on landowner's duty, not child's contributory negligence.]

Commonwealth v. Guilfoyle, 402 Mass. 130, 521 N.E.2d 984 (1988).
[Not relevant. Just lists our statute as one example of special treatment accorded to juveniles.]

McDonald v. Consolidated Rail Corp., 399 Mass. 25, 502 N.E.2d 521 (1987).
16 year old walking on railroad trestle was hit by a train. Child was unable to satisfy the element of "because of his youth" being unable to appreciate the danger. [Probably not include because of plaintiff's age and the obvious danger of walking on a railroad trestle.]

~Briggs. v. Taylor, 397 Mass. 1010, 494 N.E.2d 1023 (1986).
9 year old injured when fell into 5 foot deep excavation and landed on spikes protruding from a sheet metal sign. Verdict for defendants, affirmed. There was no evidence that the defendants had put the sign in the hole nor that they knew it was there.
[May want to use as analogous situation of a young child falling into a "pit" with a hidden danger. Here a sign; in our client's case the moonlight on the paint.]

~Oldham v. Nerolich, 389 Mass. 1005, 452 N.E.2d 225 (1983).
Defendant left his 10 year old nephew and the 11 year old plaintiff on the front steps. The boys reentered the house, removed a loaded rifle, and were injured. The court found the defendant acted reasonably in leaving the boys outside and in assuming they would not reenter the house.
[Exclude - the boys were older and known visitors. Include - could be used to argue by analogy Mr. Baker had no way of knowing boys would enter his yard.]

~Bouchard v. DeGagne, 368 Mass. 45, 329 N.E.2d 114 (1975)
2 1/2 year old fell through open sliding doors. Defendant was found negligent in that the presence of small children was a frequent occurrence; there was a drop of 8 feet to the ground; former barriers had been removed; the doors were easily opened; it was reasonably foreseeable someone would leave the doors open.
[Exclude - Invited children/not trespassers; prior to enactment of statute. Include - now that court has adopted rule of negligence for child trespassers, facts of this case could form basis for argument for Mr. Baker's failure to take precautions.]

Forbush v. City of Lynn, 35 Mass. App. Ct. 696, 625 N.E.2d 1370 (1994).
Child hurt on playground. Torts Claims Act exemption for intentional torts did not provide immunity from allegation of willful, wanton or reckless conduct. Court noted that it is anomalous that a city owes more care to trespassing child (reasonable care) than to one lawfully playing on public recreational land (to refrain from reckless conduct).   [Not relevant.]

Gage v. Westfield, 26 Mass. App. Ct. 681, 532 N.E.2d 62 (1988).
16 & 18 year olds killed by train could realize risks of standing on tracks.
[Not relevant as again deals with specifics of a train accident.]

Jad v. Boston & Main Corp., 26 Mass. App. Ct. 564, 530 N.E.2d 197 (1988)
14 year old, walking on railroad tracks was hit and killed by a commuter train.
Separate statute protects railroads from liability. This provides an exception to the
general rule of liability to child trespassers. Therefore, court affirmed trial court's
granting of summary judgment to the railroad.
[Not relevant as deals with specific exemption granted to railroads.]

Callahan v. Boston Edison Co., 24 Mass. App. Ct. 950, 509 N.E.2d 1208 (1987).
It is proper to charge that the defendant may have no duty to remedy a hazard that
is open and obvious.
[Irrelevant on the facts; dealt with injured employee who slipped and fell while
removing debris from a boiler.]

~Puskey v. Western Mass. Elec. Co., 21 Mass. App. Ct. 972, 489 N.E.2d 1025
(1986).
15 year old climbed power transmission line tower. Court affirmed trial court
decision that defendant was not negligent. Here the tower was in a remote area, it
bore warning signs, and the power company had adopted a program of cautionary
education. Also, the child knew of the dangers. Finally, the burden of eliminating
the danger was unreasonable.
[Exclude because of plaintiff's age or include as an example of when a landowner
was not found liable.]

Gaines v. General Motors Corp., 789 F. Supp. 38 (D. Mass. 1991).
16 year old boy stole car, crashed into tree, and died. Owner of lot from which the
boy stole the car was found not liable.
[As this is a federal case, the students will not be able to locate it in our library.]

3)   the citation and a brief (1-2 paragraph summary) of information that you locate in each
of the following secondary sources: Am. Jur. 2d; Mass. Practice; and Mass. Jur.;

[Note: 15 points total; 5 points each]
Am. Jur. 2d
62 Am. Jur. 2d 377, Premises Liability, Swimming Pools
Courts have allowed for recover of children injured in private swimming pools
under the attractive nuisance doctrine. While owners do not have to make it
impossible for children to get into the pool, safeguards must be reasonable. The
section then listed a set of facts which would tend to show whether a pool was an
attractive nuisance. Section 378 states that liability could be grounded on a finding
that a pool was inadequately fenced.

Mass. Practice
Torts, § 375 Attractive Nuisance
Massachusetts refused to recognize the doctrine of attractive nuisance beginning in 1891 through 1973, although the Restatement had given recognition to the doctrine. In 1977, the Legislature, enacted Mass. Gen. Laws ch. 231, § 85Q.

Mass. Jur.
Personal Injury, § 31:5 Child Trespassers
Although Massachusetts had not adopted the attractive nuisance doctrine, it did adopt the Restatement of Torts 2d, § 339, version of that doctrine, as outlined in Massachusetts General Laws ch. 231, § 85Q. If the legislature had not adopted this statute, the SJC was ready to apply the Restatement rule.

Personal Injury, § 31:7 - Conditions on recovery
All five conditions must be satisfied. This section points out that "there must be evidence to show that a particular defendant knew or should have known about the dangerous condition." Also, because of their youth, the child trespasser must not have discovered the condition or realized the risk involved. Finally, the court must examine whether the safety measures recommended by plaintiff's counsel would unreasonably encumber the owner's ability to use the property.

4)   a list of the digest topics and key numbers that are most relevant to Mr. Baker's problem; and
[Note: 5 points; looking especially for first two listed]
Negligence, 33(3)   Care as to trespassers, children
Negligence, 39   Places attractive to children.
Negligence, 134(5)   Actions, Evidence, Weight and Sufficiency, Buildings
Negligence, 136(19)   Actions, Trial, Questions for jury, Machinery and places attractive to children

5)   an outline of the issues that will have to be resolved in order to determine whether Mr. Baker will be liable.

[Note: 25 points total; 5 points for each issue. For grading purposes, the students only needed to list the issues. I have included some potential arguments that could form the basis for a classroom discussion prior to their writing their analysis.]
        Whether a swimming pool is an artificial condition and whether Jim was a trespassing child are clearly satisfied and so are not issues.

1) Whether Mr. Baker knew or had reason to know children were likely to trespass when he lived in a retirement community.
        No - No children living in the neighborhood
        Yes - Likely children will visit grandparents; these boys had been in the neighborhood for two weeks.
2) Whether the empty swimming pool involved an unreasonable risk of death or

serious bodily harm to children and Mr. Baker knew or had reason to know this.

> No - The real danger here was the way the moon reflected off the pool and Mr. Baker could have had no way of knowing this.

> Yes- Danger was of an empty pool with inadequate fencing.

3) Whether because Jim was only six years old he did not discover the condition or realize the risk;

> No - Even if acted too impetuously, should have realized dangers of jumping into even a full pool of water.

> Yes - Because of his age, he did not take time to closely examine the pool. If he had, he would have seen it was empty.

4) Whether the utility of maintaining the pool and the burden of eliminating the danger are slight as compared to the risk.

> No - It would have cost an additional $2000 to erect the higher fence. It would cost even more to fill in the pool, the only real safeguard.

> Yes - $2000 is a small price to pay compared to a child's death. Also, since it appears Mr. Baker never intends to use the pool, he should have either covered it, filled it in, or built a better fence.

5) Mr. Baker failed to exercise reasonable care to eliminate the danger or otherwise to protect the children.

> No - By draining the pool, he had done all that was necessary.

> Yes - Given great danger of empty pool and foreseeability of children trespassing, should have done more than erect easily climbable short fence. If anything, draining the pool, increased its risk to children.

For this assignment, please brief <u>Soule v. Massachusetts Elec. Co.</u>. Follow the format that we have used in the past: Citation, Facts, Rule, Issue, Holding, Reasoning, and Criticism. In your holding section, you should give two holdings: first, a very specific holding based upon the facts of the case and then second, a broader holding stating the new general legal principle arising out of this case. In your criticism section, include your criticism but also include a brief discussion of the two concurrences.

---

5   <u>Soule v. Massachusetts Elec. Co.</u>, 378 Mass. 177, 390 N.E.2d 716 (1979)

Facts: 8 year old Philip and a friend were playing on town land, as they did several times each week. Seeing a switching station, maintained by the defendant power company, that was enclosed in a wooden structure, the boys decided it would "be a good lookout tower." The station was not enclosed in a fence, and there were

15   no warning signs. Philip climbed the pole, stuck his head through the opening, came into contact with a high voltage wire that was only 6-12" above the opening, and was knocked to the ground, receiving serious injuries. The trial judge entered judgment for the defendant power company notwithstanding the jury verdict in favor of the child plaintiff. Request for direct appellate review granted; reversed and jury verdict reinstated.

Rule:
10   Landowners owe no duty toward child trespassers except to refrain from wanton and wilful misconduct. [p. 718]

Issue: Whether despite the common law rule that landowners owe no duty toward child trespassers except to refrain from wanton and wilful misconduct, the defendant power company should be held liable when

10   children frequented the area, there were no warnings nor fencing and an eight year old trespassing boy climbed the wooden enclosure surrounding defendant's switching station and was injured when he touched an uninsulated high voltage wire.

Holding: Yes, despite the common law rule that landowners owe no duty toward child trespassers except to refrain from wanton and wilful misconduct, the defendant power company should be held liable when children frequented

10   the area, there were no warnings nor fencing and an eight year old trespassing boy climbed the wooden enclosure surrounding defendant's switching station and was injured when he touched an uninsulated high voltage wire.

Also O.K. - a broader statement of the holding such as ....

A landowner owes a common law duty of reasonable care to prevent harm to a foreseeable child trespasser, but this protection is not extended to adult trespassers.

Reasoning:

20

Although Mass. Gen. Laws ch. 231, § 85Q had been enacted by the time of this lawsuit, it was not in effect at the time of the accident. However, the court stated that it was still <u>open to them to change the common law</u> to hold that a landowner owes a duty to prevent harm to foreseeable child trespassers. The court maintained that where the child is "unable to appreciate danger as intelligently as an adult, . . . the child's presence is foreseeable," and "where the burden of undertaking precautions is not great compared to the magnitude of the risk involved," then the landowner owes a duty of reasonable care to the child. <u>The right of property owners should no longer be seen as superior to that of the safety of trespassing children.</u>

<u>In this case,</u> the jury was entitled to find a breach of reasonable care in the "defendant's failure to fence in the station, post a warning sign, or elevate the high-voltage wires hired above the floor of the station." While the court thought the common law approach to differentiating based upon the status of the entrant should be abolished as to child trespassers, it withheld its judgment as to adult trespassers.

Criticism:

5

In two concurrences the judges noted that the court left the status of adult trespassers unsettled. Hennessey wanted to make it clear there should be no liability towards an adult trespasser. Kaplan would eliminate all labels.

[Personal criticism - could agree case should be extended to adults; could feel the criteria for determining liability are too onerous on landowners; could think children who trespass should not be afforded protection, etc.]

75 + 25 =100

****

ASSIGNMENT #17
ANALYSIS OF LANDOWNER'S LIABILITY

Write an analysis of the arguments regarding Mr. Baker's potential liability for Jim's death. In your analysis, please limit your references to Mass. Gen. Laws ch. 231, § 85Q, *Phachansiri*, and *Soule*.

Prior to writing your analysis, think about how Mr. Baker's attorney would argue that the situation is analogous to *Phachansiri* and distinguishable from *Soule*. Also think about how the boy's attorney would argue just the opposite. You may want to develop a chart in which you outline the facts of each situation to help you see the differences and similarities among your client's facts, the facts in *Soule*, and the facts in *Phachansiri*.

Also, before beginning to write, make sure you understand the policy reasons behind the court's decisions. While your arguments should be based on the factual similarities and differences between our case and *Soule* and *Phachansiri*, a mere listing of the factual similarities and differences is not enough. Pointing to the court's reasoning, you must be sure to tell me WHY you think those similarities and differences matter.

For your analysis, start off with a roadmap paragraph that outlines the issues you will be discussing. Select **two** of the four issues we discussed in class. Using the IRAC method, discuss those two issues in separate paragraphs. [Note: You should devote at least one paragraph to each issue. If you find that you have too much to say to fit into one paragraph, it is fine to divide your arguments into two paragraphs per issue.] Then end your analysis with a concluding paragraph. Remember to use transitions to link the paragraphs together.

In your <u>A</u>nalysis discussion of each issue, you will want to give an explanation of how the law has been applied in the past. Your analysis will consist of several components:

1) The first time you mention a case, briefly discuss its facts, holding, and reasoning. Do not do this in a separate paragraph. Rather integrate your discussion with your analysis of an issue. Recall the discussion in Chapter 10 on case synthesis. Do not simply give a mini-brief of one case followed by the next. Rather, use a case to state a general proposition and then support that proposition with a discussion of that case's facts and holding.

2) For each issue, remember to give what you view as the losing argument first so that the winning argument flows right into your conclusion for that issue.

3) Your arguments should be based on the factual similarities and differences between our case and *Soule* and *Phachansiri*.

4) But remember to go beyond a mere listing of the factual similarities and differences. Tell me, based on the court's reasoning, WHY you think those factual similarities and differences matter.

5) Give **both** the landowner's and the child's arguments, i.e., how based on our facts, our case is analogous to *Phachansiri* and distinguishable from *Soule*, thereby indicating that the landowner should not be liable, but also how our case is distinguishable from *Phachansiri* and analogous to *Soule*, thereby making the landowner liable.

6) When writing your analysis, assume I have not read *Soule* and *Phachansiri*. I am aware of our client's facts, however. Therefore, you do not need to recount those facts in a separate paragraph. Rather, <u>use those facts</u> to show how our case is distinguishable from or analogous to the cited cases.

Please review Appendix C on citation form and Appendix B on writing style. Pay particular attention to the warning regarding starting paragraphs with "In the case of . . . ." Do not use contractions and do not write in first person. (Incorrect: I think the court didn't allow recovery. Correct: The court did not allow recovery.)

Proofread and double check to make sure you have not used sentence fragments nor run-ons. <u>Points will be deducted for grammar, citation, and typographical errors.</u> This is the time to make your work look as professional as possible. Thank you.

Grading Sheet
Analysis of Landowner Liability

I.   **Writing Style/Grammar - 10**

        Note: deduct one point for any major grammar error, such as a run-on or sentence fragment

II.   **Organization - 15**

        Had roadmap paragraph (4)

        Treated issues separately (3)

        Used transitions (3)

        Had a good concluding paragraph (5)

III.   **Used IRAC consistently - 10**

    A.   Stated the Issue (2)

    B.   Gave the rule (2)

    C.   Analyzed both sides (4)

    D.   Concluded on each issue (2)

IV.   **Analysis of Issues (Pick two) - 20**

    A.   Children were foreseeable

        1.   Yes (5)

        2.   No (5)

    B.   Mr. Baker knew of the unreasonable risk

        1.   Yes (5)

        2.   No (5)

    C.   Because of his youth, the child didn't realize the peril

        1.   Yes (5)

        2.   No (5)

    D.   The burden of elimination

        1.   Yes (5)

        2.   No (5)

V.   **Use of the Cases - 20**

    A.   <u>Soule</u> (10)

        1.   Facts/Holding/Reasoning

        2.   Application to our case

    B.   <u>Phachansiri</u> (10)

        1.   Facts/Holding/Reasoning

        2.   Application to our case

VI.   **Handed it in - 25**

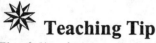 **Teaching Tip**

The following are the assignments that I use in the second semester based upon the two semester course model. I have included grading sheets that I use for most of the graded assignments (as opposed to the pass/fail assignments).

****

ASSIGNMENT #1

Please answer Discussion Questions 6 and 7, located on page 251 of your text.

[Instructor's Note: See the suggested answer given for these discussion questions in Chapter 9 earlier in this manual.]

****

ASSIGNMENT #2

Analyze the situation presented in Legal Reasoning Exercise 1, located on page 258 of your text. Be sure to base your analysis on an attorney's ethical obligations whether under the Model Code, the Model Rules, or the recently proposed changes to the Model Rules, but also include your own reasoning as to what you think the attorney should do given the differences in the situations found in *Belge, Spaulding,* and these facts.

[Instructor's Note: See the discussion of this legal reasoning exercise in Chapter 9 earlier in this manual.]

```
*********************************
```
ASSIGNMENT #3
BRIEF OF <u>WOODS</u>

Please brief <u>Woods v. Lancet</u>. It is located in your book, beginning on page 319. It is a New York Court of Appeals decision. The New York Court of Appeals is the highest appellate court in New York. (Recall from your readings last semester that New York has an odd way of naming its courts. Its trial court is called the Supreme Court, its intermediate appellate court is called the Appellate Division, and its highest appellate court is called the New York Court of Appeals.)

Please follow the briefing format that we have used in the past: citation, facts, rule, issue, holding, reasoning, and criticism. The correct citation form is to include the official and unofficial reporters.

Recall that the facts should include any fact that you think affected the court's decision as well as the main procedural facts. The rule should be the rule as it existed prior to this decision. The issue statement should contain two main components: the rule (label plus definition) and specific facts. After reading the issue, the reader should know exactly why each side thought it had a chance of convincing the court that it should win. The holding should be very specific so that your reader will know the limits that the court placed on its decision. The reasoning section should be as complete as possible so that your reader can fully understand why the court decided as it did. Finally, your criticism section should point out any logical failings or limitations in the court's thinking as well as a short description of the dissent's thoughts.

Grading Sheet for Woods Brief

Facts of Woods -

> **9 month fetus**
> **severely injured by Def.'s negl.**
> **(The case doesn't tell us, but the Def. was a landlord, and**
> **the pl.'s pregnant mother fell down a poorly maintained common stairway.)**

So a question of negligence - did he owe fetus any duty?

Procedural facts

> **N.Y. Court of Appeals - Rev'd**
> **|**
> **Appellate Division   - Aff'd**
> **|**
> **Supreme Court   - Complaint Dismissed**

RULE: <u>Drobner</u> - No recovery for fetal injury.

ISSUE: Whether or not the def. can be found liable for negligence, despite the rule that denies recovery for injury negligently caused to a fetus, when a 9 month old fetus was injured through def.'s neg. (As opposed to court's statement on page 320.)

HOLDING: Yes, recovery is possible for harm negligently caused to a fetus but the right is limited to injury to a viable fetus.

REASONING: Basis for <u>Drobner</u> no longer valid
    JURISPRUDENTIAL REASONS
       1) Lack of precedent then; plenty now (started
with a dissent);
       2) Not bound to follow own past rules; duty to
change law.
       3) Don't have to wait for legis.
  BUT NOTE: If there had been a statute, they would have had to follow it.

    ADDITIONAL REASONS
       1) Proof prob. irrelevant/ true in every negligence case
       2) No separate existence = why limited holding to
viable fetus.

CRITICISM: Any justification for limiting holding?

****

ASSIGNMENT #4
BRIEF OF <u>GREAVES</u>

Please brief <u>Greaves</u>. In <u>Greaves</u> a boy was injured while playing Ring-A-Levio. For those of you not from New York, Ring-A-Levio is a running game that does not involve water. One group of players are the chasers and the other group is chased, similar to tag. This case was decided by the same court that decided *Sauer v. Hebrew Institute of Long Island, Inc.* located on page 323 of your book. It is a New York state appellate division decision. A copy of *Greaves* is attached.

Please follow the briefing format that we have used in the past: citation, facts, rule, issue, holding, reasoning, and criticism. The A.D.2d citation is to the official reporter and the New York Supplement citation (abbreviated N.Y.S.2d) is the unofficial citation. Recall that the facts should include any fact that you think affected the court's decision as well as the main procedural facts. The rule should be the rule as it existed prior to this decision. The issue statement should contain two main components: the rule (label plus definition) and specific facts. After reading the issue, the reader should know exactly why each side thought it had a chance of convincing the court that it should win. The holding should be very specific so that your reader will know the limits that the court placed on its decision. The reasoning section should be as complete as possible so that your reader can fully understand why the court decided as it did. Finally, your criticism section should point out any logical failings or limitations in the court's thinking.

****

Richard Greaves, an Infant, by His Mother and Natural
Guardian, Adrienne Greaves, et al., Respondents, v. Bronx
Y.M.C.A., Appellant

Supreme Court of New York, Appellate Division, First
Department

87 A.D.2d 394; 452 N.Y.S.2d 27
June 24, 1982

[*394] [**28]   Defendant appeals from a judgment for the infant plaintiff after a jury trial in an action for damages sustained when the plaintiff, then nine years old, was a camper at defendant's camp. The jury, evaluating the damages as $ 250,000, found the defendant to be 60% negligent and the plaintiff 40% negligent. Following the trial court's determination that the damages awarded were excessive, plaintiff consented to a reduction to $ 150,000, resulting in a net verdict to the plaintiff of $ 90,000.

From the evidence presented by the plaintiff, the jury could reasonably have concluded that he sustained a severe injury to his elbow when he fell during the course of a [*395]   game of ring-a-levio; that both campers and counselors participated in the game, the counselors as a separate team of "catchers"; that the game was played on a sloping grass area adjacent to a swimming pool; that the plaintiff slipped on a section of the grass that was damp as a result of water spilling over from the pool and the counselors having previously hosed the campers when they had emerged from the pool.

The principal issue presented on this appeal is the legal sufficiency of the evidence, the defendant contending that the case is controlled by the decision in Sauer v Hebrew Inst. of Long Is. (17 AD2d 245, affd 13 NY2d 913) in which, in a similar factual situation, a verdict in favor of the plaintiff was reversed, on the

law and on the facts, and the complaint was dismissed.

As described in this court's decision in Sauer (supra), the plaintiff in that case, then 13 years old, was injured at a summer camp while playing a game supervised by the defendant's personnel. The game was a "water fight" between groups of campers of similar age, played on a grass-covered area in which opposing groups of boys doused each other with water from cups or water pistols. Running away from an opponent, the plaintiff in Sauer slipped on the grass and struck his head on a concrete walk on the side of the grass area.

In reversing a verdict after a nonjury trial in favor of the plaintiff, the court said (at p 246): "The defendant, as the operator of a camp for boys, could not reasonably be made responsible in damages for the consequences of every possible hazard of play activity. It was required, rather, to guard against dangers which ought to have been foreseen in the exercise of reasonable care".

Further on in the opinion, the following was said (p 246): "To impose liability in this situation is to interdict the game itself, which in turn would so sterilize camping activity for boys as to render it sedentary."

Recognizing the similarity of this case to the situation in Sauer (supra), we are not persuaded that Sauer is dispositive. The effect here of finding the evidence legally sufficient to support the jury's verdict would not be "to interdict [*396] the game itself". At issue here is not the appropriateness of the game that was played for the youngsters involved, but rather the judgment of the supervising counselors in selecting for the playing of the game a surface that might reasonably have been foreseen as adding needlessly to the risks inherent in the game itself.

It is appreciated that difficult problems of judgment may often confront counselors supervising the play activity of youngsters accustomed to strenuous physical exertions often accompanied by actions that involve some degree of risk. We appreciate the concern that a finding of liability in some camp situations may tend to "sterilize camping [activities] for boys as to render it sedentary." On the facts which the jury might reasonably have found in this case, however, we believe that a factual issue for jury determination was presented as to whether the playing of the game here on the described surface involved a foreseeable risk of unjustifiable danger. (See Quinlan [**29] v Cecchini, 41 NY2d 686, 689.)

Accordingly, the judgment of the Supreme Court, Bronx County (Callahan, J.), entered on December 12, 1980, after a jury trial in favor of plaintiff for $ 90,000 should be affirmed.

Fein, J. , Concurring

Sauer v Hebrew Inst. of Long Is. (17 AD2d 245, affd 13 NY2d 913) is distinguishable. The boys involved there were shooting water pistols at each other, an activity which would obviously make the ground on which the game was being played wet and slippery. So far as appears in Sauer, the camp counselors did not participate in the activity so that if liability were found, it would be grounded on lack of adequate supervision only.

In Sauer, this court stated (17 AD2d, at p

246): "To impose liability in this situation is to interdict the game itself, which in turn would so sterilize camping activity for boys as to render it sedentary." In our case the game was ring-a-levio, a kind of roughhouse run-hide-and-chase game in which the counselors participated as a team of "catchers" who actively chased the campers until they were caught and brought to home base. There is a basis for finding misfeasance by defendant's employees.

[*397] There is a further ground for distinguishing Sauer. The game here was played on a wet, sloping, grassy area adjacent to the swimming pool. It is plain that there are dangers in the game of ring-a-levio as there are in most sports, and they are not to be interdicted on that ground alone. However, the problem here is not basically with the game but rather with the place where it was being played, a wet, sloping, grassy area adjacent to the swimming pool. The issue is whether this was a proper place for such a game.

It is undisputed that there was a football field a short distance away on the campgrounds which would have been appropriate for the game.

In the language of Sauer (supra, p 246), it was not necessary "to interdict the game itself"; it was necessary only to use reasonable care to insure that it was played in an area which did not add to its inherent risks. This is not to make children's camping activities little more than a baby-sitting operation, as the dissent suggests. The risks of childhood are always there. Supervisory responsibility is to avoid unreasonably adding to such risks. Surely if the game of football were being played in an area such as was utilized here, instead of on the available football field, one would have little hesitancy in finding that there was at least a jury issue as to whether there was actionable negligence. After all, we are dealing with a nine-year-old boy. Each game has its own dangers. However, adding to the danger of allowing the game to be played in an inappropriate location may be negligence, a foreseeable risk of the probability and the gravity of harm.

Thus, in Eddy v Syracuse Univ. (78 AD2d 989) the game was "ultimate frisbee", played between two college teams. The game was played in a gymnasium, one wall of which was of masonry construction with glass doors. Plaintiff, in running toward that wall and looking back over his shoulder for a thrown frisbee, was unable to stop before striking one of the doors. Plaintiff's upper torso went through the door and he was severely lacerated. The defendant contended that it did not authorize use of the gym, had no foreknowledge of its use by plaintiff, could not foresee the manner in which it would be used, and finally that the gym [*398] was not defective in construction or design nor unsuited for its ordinary purposes, such as basketball. The court held: [**30] "Thus the question arises of whether defendant should have foreseen that students might use the gymnasium for the playing of games other than those for which the basketball courts had been laid out. Here again, because of the propensity of college students to engage in novel games, a jury question was presented, and if such foreseeability was found, the probability and gravity of harm was readily apparent. The jury could also reasonably have found that the risk presented by the glass doors could have been obviated without imposing an undue burden upon defendant." (Eddy v Syracuse Univ., 78 AD2d, at p 991.)

So too here it was properly a jury question whether the risk presented by participating in and allowing ring-a-levio to be played on a wet, sloping, grass-covered area adjacent to the pool presented a foreseeable risk of danger which could have been obviated by having the game played at some other portion of the campgrounds, to wit, the nearby athletic field. The duty of youth camps to the children

entrusted to their care is well settled (Willis v Young Men's Christian Assn. of Amsterdam, 28 NY2d 375). Although we now have only one standard of care, consideration of "who plaintiff is and what his purpose is upon the land are factors" in determining "what would be reasonable care under the circumstances." (Basso v Miller, 40 NY2d 233, 241.) Here we have a nine-year-old camper and his peers obviously needing supervision.

Implicit in the jury's verdict was a finding that the defendant had a duty, which was breached, to protect the youthful campers from the dangers involved in playing the game on an unsuitably, wet, sloping, grassy area.

The duty of care owed to the nine-year-old plaintiff was measured by the "risk of harm reasonably to be perceived * * * reasonable care under the circumstances whereby foreseeability shall be a measure of liability." (Basso v Miller, 40 NY2d, at p 241.)

In determining whether there is sufficient evidence to support a negligence finding to submit to a jury, the question is whether the foreseeability of risk is too remote. The court must examine the facts and weigh "the probability [*399] of the harm, the gravity of the harm against the burden of precaution, and other relevant and material considerations from which it can determine whether reasonable persons can differ as to whether the defendant was negligent" (Quinlan v Cecchini, 41 NY2d 686, 689). Only when it is concluded that there is no reasonable view of the evidence upon which to assess liability is the question one of law. Where varying inferences are possible as to what is foreseeable and what is negligence, the issue is for the jury (Derdiarian v Felix Contr. Corpage, 51 NY2d 308, 315; Palsgraf v Long Is. R.R. Co., 248 NY 339, 345).

On the facts of this case, reasonable persons can differ as to whether the defendant was negligent. Hence the jury's verdict should stand.

The spectre of entirely curtailing camp

activities, sought to be avoided by the Sauer court whose decision is relied upon by the dissent, should not be allowed to bar liability if a properly instructed jury could find, as this one did, that there was a foreseeable risk of danger or harm which was a proximate cause of the accident and which in the exercise of reasonable care, under the circumstances, could have been avoided by having the game played on a more appropriate and plainly available site. It was not necessary to anticipate the particular occurrence in order to find negligence. It was enough if there was danger of harm with foreseeable consequences. (Derdiarian v Felix Contr. Corpage, 51 NY2d, at pp 316-317; see Pagan v Goldberger, 51 AD2d 508; Willis v Young Men's Christian Assn. of Amsterdam, supra.) Although the case may be close to Sauer (supra), it is not the same case. The "idiosyncratic nature of most tort [**31] cases" makes it appropriate to leave the issue to the jury because "in the determination of issues revolving about the reasonableness of conduct", the role of the jury is significant (Havas v Victory Paper Stock Co., 49 NY2d 381, 388).

Accordingly, the judgment of the Supreme Court, Bronx County (Callahan, J.), entered on December 12, 1980, after a jury trial in favor of plaintiff for $ 90,000 should be affirmed without costs.

DISSENT: Bloom, J. (dissenting).

In August, 1976, plaintiff, then nine years of age, was enrolled in a summer day camp [*400] operated by defendant. On the day in question, plaintiff, and the others participating in the day camp, were at the Castle Hill Beach Club. In the late afternoon the campers emerged from the club pool. Their evening activity was to go to a Yankee baseball game. As they exited from the pool they were hosed down in accordance with the usual custom. They then dressed and had a typical camp supper consisting of hot dogs and hamburgers grilled at a barbecue pit. Since there was time to spare before they proceeded to the Yankee Stadium the campers and counselors engaged in a game of "ring-a-levio". The team of chasers consisted of three or four counselors while the team of those chased consisted of campers.

As the chase proceeded, plaintiff, who was dressed in jeans, a shirt, socks and sneakers, fell and injured his arm. He was taken to a hospital where it was ascertained that his elbow was broken. The arm was placed in a cast and plaintiff remained in the hospital for five days. Within three months the arm had healed and since that time plaintiff has actively engaged in athletics.

Thereafter this action was brought. It is bottomed on the claim that the "ring-a-levio" chase took place in an area surrounding the pool and that the defendant was negligent in permitting the game to be played in the vicinity of the pool. Plaintiff's fall, it is contended, resulted from the chase, during which he slipped on wet or damp grass. The jury returned a verdict in favor of the plaintiff in the sum of $ 250,000, and allocated 60% of the negligence to defendant and 40% to the infant plaintiff. Defendant thereafter separately moved for judgment notwithstanding the verdict and to reduce the verdict. The trial court denied the first motion from the Bench. It reserved decision on the second motion and, in a memorandum decision subsequently rendered, reduced the verdict to the sum of $ 150,000, leaving the apportionment as the jury had found it. It held "the total verdict in favor of the infant plaintiff to be shockingly excessive and to be in large part based on sympathy". From the judgment entered thereon defendant appeals.

We are of the opinion that this case is governed by our holding in Sauer v Hebrew Inst. of Long Is. (17 AD2d 245, [*401] affd 13 NY2d 913). Accordingly, we would reverse and dismiss the complaint. In Sauer the plaintiff was a camper at defendant's summer camp. The campers were engaged in a game of "waterfight" in which the contending teams sought to douse their adversaries with water from cups or water pistols. Plaintiff, in an endeavor to avoid being sprayed with water, ran from an opponent. In so doing he slipped on the wet grass and struck his head on a concrete area immediately adjacent to the wet grassy area on which he slipped. In exonerating the defendant from liability we noted (p 246):

"The defendant, as the operator of a camp for boys, could not reasonably be made responsible in damages for the consequences of every possible hazard of play activity. It was required, rather, to guard against dangers which ought to have been foreseen in the exercise of reasonable care * * *

"It has not been demonstrated that the water fight game was more hazardous than any ordinary camp activity involving running. It was inevitable in the game that the grass would become wet; and, indeed, in any such game among [**32] 13-year-old boys, that there would be tumbles and falls whether it was wet or dry.

"To impose liability in this situation is to interdict the game itself, which in turn would so sterilize camp activity for boys as to render it sedentary".

We do not read Eddy v Syracuse Univ. (78 AD2d 989) as requiring a different result. There the plaintiff was a participant in the game of "ultimate frisbee" which was played in defendant's gymnasium, one wall of which was of masonry construction with a glass door in the center. The two teams had been admitted to the gymnasium by the janitor who, after their admission, had locked the door. There was no proof that the janitor had authority to permit the frisbee teams to use the gymnasium. Plaintiff, while pursuing a thrown frisbee, ran toward the glass door. As he neared the door, he turned and observed it. Unable to stop, he put up his hand to grasp the handlebar across the door. Because it was locked, the glass was shattered and plaintiff's right arm was severely lacerated. Defendant argued, [*402] among other things, that it had not given the players authorization to use the gymnasium and, hence, it was not liable. In holding the defense unavailable the court noted the change wrought in the law by Basso v Miller (40 NY2d 233). In the context of the defense, it made foreseeability the criterion by which defendant's duty was to be measured. However, as Sauer (supra) makes plain, that issue is not present in the case before us. The falls and tumbles of a nine year old at play are an inherent risk of any physical, competitive game. Only by forbidding the game can the risk be guarded against. However, to interdict such games is to make children's camping activities little more than a "baby-sitting" operation. Much as the law devotes itself to the protection of children it is powerless to protect them against childhood itself.

GRADING GREAVES

5 CITE   1   1   1   1
<u>Greaves v. Bronx YMCA</u>, 87 A.D.2d 394, 452 N.Y.S.2d 27 (1st Dept. 1982)
         1

15 FACTS 9 year old camper 2 (infant = 1)
fell and got hurt 1
playing ring-a-levio or non water sport 2 (game = 1)
played by campers and counselors 1
on wet 1
sloping site 1
on site chosen by counselors 3 (or made wet by counselors
Judg for pl. 2   or knew wet)
Aff'd 2

10 RULE   Negligence (5) is the failure to guard against foreseeable danger.

15 ISSUE   Whether or not the defendant camp was negligent (2), which would mean it failed to guard against foreseeable danger (3), when the counselors selected (3) a sloping (1) wet (3) grassy area as the site for playing a running game (3)?

5 HOLDING Yes, the camp was negligent because it failed to guard against foreseeable danger when the counselors selected a sloping, wet, grassy area as the site for playing a running game.

15 REASONING   1) Distinguished *Sauer* on the facts; here it was the selection of the site (7)that added needlessly to risks inherent in game(6) and counselors participated as catchers (2)
            2) Agreed with *Sauer* on policy not to inderdict game itself but rather counselor's choice of site.

10 CRITICISM Dissent (2) - Sauer analogous; inevitable with this kind of game that there would be falls; can't protect kids against childhood itself. (3) Own criticism (5)

****
ASSIGNMENT #5
ANALYSIS OF *SAUER* AND *GREAVES*

Every year Camp Good Times holds a hike to the top of Mount Snow or to the top of Barton Hill. Of the two hikes, the one up Mount Snow is a bit more arduous, but either can be accomplished in under an hour. This past year the campers, who ranged in age from seven to twelve, voted to hike up Mount Snow. The fifty campers and two camp counselors made it to the top of the hill in about 1/2 hour with no problems. On the way back down, however, eight year old Timmy tripped over a large moss covered log lying across the path. As the result of his fall, he suffered a broken leg. His parents now want to know whether they can successfully sue the camp for Timmy's injury. Please evaluate their claim based upon *Sauer* and *Greaves*. You have already briefed *Sauer*.

Prior to writing your analysis, first think about how the parents' representative would argue that their situation is analogous to *Greaves* and distinguishable from *Sauer*. Second, think about how the camp's representative would argue just the opposite. You may want to develop a chart in which you outline the facts of each situation to help you see the differences and similarities among your client's facts, the facts in *Sauer*, and the facts in *Greaves*.

Also, before beginning to write, make sure you understand the policy reasons behind the court's decisions. While your arguments should be based on the factual similarities and differences between our case and *Sauer* and *Greaves*, a mere listing of the factual similarities and differences is not enough. Pointing to the court's reasoning, you must be sure to tell me WHY you think those similarities and differences matter.

Use the IRAC method to write your analysis. Your analysis does not have to be all in one paragraph. For example you may discuss the parent's claims in one paragraph and the camp's claims in another. However, if you have more than one paragraph, remember to use transitions to link the paragraphs together. The following is a suggested approach:

1)   Begin your analysis with a statement of the Issue you are trying to resolve. Remember that "issue" in writing an analysis is not the same as "issue" in a brief. In a brief, the issue is expected to be able to stand on its own and so must include the rule plus the facts. In an analysis, the issue is the topic sentence for your first paragraph and is a broader statement of the problem that you will be discussing.

2)   Next give a statement of the general Rule including a citation for that rule.

3)   In your Analysis section, you will want to give an explanation of how the rule has been applied in the past. Your analysis will consist of several components:

        a)   You will briefly discuss the facts, holding, and reasoning of *Greaves* and *Sauer*.

        b)   You will give **both** the camp's and the parent's arguments, i.e., how based on our facts, our case is analogous to *Greaves* and distinguishable from *Sauer*, thereby making the camp liable, but also how our case is distinguishable from *Greaves* and analogous to *Sauer*, thereby indicating that the camp should not be liable.

        c)   Remember to give what you view as the losing argument first so that the winning argument flows right into your conclusion.

        d)   Your arguments should be based on the factual similarities and difference between our case and Sauer and Greaves.

        e)   But remember to go beyond a mere listing of the factual similarities and differences. Tell me, based on the court's reasoning, WHY you think those factual similarities and differences matter.

f)   Recall the discussion in Chapter 8 on case synthesis. Do not simply give a mini-brief of one case followed by the next. Rather, use a case to state a general proposition and then support that proposition with a discussion of that case's facts and holding.

g)   When writing your analysis, assume I have not read *Sauer* and *Greaves*. I am aware of our client's facts, however. Therefore, you do not need to recount those facts in a separate paragraph. Rather, <u>use those facts</u> to show how our case is distinguishable from or analogous to the cited cases.

4)   If your analysis takes more than one paragraph, begin your second paragraph with a transition sentence to tie the two paragraphs together.

5)   Finally, give your <u>C</u>onclusion as to which side has the better argument and why.

Please review Appendix C on citation form and Appendix B on writing style. Pay particular attention to the warning regarding starting paragraphs with "In the case of . . . ." Do not use contractions and do not write in first person. (Incorrect: I think the court didn't allow recovery. Correct: The court did not allow recovery.)

Proofread and double check to make sure you have not used sentence fragments nor run-ons. <u>Points will be deducted for grammar, citation, and typographical errors.</u> This is the time to make your work look as professional as possible. Thank you.

Grading Analysis of Sauer and Greaves

6 Issue - Liable for negl when 9 year old injured on a hike

5 Rule - Negl when don't guard against foreseeable danger

7 Facts/Holding/Reasoning of <u>Sauer</u>

7 Facts/Holding/Reasoning of <u>Greaves</u>

LIABLE   15
Analogous to <u>Greaves</u>
added needlessly to danger
  Picked mountain over hill/picked spot next to pool
  Lack of supervision

Distinquishable from <u>Sauer</u>
Climbing a mountain/water game = abnormal v. normal camp activity

----

NOT LIABLE 15
Analogous to <u>Sauer</u>
Normal activity
Inevitable risks of the sport and to eliminate risks have to eliminate the sport
  Water games create wet grass/hiking creates dangers of tripping

Distinquishable from <u>Greaves</u>
Camp added water to grass/nature put the log there

Conclusion 5

Writing Style
  Grammar   10

No Run-ons/SF
No Minor errors
Organization   5
Used Transitions   75+25=100
Assignments and Grading Sheets

****

LEGAL STUDIES II
ASSIGNMENT #6
LEGAL RESEARCH ASSIGNMENT (Contracts)

1.   Where in the Massachusetts statutes is the Uniform Commercial Code, Article 2 located?
       ch. 106

2.   Find the section that deals with the exclusion or modification of warranties. In
      Massachusetts, do the UCC, Article 2 implied warranties of merchantability apply to the
      sale of human blood?
                 No
      What is the citation for the statute that gave you that answer?
             Mass. Gen. Laws Ann. ch. 106, § 2-316(5).

3.   Locate the provisions of UCC, Article 2, § 2-316A. In what ways do you think this
      significantly limits the rights of sellers regarding exclusion or modification of implied
      warranties?
             **Cannot exclude or modify any implied warranties for consumer goods and
             services, § 2-316A(2), and the provisions of this section cannot be disclaimed
             or waived by agreement, § 2-316A(5).**
      When was the last time this section was amended?
             § 5 was added in 1996.

4.   Locate the provisions of UCC, Article 2, § 2-314 dealing with breach of warranty of
      merchantability. In the case notes following the statute, look for any cases dealing with
      the sale of food.
      a.   What is the standard for determining breach of warranty of merchantability for a
            bone or other substance in food that causes harm to a consumer?
                   **The so called "reasonable expectations" test and not the "foreign
                   substance-natural substance" test. A high school student had bit into
                   a cube of white turkey meat and was injured by a small bone. The
                   case was remanded for a determination by the trial judge as to what
                   the reasonable expectations of an ordinary high school student should
                   be concerning the likely presence of a bone in his meal.**

b. What is the correct citation for the case that gave you that answer?
>   ***Phillips v. Town of West Springfield*, 405 Mass. 411, 540 N.E.2d 1331
>   (1989).**

5. Under the UCC, when must a contract be in writing to be enforceable?
>   **Sale of goods for a price of five hundred dollars or more.**
>   What is the citation for the statute that gave you that answer?
>   **Mass. Gen. Laws Ann., ch. 106, § 2-201(1)**
>   **NOTE: the students may also find ch. 106, § 1-206, Statute of Frauds for
>   Kinds of Personal Property Not Otherwise Covered, which sets the limit
>   beyond five thousand dollars.**

6. What type of contracts NOT covered by the UCC must be in writing to be enforceable?
>   **First, to charge an executor or administrator, or an assignee under an
>   insolvent law of the commonwealth, upon a special promise to answer
>   damages out of his own estate;**
>   **Second, to charge a person upon a special promise to answer for the debt,
>   default or misdoings of another;**
>   **Third, upon an agreement made upon consideration of marriage;**
>   **Fourth, upon a contract for the sale of lands, tenements or hereditaments or
>   any interest in or concerning them; or**
>   **Fifth, upon an agreement that is not to be performed within one year from
>   the making thereof.**
>   What is the citation for the statute that gave you that answer?
>   **Mass. Gen. Laws Ann., ch. 259, § 1**

7. How long do you have to bring a normal, non-personal injury, breach of contract action?
>   **Six years after the cause of action accrues**
>   What is the citation for the statute that gave you that answer?
>   **Mass. Gen. Laws Ann. ch. 260, § 2**

8. Your boss remembers the case *Zapatha v. Dairy Mart, Inc.* Please locate that decision.
>   a. What is the full and correct citation?
>   ***Zapatha v. Diary Mart, Inc.*, 381 Mass. 284, 408 N.E.2d 1370 (1980).**
>   b. In that case, Dairy Mart terminated the Zapathas' franchise. Did the court think
>   that the franchise agreement and the relationship of the parties amounted to a
>   transaction in goods?
>   **No**
>   c. On what basis did the court apply the UCC principles of good faith and
>   unconscionability to this case?
>   **Said applied by analogy**
>   d. Was the 90 day without cause termination provision unconscionable? Why?
>   **No, because there was no unfair surprise and no oppression.**
>   e. Did the court think that Dairy Mart had acted in good faith? Why?
>   **Yes, because it met both tests of honesty in fact and observance of reasonable**

commercial standards of fair dealing.

9.   Use the digest to locate cases on the law in Massachusetts regarding the right of minors to disaffirm contracts. (Note: Remember that Mass. Digest 2d covers more recent cases. For this assignment, you may also have to look for older cases in Mass. Digest.)

a.   What is the law in Massachusetts about whether a minor can disaffirm a contract? **They can even if they cannot return what they received.**

b.   What is the correct citation for the case that gave you this answer and briefly what were its facts.
    Students may find a variety of cases, such as *Adamowski v. Curtiss-Wright Flying Serv., 300 Mass. 281, 15 N.E.2d 467 (1938)* In that case a minor paid for and received instruction in aviation. On reaching his majority, he disaffirmed the contract. The court said he could get his money back even though he could not return the instruction itself. (The case was based on New York law but the court said the same would apply in Massachusetts.)

****

ASSIGNMENT #8
LEGAL ANALYSIS (Business Forms)

Please write an answer for Legal Reasoning Exercise 1, located on page 443 of your book. Be sure to start with a roadmap paragraph and to end with a concluding paragraph. In between, do not simply give me back the information you can find in the book on each of the four basic business forms. Rather analyze which form is best for each of the "friends" based on each of their unique life situations.

Grading Sheet
Business Forms

		Invest/Savings Left
Alice - 30/baker/single parent	Wants to run business	$0/$50,000
Betty - 62/retired	Wants no part in day to day	100,000/130,000
Claire - 20/student	Wants no part in day to day	invest building
Dan - 25/odd jobs	Wants to manage	5,000/5,000

Road Map Paragraph - 5
Sole Proprietorship - 5
        Advantages for all - simple to form (2)
        Disadvantage to all - liability for personal assets (3)
                        dies with owner
Partnership - 10
                Advantages - Fairly easy to form (1)
                        Each could have a say in how business is run (2)

Single taxation (1)
Disadvantages - Unlimited liability for everyone. (4)
Liable for each other's actions. (2)
& each can bind the company.
Dies with death or withdrawal of partner

Corporation - 5
Advantages - Limited liability to what invest in the company. (2)
Disadvantages - Costly to form (1)
Costly to run (1)
Double taxation. (1)
Limited Liability Company 5
Advantages - Limited Liability (appealing to all) (3)
Single Taxation (1)
Disadvantages - new form (1)

Alice - 10
Wants management control (3) so likes sole proprietorship (1) or partnership (1)
But greater worry as single mom has to be liability (3), so would prefer corp. or
LLC (2)
Betty - 10
As a retiree, her biggest concern is liability, (3) so cannot do a partnership. (3) Sole
proprietorship O.K. if really wants no say in business. If wants say or to be part of
growth of company, should choose corp. or LLC.(2) Might go for a limited
partnership. (2)
Claire - 5
Student with limited liability, (1) and no desire for control (2) but still would
probably prefer limited liability of corporation or LLC. (2)
Dan - 5
Wants management control (2) and so would not go for sole proprietorship. (1)
Young with earning power so not as concerned as others with liability. (1) Still
probably would prefer LLC. (1)

Conclusion - 5
Organization - 5
No major grammar errors - 10
Handed it in - 20

ANSWER SHEET

ASSIGNMENT #9
LEGAL RESEARCH ASSIGNMENT (Employment and Criminal Law)

EMPLOYMENT LAW (30 pts)
The Massachusetts statute, ch. 151B, covers unlawful employment discrimination practices. Locate either the Massachusetts General Laws Annotated or the Annotated Laws of Massachusetts to answer questions 1-6. REMEMBER: Check the pocket parts.

1. Look at ch. 151B, § 4(1) and 4(1B). (5 pts)
   a. What categories of persons are protected from discrimination by employers in Massachusetts?
   race, color, religious creed, national origins, sexual orientation, ancestry, and age.

   b. How does this differ from the Federal statute, Title VII?
   Adds sexual orientation and age.

2.   a. What does § 4(16) protect? (6 pts)
   Handicapped individual

   b. What are the limitations on that protection?
   1- Must be qualified - capable of performing essential job functions
   2 -Can't impose undue hardship.

3. What protections are granted by § 4(4) and 4(4A) and why do you think they are necessary? (5 pts)
   Protected if file a complaint or aid someone; so people won't be afraid to use the statute.

4. Under ch. 151B, § 1(6.) who is excluded from the definition of "employee"? (4 pts)
   Family members (parents, spouse, child); domestic servants.

5. Under ch. 151B, § 1(5.) who is excluded from the definition of "employer"? (5 pts)
   Nonprofit club and fraternal associations; fewer than 6 employees; religious organizations giving preference to members of the same religion.

6. Under ch. 151B, § 1(8.) how is age defined? (5 pts)
   Greater than 40 years.

CRIMINAL LAW (70 pts)

7. The crime of stalking is a "new" crime. (15 pts)
    a. What statute makes stalking a crime?
        ch. 265, § 43

    b. Separately list each element of the crime.
        Willfully and maliciously
        engage in a knowing
            pattern of conduct or
            series of acts
        over a period of time
        directed at a specific person
        which seriously alarms
            or annoys that person and
        would cause a reasonable person to suffer substantial emotional distress

        and

        makes a threat
        with the intent to place the person in imminent fear of death
            or serious bodily injury

    c. When was the statute enacted?
        1992

8. Take a look at ch. 234, § 28. What must a juror understand about the nature of a criminal trial? (10 pts)
        The defendant is presumed innocent until proven guilty
        That the commonwealth has the burden of proving guilt beyond a reasonable doubt
        That the defendant need not present evidence in his behalf.

9. Find the statute that defines murder. (5 pts)
    a. In Massachusetts, how is murder in the first degree defined?
        Murder committed with deliberately premeditated aforethought or
        with extreme atrocity or cruelty or
        in the commission or attempted commission of a crime punishable with death or imprisonment for life.

    b. What is the citation for the statute that gave you that answer?
        ch. 265, § 1

10. Find the case notes following the murder statute that relate to defenses. (15 pts)
    a. If a victim was found shot in the back, would that indicate the defendant acted in self-defense?   **No**

b. What is the citation for the court opinion that gave you that answer?
  Commonwealth v. Garcia, 379 Mass. 422, 399 N.E.2d 460 (1980)

c. Does the state have the burden of proving the defendant was sane or does the defendant have the burden of proving the defendant was insane?
  The Commonwealth bears the burden of proving beyond a reasonable doubt that the defendant is sane.

d. What is the citation for the court opinion that gave you that answer?
  Commonwealth v. Kappler, 416 Mass. 574, 625 N.E.2d 513 (1993)

e. In Massachusetts, what legal standard is applied to prove insanity, i.e., a lack of criminal responsibility?
  Requires existence of a mental disease or defect which causes defendant's lack of substantial capacity either to appreciate wrongfulness of his conduct or to conform his conduct to requirements of law.

f. What is the citation for the court opinion that gave you that answer?
  Commonwealth v. Johnson, 422 Mass. 420, 663 N.E.2d 559 (1996).

11.　　a. What is the statute of limitations for murder? (10 pts)
  An indictment for murder may be found at any time.
  b. What is the citation for the statute that gave you that answer?
  ch. 277, § 63

12. Find an ALR annotation that discusses whether the felony murder doctrine should be applied when the person killed was a co-felon. (15 pts)
  a. What is the citation for that annotation?
  89 ALR4th 683, Application of felony murder doctrine where person killed was co-felon.

  b. What does the annotation say is the common-law felony murder rule?
  If a person kills another in doing or attempting to do an act amounting to a felony, the killing is murder.

  c. What does the annotation say the courts have concluded as to whether the felony murder doctrine should apply when the person killed is a co-felon?
  They have come to varying conclusions as to whether the felony murder doctrine should apply where the person killed is a co-felon. Some do not if the co-felon is killed by someone other than by an accomplice.

  d. Two Massachusetts cases are cited in the annotation. According to the summary of *Balliro*, was the trial judge correct in instructing the jury that the defendants should be found guilty of murder if the victims had been killed by police bullets? **No.**

278

****
ASSIGNMENT #10
LEGAL ANALYSIS (Criminal Law)

This assignment is based upon Legal Reasoning Exercise 3. First, reread the fact scenario about Bobby and Jimmy on page 547-48. Then study the Illinois Robbery and Armed Robbery statutes on page 539 and the Model Penal Code statute on Criminal Homicide on pages 544-45. Finally, study the attached statute governing liability of accessories. Assume that all of the actions took place in a jurisdiction with statutes identical to these.

Break each of these statutes down into their elements. Decide for each of the two main characters, Jimmy and Bobby, whether their facts coupled with the statutory elements give rise to any issues. Finally, write an analysis discussing what crimes you think the state will charge Jimmy and Bobby with committing. For each crime, be sure to include the arguments that you think the prosecution would make for finding them guilty and the arguments the defense attorneys would make for finding them not guilty. Start your analysis with a road map paragraph, organize it by crime (and issues raised by each potential crime), and then end with a concluding paragraph.

NOTE: You do not have to discuss every crime, only those that you think are likely to be charged by the prosecution. For example, there is nothing in our facts suggesting that either Jimmy or Bobby assisted the store clerk with committing suicide. Therefore, you would not include a discussion of Section 210.5 in your analysis.

Answer Sheet for Bobby and Jimmy
Note: The points add up to 105. This is to give the students the leeway to miss an issue with no penalty. Also, if they don't see all of the issues, but they do a bang up job on the others, I would give them extra points for that.

Roadmap Paragraph   5

Overall Organization and use of IRAC   15

**Robbery - For both - > took property from the "presence of another"
by threat of the imminent use of force   5**

Armed Robbery - For Bobby, question is whether carried a "dangerous weapon" 5
       Yes - Realistic looking   5
            Even if thought was a water gun, said had acid in it.
       No - Only a water gun, so no potential for harm   5

Is Jimmy an Accomplice?   5
       Guilty of an offense if
            Accomplice if
                 aids another in planning and committing
      Yes - to robbery 3
      No - to armed robbery 2

Didn't know of "gun"
Can't argue terminated and called police because done after and not "prior" to commission of offense 5

Both as to Murder > Section 210.0 Must cause the death   5
Died of natural causes so not murder
But would not have died but for

Murder Section 210.2(1)(b) recklessness presumed if engaged in robbery.
Died after robbery over   5
But set in motion by robbery

Concluding paragraph - 5

No major grammar errors - 10

25 for handing it in + 80 = 105